Joanna Whitaker has lived in London for the past ten years. For most of that time she has worked in many areas of film production including research and fact-finding. As a result, friends and colleagues often ask her to find out what to do, how to get, or who to ask. She now owns dozens of reference books and is a remarkable source of diverse information. She realized that existing publications about London were inconsistent and incomplete and decided to write *London on Sunday*.

JOANNA WHITAKER

London on Sunday

PANTHER
Granada Publishing

Panther Books
Granada Publishing Ltd
8 Grafton Street, London W1X 3LA

Published by Panther Books 1985

ISBN 0-586-06390-0

Printed and bound in Great Britain by
Collins, Glasgow

Set in Ehrhardt

*Every effort has been made to ensure that the information in
this book is correct. No responsibility can be accepted for any errors.*

Contents

SPORTS & ACTIVITIES

Introduction

The idea for this book came to me one Sunday while rushing to catch the Royal Academy before it closed at 1.45 p.m. I had misread the newspaper – it's *cheaper* before 1.45 p.m. and it occurred to me then that there wasn't any way of finding out this kind of information from one book.

There are many useful books and weekly publications which provide a great deal of information about all kinds of activities and events. But what about Sunday? What time does the Tate close? Where can the kids go roller skating? Where can I buy cough mixture? Or petrol at midnight?

I began to realize that I wasn't the only one who wanted to know.

Friends began ringing me up on Sundays to find out 'Where can Uncle John have dinner tonight – everywhere seems to be closed?'; or 'Where's my nearest chemist?'; or 'There must be a pub round here with music . . ?'

I talked to friends living outside London who would happily make a day-trip to London – Sunday is an ideal day but what should they do and how do they get the most out of their visit?

There are others who get into London on Sunday evening to start work the next morning and are bored stiff by room-service sandwiches and T.V. but don't know what else to do, and many visitors from overseas who are here for a limited period of time – maybe as little as two or three days – who want to do and see as much as possible during their stay here which is likely to include a weekend.

So the idea developed, the paperwork mounted up, the files expanded and here it is – I hope you find it useful.

Acknowledgements

My thanks go to Martha Browne-Wilkinson, Ailie Collins, Lucy de Bay, Anne Jones, Sarah Seal, Isabelle Sepulchre, Anthony Whitaker and Charlotte Winer for coming to the rescue when the prospect of making three thousand telephone calls was too much for me.

My thanks also to Maggie Hanbury for her encouragement and guidance and to Lucy de Bay for her artwork.

And, more by way of a dedication, to A.N.F. whose support for me and my book has been constant, generous and wholehearted *every* day of the week.

How To Use This Book

Each section of this book is virtually self-contained regarding notes, keys to abbreviations, etc. Having said that, the layout of each section is based on the answers to the following questions:

(a) Am I prepared to cross town to see/do/buy it?
(b) Where's the nearest place round the corner where I can see/do/buy it?

I feel that in the case of, for example, museums or classical music, one would be prepared to travel a distance but once there, one would want to find a restaurant nearby.

For this reason museums are listed alphabetically while restaurants are listed by postal zone. Where appropriate, I have included a postal zone index to the information already contained within a section.

THE AREA COVERED
Those areas with a postal zone – anywhere in London from N21 to SE25 – as well as some popular places, e.g. Richmond, out of town.

POSTAL ZONES
London is divided into 119 postal districts. Throughout the book they are listed alphabetically starting with E1 and ending with WC2. There is logic in the layout of the zones but also some surprises (e.g. SE2) and they do provide the clearest definition of areas of London. If, for example, you are in SW7 and want to find somewhere to eat locally, use the map on the following pages to find out which other zones are nearby and then refer to the 'Restaurants' section of this book.

POSTAL ZONE MAP
see key on next page

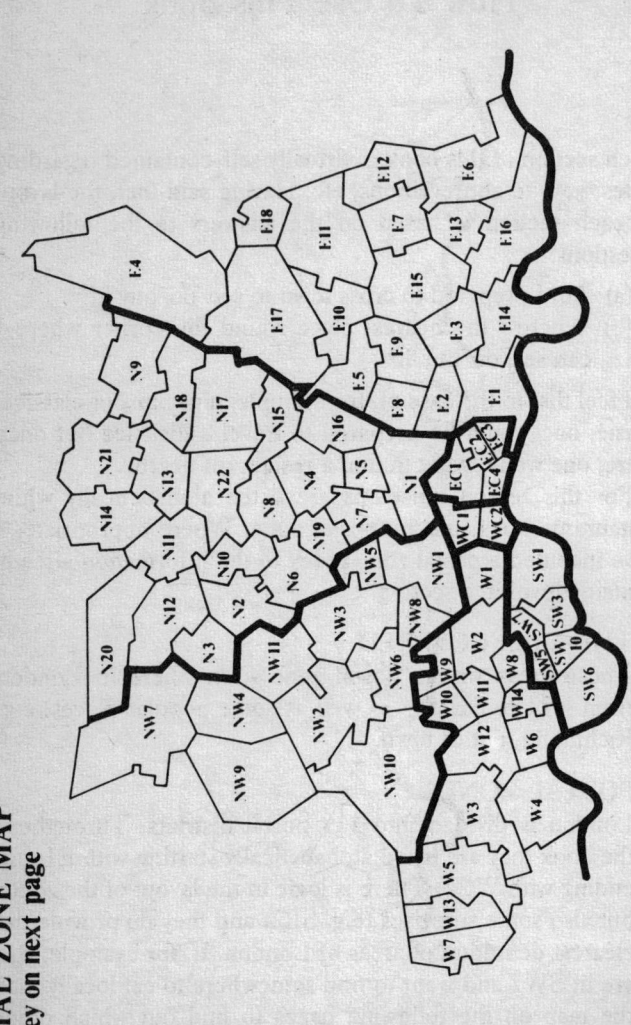

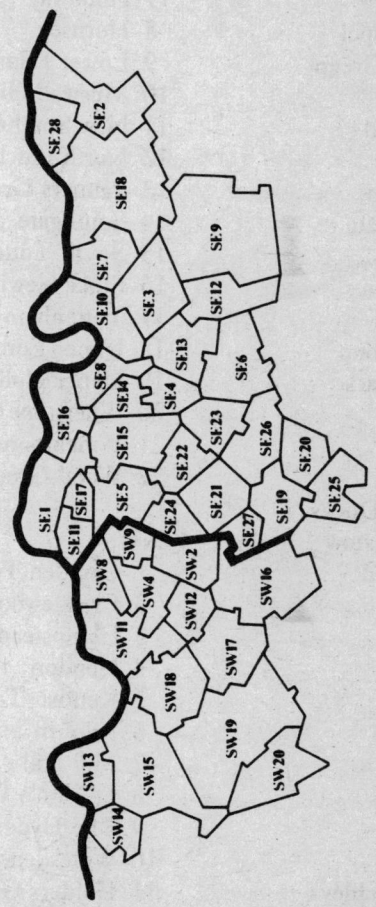

RIVER THAMES

KEY TO POSTAL ZONE MAP

E

1 Whitechapel
2 Bethnal Green
3 Bow
4 Chingford
5 Clapton
6 East Ham
7 Forest Gate
8 Hackney
9 Homerton
10 Leyton
11 Leytonstone
12 Manor Park
13 Plaistow
14 Poplar
15 Stratford
16 Victoria Docks
17 Walthamstow
18 Woodford

EC

1 City
2 of
3 London
4

N

1 Islington
2 East Finchley
3 Finchley
4 Finsbury Park
5 Highbury
6 Highgate
7 Holloway
8 Hornsey
9 Lower Edmonton
10 Muswell Hill
11 New Southgate
12 North Finchley
13 Palmers Green
14 Southgate
15 South Tottenham
16 Stoke Newington
17 Tottenham
18 Upper Edmonton
19 Upper Holloway
20 Whetstone
21 Winchmore Hill
22 Wood Green

NW

1 Camden Town
2 Cricklewood
3 Hampstead
4 Hendon
5 Kentish Town
6 Kilburn
7 Mill Hill
8 St John's Wood
9 The Hyde
10 Willesden
11 Golders Green

SE

1 Southwark
2 Abbey Wood

TELEPHONE NUMBERS
All the numbers given should be preceded by 01 if calling from outside London.

NEAREST STATION
This is indicated by ⊖ for Underground and BR for British Rail. If none is given, none is near.

CREDIT CARDS
Where it might be useful, the acceptance of credit cards is indicated as follows:

AC = Access
AX = American Express
BC = Barclaycard (Visa)
DC = Diners Club

PUBS
As a rule, they have not been included because they all open on Sunday. The ones listed in this book are those with entertainment – music, disco etc.

Pub opening hours on Sunday are Noon–2.00 p.m. & 7.00 p.m.–10.30 p.m.

ANNUAL EVENTS
Exhibitions at Earls Court, shows at Olympia etc. You can find out more from Tourist Information, Leisureline and other services (see 'Information').

BANK HOLIDAY WEEKENDS
Some places included in this book may be closed on a Sunday which falls on a Bank Holiday weekend – ring and check.

CHILDREN

It should be possible to judge from the information given whether a place is suitable for children. In general, many restaurants welcome children and a number of those listed serving traditional Sunday lunch have a reduced-price menu for children.

For a weekly recommendation of events, entertainment, etc. see 'Information'.

DISABLED

If you are planning in advance, call Artsline on 625 5666/7. They are open Monday to Friday 10.00 a.m.–4.00 p.m. and on Saturday 10.00 a.m.–2.00 p.m. and can provide information on places to go and facilities for the disabled.

FUTURE EDITIONS

At the end of this book is a form. It would be of great help in compiling a future edition if you could complete this and send it to the address shown.

RESTAURANTS

The restaurants are listed by postal zone and then alphabetically under types of cuisine. If a restaurant is part of a hotel, it is listed under the name of the hotel.

At the back of this section there are lists of restaurants under the following headings:

- Breakfast and/or Brunch
- Traditional Sunday Lunch
- Afternoon Tea
- Late Night
- Open Air Eating
- Cuisine Index

PRICE
The price guide in brackets is based on the approximate cost per head for *lunch* or *dinner* without wine.

- (A) = up to £5
- (B) = £5–£10
- (C) = £10–£15
- (D) = £15–£20
- (E) = £20–£25
- (F) = over £25

KEY

✆ or BR	nearest Underground or British Rail station
*Breakfast *Brunch *Roast lunch *Tea	self-explanatory

*Not licensed	not licensed to sell wine but, generally speaking, you may take your own
*Veg	caters for vegetarians
*T/A	take away available
*Open Air	seating available outside
*Book	advance booking advised
*AC AX BC DC	credit cards accepted: Access/ American Express/Barclaycard (Visa)/Diners Club

E1

ENGLISH

BEEFEATER (E)
Ivory House
St Katharine's Dock
408 1001
☻ Tower Hill
8.00 p.m.–11.30 p.m.
Medieval banquet with
entertainment and dancing
*Book *AC AX BC DC

DICKENS INN BY THE
TOWER
St Katharine's Way
☻ Tower Hill
– PICKWICK ROOM (D)
488 2208
Noon–2.30 p.m. all year &
7.00 p.m.–10 p.m.
June–September only
*Roast lunch *Veg
*Book *AC AX BC DC

G & T RESTAURANT (A)
17 Bethnal Green Road
739 4571

☻ Liverpool Street
7.30 a.m.–4.00 p.m.
English café
*Breakfast *T/A *AC AX BC
DC

NICK'S PLACE (B)
137 Leman Street
488 9908
☻ Aldgate East
6.00 p.m.–10.30 p.m.
Traditional pies
*T/A *AC AX BC

THE TOWER HOTEL
St Katharine's Way
481 2575
☻ Tower Hill
– THE CARVERY (B)
12.15 p.m.–3.00 p.m. & 6.00
p.m.–10.00 p.m.
*Roast lunch *Book
*AC AX BC DC
– THE PICNIC BASKET (B)
7.00 a.m.–midnight
Buttery menu
*Breakfast *Tea *Veg
*AC AX BC DC

– THE PRINCES ROOM (D)
12.30 p.m.–2.30 p.m. & 7.00
p.m.–10.30 p.m.
English/French menu
*Veg *Book *AC AX BC DC

FISH

DICKENS INN BY THE
TOWER
St Katharine's Way
✆ Tower Hill
– DICKENS ROOM (D)
488 9932
Noon–2.30 p.m. &
7.00 p.m.–10.00 p.m.
*Book *AC AX BC DC

INDIAN

CLIFTON (A)
126 Brick Lane
377 9402/247 2364
✆ Aldgate East
Noon–1.00 a.m.
*Veg *T/A *AC AX BC DC

INDIA GRILL (B)
106 Mile End Road
790 0906
✆ Whitechapel/Stepney
Green
Noon–3.00 p.m. &
6.00 p.m.–12.30 a.m.
*Veg *T/A *AC AX BC DC

SHEBA TANDOORI (B)
136 Brick Lane
247 7824
✆ Aldgate East
Noon–midnight
*Veg *T/A *Book *AC AX
BC DC

SITA TANDOORI (B)
222 Whitechapel Road
247 4936
✆ Whitechapel
Noon–3.00 p.m. &
6.00 p.m.–midnight
*Veg *T/A *Book *AC AX
BC DC

SUNAR BANGLA (A)
46 Hanbury Street
247 2417
✆ Whitechapel/Aldgate East
Noon–midnight
*Veg *T/A *AC BC

JEWISH

BLOOM'S (B)
90 Whitechapel High Street
247 6001/6835
✆ Aldgate East
11.15 a.m.–9.30 p.m.
*Veg *T/A *Book *AC BC

E2

AMERICAN

THE RINGSIDE (B)
22 Kingsland Road
739 1838
✆ Old Street
2.00 p.m.–8.00 p.m.
American/English late lunch
*Roast lunch *Veg *AC AX
BC

INTERNATIONAL

VENUS STEAK HOUSE (B)
366–368 Bethnal Green
Road
739 2650/1458
➍ Bethnal Green
6.00 p.m.–1.00 a.m.
*Book *AC AX BC DC

E4

INDIAN

MUMTAZ TANDOORI (B)
102 Station Road
529 2620
BR Chingford
Noon–3.00 p.m. &
6.00 p.m.–midnight
*Veg *T/A *AC AX BC DC

E7

INDIAN

BALA (A)
183 Upton Lane
472 6755
➍ Upton Park
Noon–3.00 p.m. &
6.30 p.m.–12.30 a.m.
*Veg *T/A *AX

RONAK (B)
317 Romford Road
534 2944/519 2110
BR Forest Gate
11.00 a.m.–10.00 p.m.
*Veg *T/A

E11

ENGLISH

**THE WOODBINE WINE
ROOMS** (B)
36 High Street, Wanstead
989 0552
➍ Wanstead
Noon–2.00 p.m.
Wine Bar
*Roast lunch *Book *AC BC

ITALIAN

GOTICO RISTORANTE (C)
62 High Street, Wanstead
530 4245
➍ Wanstead
Noon–2.30 p.m. &
6.00 p.m.–11.00 p.m.
*Veg *Book *AC AX BC DC

PAPILLON (B)
17 Cambridge Park
989 1977
➍ Wanstead
Noon–2.30 p.m. &
6.00 p.m.–11.00 p.m.
*Veg *Open Air *AC AX BC
DC

E14

CHINESE

CHINATOWN (B)
795 Commercial Road
987 2330/6720

Noon–3.30 p.m. &
6.00 p.m.–11.00 p.m.
Cantonese
*Veg *Book *AC AX BC DC

GOOD FRIENDS (B)
139 Salmon Lane
987 5541
BR Stepney East
Noon–11.30 p.m.
Cantonese
*Not licensed *Veg *T/A
*Book *AC AX BC DC

NEW FRIENDS (B)
53 West India Dock Road
987 1139/3440
BR Stepney East
Noon–11.00 p.m.
Cantonese
*Veg *T/A *AC AX BC DC

YOUNG FRIENDS
CHINESE (B)
11 Pennyfields
987 4276
BR Stepney East
11.30 a.m.–11.30 p.m.
Cantonese
*T/A *AC AX BC

E17

CHINESE

NEW CHINA
RESTAURANT (B)
178 Hoe Street
520 5918
✪ Walthamstow Central
Noon–2.30 p.m. &
6.00 p.m.–11.30 p.m.
*Veg *T/A *AC AX BC DC

ITALIAN

LA NOTTE (C)
524–528 Forest Road
520 7311
✪ Walthamstow Central
Noon–2.30 p.m. &
6.00 p.m.–11.30 p.m.
*Veg *AC AX BC DC

E18

CHINESE

DRAGON INN (C)
127 High Road
504 0581
✪ South Woodford
Noon–midnight
*T/A *Book *AX BC DC

HO HO (B)
20 High Road
989 8021
✪ South Woodford
Noon–3.00 p.m. &
6.00 p.m.–11.30 p.m.
Pekingese
*Veg *T/A *Open Air *Book
*AC AX BC DC

INDIAN

MEGHNA GRILL (B)
219 High Road
504 0923
✪ South Woodford
Noon–3.00 p.m. &
6.00 p.m.–midnight
*Veg *T/A *Book *AC AX
BC DC

EC1

ENGLISH

BARBICAN CITY HOTEL
Central Street
251 1565
⊖ Old Street
7.00 a.m.–10.00 a.m.
*Breakfast
– THE CARVERY   (B)
12.30 p.m.–2.30 p.m. & 6.00
p.m.–10.00 p.m.
*Roast lunch *Book *AC BC

CAFÉ ST PIERRE   (B)
29 Clerkenwell Green
251 6606
⊖ Farringdon
11.00 a.m.–5.00 p.m.
Restaurant/Wine Bar
French-inspired cuisine
*Roast lunch *Open Air
*Book *AC AX BC DC

RUDLAND & STUBBS   (B)
35–37 Greenhill Rents
Cowcross Street
253 0148
⊖ Farringdon
Noon–3.00 p.m.
*Roast lunch *Veg *Open Air

INDIAN

THE JAMUNA   (B)
164 Clerkenwell Road
278 8674
⊖ Farringdon
6.00 p.m.–midnight
*Veg *T/A *AC AX BC DC

JEWISH

HATCHETT'S   (A)
5 Clerkenwell Road
251 2587/253 8133
⊖ Farringdon
10.30 a.m.–3.30 p.m.
*Veg *T/A *BC

EC2

ENGLISH

BARBICAN CENTRE
Silk Street
⊖ Moorgate
– THE CUT ABOVE   (B)
(Level 7)
588 3008
Noon–3.00 p.m. &
6.00 p.m.–30 minutes after end
of last performance
Carvery or cold buffet
*Roast lunch *Book
*AC AX BC DC

THE GREAT EASTERN
HOTEL
Liverpool Street
283 4363
⊖ Liverpool Street
8.00 a.m.–10.00 a.m.
*Breakfast
– CITY GATES
RESTAURANT   (B)
Noon–2.00 p.m. &
7.00 p.m.–9.30 p.m.
Carvery
*Roast lunch *Book
*AC AX BC DC

CHINESE

EAT & DRINK (B)
169 Bishopsgate
247 1313
✆ Liverpool Street
Noon–10.30 p.m.
*Veg *T/A *AC AX BC DC

INTERNATIONAL

BARBICAN CENTRE
Silk Street
✆ Moorgate
– THE WATERSIDE
CAFÉ (A)
(Level 5)
638 4141
Noon–8.00 p.m.
Hot and cold snack menu
*Tea *Veg *Open Air
*AC AX BC DC

CHUBBIES (A)
22–23 Liverpool Street
283 3504
✆ Liverpool Street
8.00 a.m.–3.00 p.m.
Café
*Breakfast *Not licensed

EC4

ENGLISH

CITY OF LONDON
TAVERN (A)
Blackfriars Lane
408 1001
✆ Blackfriars
6.30 p.m.–1.00 a.m.

Pub evening with games,
entertainment and dancing
*AC AX BC DC

INDIAN

TEMPLE BAR
TANDOORI (B)
23–28 Fleet Street
583 4673
✆ Blackfriars
Noon–10.00 p.m.
*Veg *T/A *AC AX BC DC

N1

CHINESE

YOUNGS (B)
19 Canonbury Lane
226 9791/0274
✆ Highbury & Islington
Noon–2.30 p.m. &
6.00 p.m.–11.00 p.m.
*Veg *T/A *Book *AC AX
BC

ENGLISH

Mr BUMBLE (B)
23 Islington Green
354 1952
✆ Angel
12.30 p.m.–3.00 p.m.
*Roast lunch *Open Air
*Book *AC AX BC DC

INDIAN

GOAN RESTAURANT (B)
16 York Way
837 7517

◒ King's Cross
Noon–midnight
*Veg *T/A *AC AX BC DC

MANZIL TANDOORI (B)
18 York Way
837 8042
◒ King's Cross
Noon–midnight
*Veg *Book *AX BC DC

PARVEEN TANDOORI (B)
6 Theberton Street
226 0504
◒ Angel
Noon–3.00 p.m. &
6.00 p.m.–12.30 a.m.
*T/A *AC BC

SONAR GAON (B)
46 Upper Street
226 6499
◒ Angel
Noon–2.30 p.m. &
6.00 p.m.–midnight
*Veg *T/A *AC AX BC DC

INTERNATIONAL

SERENDIPITY (B)
The Mall, Camden Passage
359 1932
◒ Angel
Noon–11.00 p.m.
Restaurant/Wine Bar with live
jazz most Sundays
*Brunch *Tea *AC BC

UPPERS BISTRO (B)
349 Upper Street
226 5650
◒ Angel
12.30 p.m.–3.00 p.m. &
7.00 p.m.–11.00 p.m.

*Roast lunch *Veg *Book
*AC AX BC

VARNAMS (C)
2 Greenman Street
359 6707
◒ Highbury & Islington
Noon–3.00 p.m.
*Open Air *AC AX BC DC

ITALIAN

PIZZA EXPRESS (A)
335–337 Upper Street
226 9542
◒ Angel
11.30 a.m.–midnight
*Veg *T/A

TURKISH

HODJA NASREDDIN (A)
53 Newington Green Road
226 7757
◒ Highbury & Islington
11.00 a.m.–3.00 a.m.
*Veg *T/A *Book

SULTAN AHMET (B)
326 Essex Road
226 1986
◒ Angel
Noon–2.30 a.m.
*Not licensed *Veg

SULTAN'S DELIGHT (A)
301 Upper Street
226 8346
◒ Angel
6.00 p.m.–1.00 a.m.
*T/A *AC AX BC DC

N3

GREEK

SPARTA RESTAURANT (B)
225–227 Regent's Park Road
346 0854
⊖ Finchley Central
6.00 p.m.–midnight
*Veg *Book *AC BC

N4

VEGETARIAN

SEASONS (A)
3 Chatterton Road
359 0341
⊖ Arsenal
10.00 a.m.–2.00 p.m. &
7.00 p.m.–11.00 p.m.
*Breakfast/brunch *Book

WEST INDIAN

BEEWEES (B)
96 Stroud Green Road
263 4004
⊖ Finsbury Park
5.00 p.m.–10.00 p.m.
*Veg *T/A *Book

N6

CHINESE

NEW DRAGON (B)
66 Highgate High Street
348 6160
⊖ Archway

Noon–midnight
*Veg *T/A *Book *AC AX
BC DC

ENGLISH

THE ORANGERY (A)
Lauderdale House,
Waterlow Park
341 4807
⊖ Archway
10.00 a.m.–5.00 p.m.
Coffee, snacks and lunches
*Roast lunch *Tea *T/A
*Open Air *Book

FRENCH

ONE HAMPSTEAD
LANE (C)
1 Hampstead Lane
340 4444
⊖ Archway/Highgate
12.30 p.m.–3.00 p.m.
French/English cuisine
*Roast lunch *Veg *Open Air
*Book *AC BC DC

ITALIAN

SAN CARLO (D)
2 Highgate High Street
340 5823
⊖ Archway/Highgate
12.30 p.m.–3.00 p.m. &
7.00 p.m.–11.00 p.m.
*Veg *Open Air *Book
*AC AX BC DC

WHOLEFOOD

EARTH EXCHANGE (A)
213 Archway Road
340 6407

● Highgate
Noon–4.00 p.m. &
6.00 p.m.–10.30 p.m.
*Veg *T/A *Open Air *Book

N7

INDIAN

TAJ MAHAL (B)
35 Holloway Road
607 2980
● Highbury & Islington
Noon–3.00 p.m. &
6.00 p.m.–12.30 a.m.
*Veg *T/A *AC BC

N8

FAR EASTERN

PENANG SATAY HOUSE (B)
27 Turnpike Lane
340 8707
● Turnpike Lane
6.00 p.m.–10.45 p.m.
Malaysian/Singaporean
*Veg *T/A *Book

GREEK

AROCARIA (B)
48c The Broadway
340 0580
● Finsbury Park
6.00 p.m.–11.30 p.m.
*Open Air *Book *AC AX BC

INDIAN

JALALIAH (A)
163 Priory Road
348 4756
● Turnpike Lane
1.00 p.m.–3.00 p.m. &
6.00 p.m.–midnight
*Veg *T/A *AC BC

INTERNATIONAL

CRITERION STEAK
HOUSE (B)
4 Queens Parade,
Green Lanes
348 6945
● Turnpike Lane
Noon–2.00 a.m.
Mainly English dishes
*Veg *Book *BC DC

N9

INTERNATIONAL

GATTO BLU
INTERNATIONAL (B)
52 Church Street
803 0315
BR Lower Edmonton
Noon–4.00 p.m.
Live organ/guitar music
*Roast lunch *Veg *Book
*AC AX BC

N10

INDIAN

CURRY & TANDOORI
GARDEN (B)
291 Muswell Hill Broadway
883 0557
◉ East Finchley
Noon–2.30 p.m. &
6.30 p.m.–11.00 p.m.
*Veg *T/A *AC AX BC DC

ITALIAN

GUIDEBERRY (A)
265 Muswell Hill Broadway
883 1500
◉ East Finchley
11.00 a.m.–10.00 p.m.
Italian/American food
*Brunch *T/A *Book *AC BC

N13

INDIAN

DIPALI RESTAURANT (B)
82 Alderman's Hill
886 4985/2221
◉ Arnos Grove
6.00 p.m.–midnight
*Veg *T/A *AC AX BC DC

N14

FRENCH

L'OISEAU NOIR (C)
163 Bramley Road
367 1100

◉ Oakwood
Noon–2.30 p.m.
English menu on Sundays
*Roast lunch *Veg *Book
*AC AX BC DC

INDIAN

EMPEROR OF INDIA (B)
49 Cannon Hill
882 3754
◉ Southgate
Noon–3.00 p.m. &
6.00 p.m.–midnight
*Veg *T/A *Book
*AC AX BC DC

STANDARD (B)
106 Crown Lane
886 1124
◉ Southgate
Noon–2.30 p.m. &
6.00 p.m.–midnight
*Veg *T/A *Book
*AC AX BC DC

N15

VEGETARIAN

DEENS (A)
418 West Green Road
889 8748
◉ Turnpike Lane
5.30 p.m.–11.00 p.m.
*T/A *Open Air *Book

N16

CHINESE

ELEGANZA (B)
70 Stoke Newington High
Street
254 1950
BR Stoke Newington
6.30 p.m.–midnight
Pekingese
*T/A *AC AX BC DC

INTERNATIONAL

CRAZY HORSE (B)
50 Stoke Newington Road
249 4895
BR Dalston Junction
3.00 p.m.–12.45 a.m.
*Veg *T/A *Open Air

FOX'S WINE BAR (A)
176 Stoke Newington Church
Street
254 2709
BR Stoke Newington
Noon–2.00 p.m. & 7.00
p.m.–10.30 p.m.
Barbecues in summer
*Veg *Open Air *AC BC

N19

PORTUGUESE & SPANISH

LA PARRA (B)
114 Junction Road
272 4009/0494
● Tufnell Park/Archway

Noon–3.00 p.m. &
6.00 p.m.–midnight
Disco in basement at night
*Veg *Open Air *Book

N21

INDIAN

RAJ OF INDIA (A)
10 Station Road
360 9543
● Southgate
Noon–2.30 p.m. &
6.00 p.m.–midnight
*Veg *T/A *AC AX BC DC

N22

INDIAN

EASTERN EYE (A)
19 Westbury Avenue
889 6963
● Turnpike Lane
Noon–3.00 p.m.
& 6.00 p.m.–midnight
*Veg *AC AX BC DC

NW1

CHINESE

GALLERY BOAT (C)
opposite 15 Prince Albert Road
485 8137
● Camden Town
Noon–11.00 p.m.
*Veg *T/A *Book *AX DC

ENGLISH

CHALK & CHEESE (B)
14 Chalk Farm Road
267 9820
● Camden Town
Noon–3.00 p.m.
*Veg *Open Air *Book
*AC AX BC DC

MUSTOE BISTRO (C)
73 Regent's Park Road
586 0901
● Chalk Farm
1.00 p.m.–3.00 p.m. &
6.30 p.m.–10.45 p.m.
English/French cuisine
*Roast lunch *Book

MY FAIR LADY (B)
embarkation point at:
250 Camden High Street
485 4433
● Camden Town
Boarding from 12.30 p.m.
Returning 3.30 p.m.
Lunch cruise on canal
*Roast lunch *Book *AC BC

THE ONE LEGGED GOOSE
(C)
17 Princess Road
722 9665
● Camden Town/Chalk
Farm
Noon–2.30 p.m. &
7.00 p.m.–10.30 p.m.
English food and pasta
*Veg *Open Air *Book *AC
BC

FRENCH

CHALCOT'S (B)
49 Chalcot Road
722 1956
● Chalk Farm
12.30 p.m.–2.30 p.m.
*Book *AC BC DC

**LA CRÊPERIE DE
L'ECLUSE** (B)
3 Chalk Farm Road
267 8116
● Camden Town
10.30 a.m.–11.30 p.m.
*Veg *T/A *AC AX BC

LE BISTROQUET (C)
273–275 Camden High
Street
485 9607
● Camden Town
9.00 a.m.–11.00 p.m.
Brasserie
*Breakfast *Tea *Veg
*Open Air *Book *AC AX BC

LE ROUTIER (C)
13 Camden Lock Place
485 0360
● Camden Town/Chalk
Farm
12.30 p.m.–2.30 p.m. &
7.00 p.m.–10.45 p.m.
Two sittings for English lunch
*Roast lunch *Veg *Open air
*Book *AC AX BC DC

PRATTS (B)
Camden Lock Place
485 9987/6044
● Camden Town
9.00 a.m.–11.30 p.m.

Restaurant/brasserie
*Breakfast *Roast lunch
*Tea *Veg *Book *AC AX BC
DC

GREEK

ANDY'S KEBAB HOUSE (B)
81a Bayham Street
485 9718
◉ Camden Town
6.00 p.m.–midnight
*Veg *T/A *AC BC

ARARAT (B)
249 Camden High Street
267 0319
◉ Camden Town
Noon–3.00 p.m. &
6.00 p.m.–midnight
Greek/Armenian food
*T/A *Open Air *AC AX BC
DC

TRIMITHI (A)
33 Pratt Street
267 1147
◉ Camden Town
6.00 p.m.–11.00 p.m.

INDIAN

DIWANA BHEL-POORI
HOUSE (A)
121 Drummond Street
387 5556
◉ Euston
Noon–11.00 p.m.
*Not licensed *Veg *T/A
*AC BC DC

LIGHT OF INDIA (B)
59 Park Road
723 6753

◉ Baker Street
Noon–3.00 p.m. &
6.00 p.m.–midnight
*Veg *T/A *Book *AC AX
BC DC

MUMTAZ (C)
4 Park Road
723 0549
◉ Baker Street
Noon–3.00 p.m. &
6.00 p.m.–11.00 p.m.
*Veg *T/A *Book *AC AX
BC DC

RANA OF CAMDEN (B)
31 Parkway
485 1313
◉ Camden Town
Noon–3.00 p.m. &
6.00 p.m.–midnight
*Veg *T/A *Book *AC AX
BC DC

RAVI SHANKAR (B)
133–135 Drummond Street
388 6458
◉ Euston/Euston Square
Noon–11.00 p.m.
South Indian vegetarian
*Veg *T/A *AC AX BC DC

SAGARMATHA (B)
339 Euston Road
387 6531
◉ Warren Street
Noon–3.00 p.m. &
6.00 p.m.–midnight
*Veg *T/A *Book *AC AX
BC DC

TANDOOR MAHAL (B)
321 Euston Road
387 2995

✪ Warren Street
Noon–midnight
*Veg *T/A *Book *AC AX
BC DC

VICEROY OF INDIA   (C)
3–5 Glentworth Street
486 3515
✪ Baker Street
Noon–3.00 p.m. &
6.00 p.m.–11.00 p.m.
*Veg *T/A *AC AX BC DC

INTERNATIONAL

CAMDEN BRASSERIE   (A)
216 Camden High Street
482 2114
✪ Camden Town
Noon–3.00 p.m.
*Veg *Book *AC AX BC DC

FERDINAND'S
RESTAURANT &
COCKTAIL BAR   (B)
48 Chalk Farm Road
267 5939
✪ Chalk Farm
12.30 p.m.–3.30 p.m. &
7.00 p.m.–11.30 p.m.
*Veg *Book *AC AX BC DC

HAREWOOD HOTEL
Harewood Row
262 2707
✪ Marylebone
7.30 a.m.–10.30 a.m.
*Breakfast
– STREETCARS   (B)
Noon–3.00 p.m. &
6.00 p.m.–11.00 p.m.
*T/A *Open Air *AC AX BC
DC

PRIMROSE   (A)
64 Parkway
485 0678
✪ Camden Town
11.00 a.m.–midnight
*Veg *T/A *Book *AC AX
BC DC

MIDDLE EASTERN

ALI BABA   (A)
32 Ivor Place
723 5805
✪ Baker Street
Noon–midnight
Egyptian food
*Veg *T/A

NW2

ENGLISH

QUINCY'S   (B)
675 Finchley Road
794 8499
✪ Golders Green
12.30 p.m.–2.00 p.m.
*Roast lunch *Open Air
*Book *AC BC

INDIAN

CRICKLEWOOD
TANDOORI   (B)
96 Cricklewood Broadway
450 4081
✪ Kilburn
6.00 p.m.–midnight
*Veg *T/A *AX BC DC

SHAMA TANDOORI   (A)
66 Cricklewood Broadway
450 9052

✆ Kilburn
Noon–3.00 p.m. &
5.30 p.m.–midnight
*Not licensed *Veg *T/A
*Book *AC BC

YETI TANDOORI (B)
68 Cricklewood Broadway
452 4789
✆ Kilburn
Noon–3.00 p.m. &
6.00 p.m.–midnight
*Veg *T/A *AC AX BC DC

INTERNATIONAL

MARTHA'S VINEYARD (A)
424 Finchley Road
435 2788
✆ Golders Green/Hampstead
Noon–2.00 p.m. &
7.00 p.m.–midnight
Live music from 9.00 p.m.
*Veg

PAPILLON WINE BAR &
BRASSERIE (B)
54 Cricklewood Lane
452 7856
✆ Willesden Green
7.00 p.m.–11.30 p.m.
*Veg *AC BC DC

NW3

AMERICAN

MAXWELL'S (A)
76 Heath Street
794 5450
✆ Hampstead
12.30 p.m.–midnight
*T/A *Open air *AC BC

SIMPLY STEAKS (B)
66 Heath Street
794 6775
✆ Hampstead
7.00 p.m.–11.00 p.m.
*Book *AC BC

AUSTRIAN

THE THIRD MAN (B)
30 Englands Lane
586 8619
✆ Belsize Park
Noon–midnight
Austrian/International menu
String quartet plays at lunch
Dinner/dance evenings
*Roast lunch *Veg *Book
*AC AX BC

CHINESE

DYNASTY OF
HAMPSTEAD (B)
291 Finchley Road
794 5920/5945
✆ Finchley Road
1.00 p.m.–11.00 p.m.
*Veg *T/A *Book *AC AX
BC DC

GOURMET RENDEZVOUS
(B)
263 Finchley Road
435 0755
✆ Finchley Road
Noon–3.00 p.m. &
6.00 p.m.–midnight
*Veg *T/A *Book *AC AX
BC DC

THE GREEN COTTAGE (C)
122a Finchley Road
794 3833/3969
● Finchley Road
Noon–3.00 p.m. &
6.00 p.m.–11.00 p.m.
Vegetarian food only
*Veg *Book *AC AX BC DC

THE GREEN COTTAGE (B)
9 New College Parade,
Finchley Road
722 5305
● Finchley Road/Swiss
Cottage
Noon–11.30 p.m.
Cantonese
*T/A

MANDARIN (B)
279c Finchley Road
794 6119
● Finchley Road
6.00 p.m.–11.30 p.m.
*Veg *T/A

MOONLIGHT (C)
42 Hampstead High Street
435 7632
● Hampstead
Noon–11.30 p.m.
*Veg *T/A *Book *AC AX
BC DC

WELCOME (B)
68 Belsize Lane
794 9217
● Belsize Park/Swiss Cottage
12.30 p.m.–2.30 p.m. &
6.00 p.m.–11.30 p.m.
*T/A *Book *AX DC

WENG WAH HOUSE (B)
240 Haverstock Hill
794 5123
● Belsize Park
Noon–midnight
*Veg *T/A *AC AX DC

ENGLISH

FARQUHARSONS (A)
1b Hampstead High Street
435 8278
● Hampstead
10.00 a.m.–midnight
Snacks and hot meals
*Breakfast *Tea *Veg *T/A
*Open air

FINCHES (B)
250 Finchley Road
435 8622
● Swiss Cottage
Noon–2.30 p.m. &
6.30 p.m.–midnight
English/French cuisine
*Roast lunch *Veg *T/A
*Book *AC AX BC DC

KENWOOD HOUSE
Hampstead Lane
348 8876
● Archway/Golders Green
– THE COACH HOUSE (A)
10.00 a.m.–5.30 p.m.
(4.15 p.m. in winter)
Cafeteria
*Roast lunch *Tea
*Not licensed *Open air *BC
– THE OLD KITCHEN (B)
Noon–4.30 p.m.
*Roast lunch *Tea *Book *BC

TURPIN'S   (C)
118 Heath Street
435 3791
♻ Hampstead
12.15 p.m.–2.30 p.m.
*Roast lunch *Open air
*Book *AC AX BC DC

FISH

LA GAFFE   (B)
107 Heath Street
435 8965/4941
♻ Hampstead
12.30 p.m.–3.00 p.m. &
7.00 p.m.–11.00 p.m.
Piano music and Sunday lunch
*Roast lunch *Open air
*Book *AC AX BC DC

FRENCH

BUNNY'S   (C)
7 Pond Street
435 1541
♻ Belsize Park
12.30 p.m.–2.30 p.m. &
7.00 p.m.–10.30 p.m.
Serves English lunch
*Roast lunch *Veg *Book
*AX DC

DOME   (B)
38 Hampstead High Street
435 4240
♻ Hampstead
9.00 a.m.–10.30 p.m.
Brasserie with occasional live
music
*Breakfast *Tea *Veg

FAGIN'S KITCHEN   (C)
82 Hampstead High Street
435 3608

♻ Hampstead
12.30 p.m.–2.30 p.m. &
7.00 p.m.–11.00 p.m.
*Roast lunch *Veg *Book
*AC AX BC DC

LE CELLIER DU MIDI   (C)
28 Church Row
435 9998
♻ Hampstead
Noon–2.00 p.m. &
7.00 p.m.–10.30 p.m.
*Book *AC AX BC DC

GREEK

SKORPIOS   (B)
559 Finchley Road
794 4179
♻ Golders Green
6.00 p.m.–2.00 a.m.
*Veg *T/A *AX BC

INDIAN

BEER & CURRY   (A)
58 Belsize Lane
794 8643
♻ Belsize Park/Swiss Cottage
Noon–midnight
Also Chinese/English food
*Veg *T/A *AC AX BC DC

BOMBAY   (B)
2 Elm Terrace,
Constantine Road
485 9921
♻ Belsize Park
Noon–11.00 p.m.
*Veg *T/A *AC AX BC DC

BULLOCK CART   (B)
77 Heath Street
435 3602

✪ Hampstead
12.30 p.m.–3.00 p.m. &
6.00 p.m.–midnight
*Veg *T/A *Book *AC AX
BC DC

GULISTAN TANDOORI (B)
73 Heath Street
435.3413
✪ Hampstead
Noon–11.00 p.m.
*T/A *Book *AC AX BC DC

HAWELLI (B)
102 Heath Street
431 0172/794 8057
✪ Hampstead
Noon–2.30 p.m. &
6.00 p.m.–11.30 p.m.
*Veg *T/A *Book *AC AX
BC DC

THE LIGHT OF KASHMIR
(B)
98 Fleet Road
485 6908
✪ Belsize Park
Noon–2.30 p.m. &
5.30 p.m.–11.00 p.m.
*Veg *T/A *AC AX BC DC

OM (B)
321 Finchley Road
794 0331
✪ Finchley Road
Noon–3.00 p.m. &
6.00 p.m.–11.00 p.m.
Vegetarian food only
*Veg *T/A *Book *AC AX
BC DC

RAJ OF HAMPSTEAD (B)
152 Haverstock Hill
722 5047

✪ Belsize Park
Noon–2.30 p.m. &
6.00 p.m.–midnight
*Veg *T/A *AC AX BC DC

INTERNATIONAL

HAMPSTEAD PÂTISSERIE
& TEA ROOMS (A)
9 South End Road
435 9563
✪ Belsize Park
9.30 a.m.–8.00 p.m.
*Breakfast *Tea
*Not licensed *Veg *T/A

HILL HOUSE (B)
216 Haverstock Hill
794 4125
✪ Belsize Park
Noon–10.30 p.m.
*Roast lunch *Veg *T/A
*Open air *Book *AC AX DC

LOUIS PÂTISSERIE (A)
12 Harben Parade,
Finchley Road
722 8100
✪ Swiss Cottage
and
32 Heath Street
435 9908
✪ Hampstead
9.30 a.m.–6.00 p.m.
Tea, coffee, pastries, cakes
*Tea *Not licensed *Veg *T/A

MARINE ICES (A)
8 Haverstock Hill
485 5298
✪ Chalk Farm
11.00 a.m.–10.00 p.m.
Ice cream only

THE MILK CHURN (B)
70 Heath Street
435 8444
✆ Hampstead
11.30 a.m.–midnight
Meals and ice cream
*Veg

PARKS (B)
83–84 Hampstead High
Street
435 6434
✆ Hampstead
11.00 a.m.–midnight
*Book *AC BC

PEPPERCORNS (B)
58–62 Heath Street
431 2439
✆ Hampstead
11.00 a.m.–1.00 a.m.
*Open air *AC AX BC DC

RUMBOLD'S TEA ROOMS
(A)
45 South End Road
435 4998
✆ Belsize Park/Hampstead
10.00 a.m.–6.00 p.m.
*Breakfast *Tea *Not licensed
*Veg *T/A

TINOT'S WINE BAR (B)
34 Rosslyn Hill
435 5203
✆ Belsize Park/Hampstead
7.00 p.m.–10.00 p.m.
Accordion music
*Veg *Open air *AX BC DC

ITALIAN

CIAO (B)
50 Belsize Lane
794 4981
✆ Belsize Park
6.00 p.m.–11.30 p.m.
Pasta/Wine Bar
*Veg *Open air *Book
*AC AX BC DC

LA BAITA (C)
200 Haverstock Hill
794 4126/2143
✆ Belsize Park
Noon–2.30 p.m. &
6.00 p.m.– 11.30 p.m.
*Veg *Open air *AC AX BC
DC

LA SORPRESA (C)
3 Heath Street
435 0024/794 4289
✆ Hampstead
12.30 p.m.–2.30 p.m. &
7.00 p.m.–11.30 p.m.
*Book *AC BC

PIZZA EXPRESS (A)
64 Heath Street
435 6722
✆ Hampstead
and
227 Finchley Road
794 5100
✆ Swiss Cottage
11.30 a.m.–midnight
*Veg *T/A

JAPANESE

WAKABA (D)
31 College Crescent
722 3854

⊖ Swiss Cottage
6.00 p.m.–11.00 p.m.
*T/A *Book *AC AX BC DC

JEWISH

FAY SCHNEIDER   (B)
7 New College Parade,
Finchley Road
722 7116
⊖ Finchley Road/Swiss
Cottage
11.30 a.m.–9.45 p.m.
*Veg *T/A *Open air *Book
*AC AX BC DC

VEGETARIAN

MANNA   (B)
4 Erskine Road
722 8028
⊖ Chalk Farm
6.30 p.m.–11.30 p.m.
*T/A

ZORBA THE BUDDHA
RAJNEESH   (B)
81 Belsize Park Gardens
722 6404/8220
⊖ Belsize Park/Swiss Cottage
8.00 a.m.–10.30 p.m.
*Breakfast *AX

NW4

INTERNATIONAL

CHAGLAYAN KEBAB
HOUSE   (B)
86 Brent Street
202 8575

⊖ Hendon Central
7.00 p.m.–midnight
Cypriot/Continental menu
*Veg *T/A *AC BC DC

JAPANESE

FUJII   (C)
27 Finchley Lane
203 0750
⊖ Hendon Central
6.00 p.m.–10.45 p.m.
*Veg *T/A *AC AX BC DC

NW5

FRENCH

LE PETIT PRINCE   (B)
5 Holmes Road
267 0752
⊖ Kentish Town
7.00 p.m.–11.15 p.m.
French/Algerian food
*Book

NW6

ENGLISH

ARCHES WINE BAR   (B)
7 Fairhazel Gardens
624 1867
⊖ Swiss Cottage
Noon–2.30 p.m.
*Roast lunch *Veg *Open Air
*Book *BC

PETER'S   (B)
65 Fairfax Road
624 5804

✆ Swiss Cottage/Finchley
Road
12.30 p.m.–3.00 p.m.
*Roast lunch *Veg *Open Air
*Book *AC AX BC DC

FRENCH

LA CLOCHE (B)
304 Kilburn High Road
328 0302
✆ Kilburn
Noon–3.00 p.m. &
7.00 p.m.–11.00 p.m.
*Veg *Book *BC

THE LANTERN (B)
23 Malvern Road
624 1796
✆ Maida Vale/Kilburn Park
Noon–3.00 p.m. &
7.00 p.m.–11.00 p.m.
*Veg *Open air *Book

INDIAN

BANGLADESH CUISINE (B)
327 West End Lane
435 3327
✆ West Hampstead
Noon–3.00 p.m. &
6.00 p.m.–midnight
*Veg *T/A *AC AX BC DC

GEETA (A)
57 Willesden Lane
624 1713
✆ Kilburn
Noon–3.00 p.m. &
6.00 p.m.–11.00 p.m.
*Veg *T/A *Book *AC BC

GULMARG (B)
227 Kilburn High Road
328 4351
✆ Kilburn
Noon–3.00 p.m. &
6.00 p.m.–11.30 p.m.
*Veg *T/A *Book *AC AX
BC DC

KILBURN TANDOORI (A)
22 Kilburn High Road
624 3154
✆ Kilburn Park
6.00 p.m.–midnight
*Veg *T/A *AC AX BC DC

LAL BHAG (B)
51 Kilburn High Road
624 5289
✆ Kilburn Park
Noon–3.00 p.m. &
6.00 p.m.–11.30 p.m.
*Veg *T/A *Book *AC AX
BC DC

RAFFLES (B)
391 Kilburn High Road
328 9070
✆ Kilburn
Noon–midnight
*Veg *T/A *AX BC DC

VIJAY (A)
49 Willesden Lane
328 1087
✆ Kilburn
Noon–2.45 p.m. &
6.00 p.m.–10.45 p.m.
*Veg *T/A *Book *AC AX
BC DC

INTERNATIONAL

HOBNOBS (A)
280 West End Lane
794 5857
✪ West Hampstead
7.00 p.m.–10.30 p.m.
Wine Bar
*Open air *AC BC

JOCKEY'S CLUB (B)
1 Broadhurst Gardens
328 0928
✪ Finchley Road
9.00 p.m.–3.00 a.m.
Restaurant/disco
*AC AX BC DC

No 77 WINE BAR (B)
77 Mill Lane
435 7787
✪ West Hampstead
7.00 p.m.–10.30 p.m.
*Veg *Open air * AC BC DC

TROTTERS (B)
2 Canfield Gardens
328 0340
✪ Finchley Road
7.00 p.m.–10.30 p.m.
*AC AX BC DC

NW7

CHINESE

GOOD EARTH (C)
143 The Broadway
959 7011
12.30 p.m.–2.45 p.m. &
6.00 p.m.–10.45 p.m.
*Veg *T/A *Book *AC AX
BC DC

TAI COON (B)
655 Watford Way
906 2632
Noon–midnight
*Veg *T/A *Book *AC AX
BC DC

NW8

CHINESE

LORD'S RENDEZVOUS (D)
24 Finchley Road
722 4750
✪ St John's Wood
Noon–2.00 p.m. &
7.00 p.m.–11.00 p.m.
*Veg *T/A *AC AX BC DC

ENGLISH

**KNIGHTS ON THE
PARK** (B)
41 Mackennal Street
722 5009
✪ St John's Wood
Noon–3.00 p.m. &
7.00 p.m.–10.30 p.m.
*Open air *AC AX BC DC

**LADBROKE
WESTMORELAND
HOTEL**
18 Lodge Road
722 7722
✪ St John's Wood
– LORD'S CARVER
RESTAURANT (C)
12.30 p.m.–2.00 p.m. &
6.00 p.m.–10.00 p.m.
*Roast lunch *AC AX BC DC

FRENCH

AU BOIS ST JEAN　　(C)
122 St John's Wood High
Street
722 0400
✪ St John's Wood
Noon–2.00 p.m. &
7.00 p.m.–10.30 p.m.
*Book *AC AX BC DC

INDIAN

MEGHNA GRILL　　(A)
113 Boundary Road
624 2595
✪ St John's Wood
Noon–2.30 p.m. &
6.00 p.m.–11.30 p.m.
*Veg *T/A *Book *AC AX
BC DC

INTERNATIONAL

BARACCA　　(B)
3 Circus Road
722 9303/1592
✪ St John's Wood
Noon–3.00 p.m. &
6.00 p.m.–10.30 p.m.
*Open Air *Book *AC AX BC
DC

**OSLO COURT
RESTAURANT**　　(C)
Prince Albert Road
722 8795
✪ St John's Wood
Noon–3.00 p.m.
*Roast lunch *Veg *Open Air
*Book *AC AX BC DC

ITALIAN

FONTANA AMOROSA　　(C)
1 Blenheim Terrace
328 5014
✪ St John's Wood
12.30 p.m.–2.30 p.m.
*Roast lunch *Veg *Open Air
*AC AX BC DC

ROSSETTI　　(B)
23 Queen's Grove
722 7141
✪ St John's Wood
12.30 p.m.–2.45 p.m. &
7.00 p.m.–11.00 p.m.
*Open Air *Book *AC AX BC
DC

JEWISH

HARRY MORGAN'S　　(B)
31 St John's Wood High Street
722 1869
✪ St John's Wood
Noon–10.00 p.m.

SPANISH

DON PEPE　　(B)
99 Frampton Street
262 3834/723 9749
✪ Edgware Road
Noon–2.30 p.m. &
7.00 p.m.–10.30 p.m.
Guitar music
*Veg *Book *AC BC DC

NW10

AMERICAN

MEAN FIDDLER (B)
28a Harlesden High Street
961 5490
✪ Willesden Junction
Noon–2.00 p.m. &
9.00 p.m.–1.00 a.m.
Live music – folk/country
*Book *AC

CHINESE

KUO YUAN (B)
217 High Road
459 2297
✪ Dollis Hill
Noon–2.30 p.m. &
6.00 p.m.–11.00 p.m.
*T/A *Book

INDIAN

KHAS TANDOORI (A)
39 Chamberlayne Road
969 2537
✪ Queen's Park/Kensal
Green
Noon–3.00 p.m. &
6.00 p.m.–midnight
*Veg *T/A *AC AX BC DC

SAB-RAS (B)
263 High Road
459 0340
✪ Dollis Hill
12.30 p.m.–9.15 p.m.
*Not licensed *Veg *T/A
*Book *AC AX BC DC

NW11

CHINESE

PEKING DUCK (B)
30 Temple Fortune Parade,
Finchley Road
455 9444
✪ Golders Green
Noon–2.30 p.m. &
6.00 p.m.–11.30 p.m.
*T/A *Book *AC AX BC DC

INDIAN

MOGUL ROOM (B)
757 Finchley Road
455 9497
✪ Golders Green
Noon–3.00 p.m. &
5.30 p.m.–midnight
*Veg *T/A *Book *AC AX
BC DC

ITALIAN

CAPRICCIO (B)
20 Temple Fortune Parade,
Finchley Road
455 4432
✪ Golders Green
Noon–2.30 p.m. &
6.00 p.m.–11.00 p.m.
Italian/French cuisine
*Book *AC AX BC DC

IL CAVALIERE (B)
14 North End Road
455 3849
✪ Golders Green
Noon–3.00 p.m. &
6.00 p.m.–11.30 p.m.
*Book *AC AX BC DC

VILLA DEI FIORE (C)
38 North End Road
458 6344
✆ Golders Green
12.15 p.m.–2.15 p.m. &
6.30 p.m.–11.00 p.m.
Piano music at night
*Book *AC AX BC DC

JEWISH

BLOOM'S (B)
130 Golders Green Road
455 3033
✆ Golders Green
9.30 a.m.–9.30 p.m.
*T/A *Book *AC BC

ZAKI'S (C)
634 Finchley Road
458 2012
✆ Golders Green
Noon–2.30 p.m. &
6.00 p.m.–11.00 p.m.
*Veg *Book *AC AX BC DC

SE1

INDIAN

CASTLE TANDOORI (B)
200 Elephant & Castle
Shopping Centre
703 9130
✆ Elephant & Castle
4.00 p.m.–midnight
*Veg *T/A *Book *AX BC
DC

INTERNATIONAL

ROYAL FESTIVAL HALL
Belvedere Road
Recorded information: 928
3002
✆ Waterloo/Embankment
*AC AX BC DC
– COFFEE LOUNGE (A)
(Level 2)
10.00 a.m.–10.30 p.m.
*Tea
– FESTIVAL BUFFET (B)
(Level 2)
12.30 p.m.–2.30 p.m. &
5.30 p.m.–10.30 p.m.
– PIZZA & SALT BEEF BAR
(A)
(Level 2)
Noon–3.00 p.m.
& 5.30 p.m.–7.30 p.m.
– RIVERSIDE CAFÉ (B)
(Level 1)
10.00 a.m.–10.00 p.m.
Jazz in the evening

SE3

FRENCH

LA GOULUE (C)
17 Montpelier Vale
852 9226
BR Blackheath
7.00 p.m.–10.30 p.m.
*Book

INDIAN

SOPNA TANDOORI (B)
39 Tranquil Vale
852 7872

BR Blackheath
Noon–3.00 p.m. &
6.00 p.m.–midnight
*Veg *T/A *Book *AC AX
BC DC

SE4

INDIAN

INDIANA TANDOORI   (A)
14a Brockley Close
692 9040
BR Brockley
5.30 p.m.–midnight
*Veg *T/A *AC AX BC DC

SE5

INTERNATIONAL

BARTHOLOMEW'S WINE
BAR   (A)
54 Camberwell Church Street
708 1097
❷ Oval
7.00 p.m.–10.30 p.m.
*Veg *AC AX BC DC

ITALIAN

NEW LA BELLE ITALIA (B)
163 Camberwell Road
701 8760
BR Denmark Hill
Noon–midnight
*Veg *T/A *Book *AC BC

SE8

TURKISH

MARMARA   (B)
166 Evelyn Street
692 5557
❷Surrey Docks
6.00 p.m.–12.30 a.m.
*Veg *Book *AC BC

SE9

INTERNATIONAL

MELLINS   (A)
90 Eltham High Street
850 4462
BR Eltham Well Hall
7.00 p.m.–10.30 p.m.
Wine Bar
*AC AX BC DC

SE10

CHINESE

Mr CHUNG   (B)
166 Trafalgar Road
858 6424/4245
BR Maze Hill
1.00 p.m.–midnight
*Veg *T/A *Book *AC AX
BC DC

FRENCH

BRANDIES   (B)
13 Nelson Road
853 4385

BR Greenwich
Noon–midnight
Many fish dishes served
*Roast lunch *Book
*AC AX BC DC

GACHON'S (B)
269 Creek Road
853 4461
BR Greenwich
11.30 a.m.–4.30 p.m.
French/English food
*T/A *Book

LE PREMIER CRU (B)
328 Creek Road
858 9222
BR Greenwich
Noon–3.00 p.m.
French/English food
*Book *AC AX BC DC

INDIAN

GREENWICH TANDOORI
(B)

17 Colomb Street
858 1913
BR Maze Hill
Noon–2.30 p.m. &
6.00 p.m.–midnight
*Veg *T/A *Book *AC AX
BC

MOGUL (B)
10 Greenwich Church Street
858 6790
BR Greenwich
Noon–2.30 p.m. &
6.00 p.m.–11.30 p.m.
*Veg *T/A *AC AX BC DC

INTERNATIONAL

BAR DU MUSÉE (B)
17 Nelson Road
858 4710
BR Greenwich
Noon–1.45 p.m. &
7.00 p.m.–10.00 p.m.
*Open air *Book *AC AX BC
DC

MEANTIME (B)
47 Greenwich Church Street
858 8705
BR Greenwich
Noon–2.30 p.m.
*Brunch *AC AX BC DC

ORTON'S KITCHEN (B)
16 Nelson Road
858 3877
BR Greenwich
Noon–3.00 p.m. &
6.00 p.m.–11.00 p.m.
*Veg *Book *AC AX BC DC

SE11

INDIAN

GANDHI'S (B)
347a Kennington Road
735 9015
● Oval
Noon–2.30 p.m. &
6.00 p.m.–11.45 p.m.
*Veg *T/A *AC AX BC DC

SE13

INDIAN

CURRY GARDEN (B)
318 Lee High Road
852 9891
BR Lewisham
Noon–2.30 p.m. &
6.00 p.m.–midnight
*Veg *T/A *AC AX BC DC

SE16

ENGLISH

DOWNTOWN (B)
4 Odessa Street
231 8838
✆ Rotherhithe/Surrey Docks
12.30 p.m.–2.45 p.m.
*Roast lunch *Veg *Open air
*Book *AC AX BC DC

SE21

INTERNATIONAL

LONDON STEAK HOUSE
(B)
96 Dulwich Village
693 6880
BR West Dulwich
Noon–3.00 p.m. &
7.00 p.m.–10.00 p.m.
*Veg *Book *AC AX BC DC

SE22

CHINESE

Mr LIU (B)
148 Lordship Lane
693 8266
5.30 p.m.–10.30 p.m.
*T/A *Book *AX BC DC

FRENCH

LE MOULIN (B)
377 Lordship Lane
693 7600
Noon–2.30 p.m. &
7.00 p.m.–11.30 p.m.
French/English menu
*Roast lunch *Veg *Open Air
*Book *AC AX BC DC

THE PYRAMID (B)
78 East Dulwich Grove
693 0372
BR East Dulwich
Noon–3.00 p.m.
French/English menu
*Roast lunch *Open Air
*Book *AC AX BC

INDIAN

DULWICH TANDOORI (A)
54 Lordship Lane
693 3012
Noon–3.00 p.m. &
6.00 p.m.–midnight
*Veg *T/A *Book *AC AX
BC DC

SE23

INDIAN

DEWANIAM (B)
133 Stanstead Road
291 4778
BR Forest Hill
Noon–2.30 p.m. &
5.30 p.m.–midnight
*Veg *T/A *Book *AC AX
BC DC

SE24

FRENCH

BON TON ROULET (B)
127 Dulwich Road
733 8701
⊖ Brixton
12.30 p.m.–2.30 p.m.
Two sittings for English lunch
*Roast lunch *Not licensed
*Veg *Book

SE26

ENGLISH

DELVINO'S (B)
124 Kirkdale
699 9946
BR Sydenham
Noon–4.00 p.m.
*Roast lunch *Veg *Book
*AX BC

INTERNATIONAL

MISTER MOON'S (B)
82 Sydenham Road
659 2030
BR Sydenham
12.15 p.m.–2.00 p.m.
*Roast lunch *Veg *Open Air
*Book *AC AX BC DC

SW1

AMERICAN

HAMBURGER HEAVEN (A)
11 Knightsbridge
235 5550
⊖ Hyde Park Corner
10.00 a.m.–midnight
part of Pizza On The Park
*T/A *AX

SLOANES 208 (B)
116 Knightsbridge
589 6520
⊖ Knightsbridge
Noon–midnight
*T/A *AC AX BC DC

CHINESE

Mr CHOW (D)
151 Knightsbridge
589 7347
⊖ Knightsbridge
12.30 p.m.–2.45 p.m. &
7.00 p.m.–midnight
*Veg *Book *AC AX BC DC

ENGLISH

CHIMES (B)
26 Churton Street
821 7456
✪ Pimlico/Victoria
Noon–2.30 p.m. &
7.00 p.m.–10.00 p.m.
*Roast lunch *Veg *Book
*AC AX BC

DUKES HOTEL
35 St James's Place
491 4840
✪ Green Park
– THE RESTAURANT (C)
12.30 p.m.–2.00 p.m. &
7.00 p.m.–10.00 p.m.
English/French cuisine
*Veg *Book *AC AX BC DC

GORING HOTEL
15 Beeston Place
834 8211
✪ Victoria
4.00 p.m.–5.00 p.m.
*Tea
– THE RESTAURANT (C)
12.30 p.m.–3.00 p.m. &
6.30 p.m.–9.30 p.m.
*Roast lunch *Book
*AC AX BC DC

GRANDMA LEE'S (A)
2 Bridge Street
839 1319
✪ Westminster
7.00 a.m.–9.00 p.m.
*Breakfast *Tea *Veg *T/A

GRUMBLES (B)
35 Churton Street
834 0149

✪ Pimlico/Victoria
1.00 p.m.–3.00 p.m.
*Roast lunch *Open Air
*Book *AC AX BC DC

HOLIDAY INN
17 Sloane Street
235 4377
✪ Knightsbridge
7.00 a.m.–11.30 a.m.
*Breakfast
– PAPILLON (C)
Noon–3.00 p.m. &
7.00 p.m.–10.30 p.m.
*Roast lunch *Book
*AC AX BC DC

HYDE PARK HOTEL
66 Knightsbridge
235 2000
✪ Knightsbridge
(see also 'International')
– THE GRILL ROOM (D)
12.30 p.m.–2.30 p.m. &
7.00 p.m.–10.00 p.m.
*Roast lunch *Veg *Book
*AC AX BC DC

METHUSELAH'S (B)
29 Victoria Street
222 0424
✪ St James's Park
10.00 a.m.–5.00 p.m.
Brasserie
*Veg *Open Air *AC AX BC
DC

ST ERMIN'S HOTEL
Caxton Street
222 7888
✪ St James's Park
3.00 p.m.–6.00 p.m.
*Tea

– THE CARVERY (B)
12.30 p.m.–2.30 p.m. &
6.00 p.m.–9.30 p.m.
English/French food
*Roast lunch *Veg *Book
*AC AX BC DC

SHERATON PARK
TOWER HOTEL
101 Knightsbridge
235 8050
◉Knightsbridge
8.00 a.m.–noon
*Breakfast
3.00 p.m.–5.30 p.m.
*Tea
–THE RESTAURANT (D)
Noon–3.00 p.m. &
6.00 p.m.–midnight
*Brunch *Veg *Book
*AC AX BC DC

UPPER CRUST IN
BELGRAVIA (B)
9 William Street
235 8444
◉ Knightsbridge
10.00 a.m.–6.00 p.m.
*Breakfast *Roast lunch *Tea
*Veg *Open Air *Book
*AC AX BC DC

FISH

CARAFE (C)
15 Lowndes Street
235 2525
◉ Knightsbridge
12.30 p.m.–2.20 p.m. &
7.00 p.m.–10.20 p.m.
*Veg *Open Air *Book
*AC AX BC DC

FRENCH

THE BERKELEY HOTEL
Wilton Place
235 6000
◉ Hyde Park Corner
– THE RESTAURANT (E)
12.45 p.m.–2.15 p.m. &
7.00 p.m.–10.15 p.m.
*Book *AC AX BC

HYATT CARLTON
TOWER HOTEL
2 Cadogan Place
235 5411
◉ Knightsbridge
(see also 'International')
3.00 p.m.–5.30 p.m.
*Tea
– THE CHELSEA ROOM (D)
Noon–3.00 p.m. &
7.00 p.m.–10.00 p.m.
Piano music in the evening
*Veg *Book *AC AX BC DC

LA BRASSERIE AT
DOLPHIN SQUARE (A)
Dolphin Square
828 3207
◉ Pimlico
7.30 a.m.–11.30 a.m. (only)
*Breakfast

LE CAPRICE (D)
Arlington House
Arlington Street
629 2239
◉ Green Park
Noon–3.00 p.m. &
7.00 p.m.–midnight
Piano music in the evening
*Brunch *Veg *Book
*AC AX BC DC

MAXINE'S DES CHAMPS
ELYSÉES (D)
142 Victoria Street
828 0512
✪ Victoria
11.00 a.m.–midnight
*Veg *Book *AC AX BC DC

ROYAL HORSEGUARDS
HOTEL
2 Whitehall Court
839 3400
✪ Embankment
– COFFEE CORNER (A)
11.00 a.m.–11.15 p.m.
Snacks and light meals
*Tea
– GRANBY'S (C)
12.30 p.m.–2.30 p.m. &
6.00 p.m.–10.30 p.m.
*Veg *Book *AC AX BC DC

GREEK

ACROPOLIS KEBAB
HOUSE (B)
1 Denbigh Street
828 2471
✪ Victoria
6.00 p.m.–10.30 p.m.
Greek/Turkish/English food
*Veg *Book *AC AX BC DC

INDIAN

PIMLICO TANDOORI (B)
38 Moreton Street
834 3375
✪ Pimlico
Noon–3.00 p.m. &
6.00 p.m.–midnight
*Veg *T/A *Book *AC AX
BC DC

YASMINE (C)
278 Vauxhall Bridge Road
834 5413
✪ Victoria
Noon–3.00 p.m. &
6.00 p.m.–midnight
*Veg *T/A *AC BC DC

INTERNATIONAL

A L'ÉCU DE FRANCE (D)
111 Jermyn Street
930 2837
✪ Piccadilly Circus
7.00 p.m.–10.30 p.m.
Piano music
*Veg *Book *AC AX BC DC

BELGRAVIA SHERATON
HOTEL
20 Chesham Place
235 6040
✪ Knightsbridge/Hyde Park
Corner
8.00 a.m.–10.00 a.m.
*Breakfast
3.00 p.m.–5.30 p.m.
*Tea
– THE RESTAURANT (C)
12.30 p.m.–2.30 p.m. &
7.00 p.m.–10.30 p.m.
Piano music in the evening
*Veg *Book *AC AX BC DC

CADOGAN HOTEL
75 Sloane Street
235 7141
✪ Sloane Square/
Knightsbridge
*Tea
– LILLIE'S (B)
11.30 a.m.–10.00 p.m.
*Book *AC AX BC DC

THE CAVENDISH HOTEL
Jermyn Street
930 2111
♦ Piccadilly Circus/Green
Park
3.00 p.m.–5.30 p.m.
*Tea
– THE CAVENDISH   (D)
12.30 p.m.–3.00 p.m. &
7.00 p.m.–11.00 p.m.
American jazz lunch
French menu in evening
*Brunch *Veg *Book
*AC AX BC DC

DRONES   (D)
1 Pont Street
235 9638
♦ Knightsbridge
12.30 p.m.–3.00 p.m. &
7.30 p.m.–11.00 p.m.
*Veg *T/A *Book *AC AX
BC DC

EBURY WINE BAR   (B)
139 Ebury Street
730 5447
♦ Victoria/Sloane Square
Noon–2.30 p.m. &
7.00 p.m.–10.00 p.m.
Traditional music
*Veg *Book *AC AX BC DC

HYATT CARLTON
TOWER HOTEL
2 Cadogan Place
235 5411
♦ Knightsbridge
(see also 'French')

– THE RIB ROOM   (E)
12.30 p.m.–2.30 p.m. &
7.00 p.m.–10.30 p.m.
*Book *AC AX BC DC

HYDE PARK HOTEL
66 Knightsbridge
235 2000
♦ Knightsbridge
(see also 'English')
7.30 a.m.–11.00 a.m.
*Breakfast
3.45 p.m.–6.00 p.m.
Piano music from 4.00 p.m.
*Tea
– THE PARK ROOM   (D)
12.30 p.m.–2.30 p.m. &
7.00 p.m.–11.00 p.m.
Buffet lunch
French/English menu and
piano music in the evening
*Veg *Book *AC AX BC DC

L'EXPRESS   (A)
16 Sloane Street
235 9869
♦ Knightsbridge
11.00 a.m.–6.00 p.m.
Café
*Not licensed *Veg
*AC AX BC DC

ROWLEY'S   (B)
113 Jermyn Street
930 2707
♦ Piccadilly Circus
Noon–2.30 p.m. &
6.00 p.m.–11.00 p.m.
*AC AX BC DC

THE STOCKPOT   (A)
40 Panton Street
839 5142

✪ Piccadilly Circus
Noon–10.00 p.m.
*Veg *T/A

THE TENT (C)
15 Eccleston Street
730 6922
✪ Victoria
12.30 p.m.–3.00 p.m. &
7.00 p.m.–11.00 p.m.
*Book *AC AX BC

THE WREN AT
ST JAMES'S (A)
35 Jermyn Street
437 9419
✪ Piccadilly Circus
10.30 a.m.–4.00 p.m.
Snacks and salads
*Not licensed *Veg
*Open Air

ITALIAN

LA FONTANA (C)
101 Pimlico Road
730 6630
✪ Sloane Square
Noon–2.30 p.m. &
7.00 p.m.–11.00 p.m.
*Veg *Book *AX BC DC

PIZZA EXPRESS (A)
154 Victoria Street
828 1477
✪ Victoria
11.30 a.m.–midnight
*Veg *T/A

PIZZA ON THE PARK (A)
11 Knightsbridge
235 5550

✪ Hyde Park Corner
11.30 a.m.–midnight
*Veg *T/A *AX

SIGNOR CAMPARI (C)
22 Brompton Road
589 8772
✪ Knightsbridge
Noon–2.30 p.m. &
7.00 p.m.–11.00 p.m.
*Veg *Book *AC AX DC

VILLA DEI CESARI (F)
135 Grosvenor Road
834 9872
✪ Pimlico
8.00 p.m.–2.00 a.m.
Dinner/dance
*Veg *Book *AC AX BC DC

SW2

ITALIAN

PIZZA PLUS (A)
96 Streatham Hill
674 1519
BR Streatham Hill
Noon–midnight
*Veg *T/A *AC BC

SW3

AMERICAN

THE AMERICAN
HAMBURGER
RESTAURANT (C)
190 King's Road
352 7182

⊖ Sloane Square
11.30 a.m.–11.30 p.m.
*T/A *AC AX BC DC

HENRY J. BEAN'S (B)
195 King's Road
352 9255
⊖ Sloane Square
Noon–10.30 p.m.
*Tea *Veg *Open Air

WOLFE'S (B)
25 Basil Street
589 8444
⊖ Knightsbridge
11.30 a.m.–midnight
*T/A *Open Air *AC AX BC
DC

CHINESE

CHELSEA RENDEZVOUS
(D)
4 Sydney Street
352 9519
⊖ South Kensington
Noon–2.30 p.m. &
7.00 p.m.–11.30 p.m.
*T/A *Book *AC AX BC DC

CHOY'S (B)
172 King's Road
352 9085
⊖ Sloane Square
Noon–midnight
*Veg *T/A *Book *AC AX
BC DC

DUMPLING HOUSE (B)
9 Beauchamp Place
589 8240
⊖ Knightsbridge

Noon–midnight
*Veg *T/A *Book *AC AX
BC DC

GOOD EARTH (C)
233 Brompton Road
584 3658
⊖ South Kensington
and
91 King's Road
352 9231/4692
⊖ Sloane Square
12.30 p.m.–2.45 p.m. &
6.00 p.m.–10.45 p.m.
*Veg *T/A *Book *AC AX
BC DC

HO LEE FOOK (B)
368 King's Road
352 6797
⊖ Sloane Square
Noon–11.15 p.m.
*T/A *AC AX BC DC

TAI-PAN (D)
8 Egerton Gardens Mews
589 8287
⊖ South Kensington
Noon–2.30 p.m. &
7.00 p.m.–11.30 p.m.
*Veg *T/A *Book *AC AX
BC DC

ZEN (C)
Chelsea Cloisters,
Sloane Avenue
589 1781
⊖ South Kensington
Noon–11.00 p.m.
*Book *AC AX BC DC

ENGLISH

DRAKES (D)
2a Pond Place
584 4555
✆ South Kensington
12.30 p.m.–2.30 p.m. &
7.30 p.m.–10.30 p.m.
*Roast lunch *Veg *Book
*AC AX BC DC

THE ENGLISH GARDEN (E)
10 Lincoln Street
584 7272
✆ Sloane Square
12.30 p.m.–2.00 p.m. &
7.30 p.m.–11.15 p.m.
*Veg *Book *AC AX BC DC

THE ENGLISH HOUSE (D)
3 Milner Street
584 3002
✆ South Kensington
12.30 p.m.–2.30 p.m. &
7.30 p.m.–9.00 p.m.
*Roast lunch *Veg *Book
*AC AX BC DC

NINETEEN (B)
19 Mossop Street
589 4971
✆ South Kensington
Noon–3.00 p.m. &
7.00 p.m.–11.45 p.m.
*Roast lunch

REFLECTIONS (C)
85 King's Road
352 1008
✆ Sloane Square
Noon–4.00 p.m.
*Roast lunch *Book
*AC AX BC DC

WALTONS (E)
121 Walton Street
584 0204
✆ South Kensington
12.30 p.m.–2.00 p.m. &
7.30 p.m.–10.30 p.m.
*Roast lunch *Book
*AC AX BC DC

FISH

LE SUQUET (D)
104 Draycott Avenue
581 1785
✆ South Kensington
12.30 p.m.–3.00 p.m. &
7.30 p.m.–11.30 p.m.
*Open Air *Book *AX

FRENCH

ASTRIX (A)
329 King's Road
352 3891
✆ Sloane Square
Noon–midnight
Crêperie
*Veg

BEWICKS (E)
78–79 Walton Street
584 6711
✆ South Kensington/
Knightsbridge
7.30 p.m.–10.30 p.m.
*AC AX BC DC

BRASSERIE DES AMIS (D)
27 Basil Street
584 9012
✆ Knightsbridge
11.30 a.m.–3.00 p.m. &
5.30 p.m.–10.00 p.m.
*Open Air *AC AX BC DC

BRASSERIE ST QUENTIN (D)
243 Brompton Road
589 8005
☻ South Kensington
10.00 a.m.–11.00 a.m.
*Breakfast
4.00 p.m.–6.00 p.m.
*Tea
Noon–4.00 p.m. &
7.00 p.m.–11.30 p.m.
*Veg *Book *AC AX BC DC

CAFÉ BOUCHON (C)
362 King's Road
352 0074
☻ Sloane Square
Noon–2.30 p.m. &
7.00 p.m.–11.30 p.m.
*Open Air *AC AX BC DC

CAPITAL HOTEL
22 Basil Street
589 5171
☻ Knightsbridge
7.00 a.m.–10.00 a.m.
*Breakfast
2.00 p.m.–6.00 p.m.
*Tea
– THE RESTAURANT (E)
12.30 p.m.–1.45 p.m. &
7.00 p.m.–9.45 p.m.
*Book *AC AX BC DC

DOMINIC'S (C)
249 King's Road
352 1918
☻ Sloane Square
Noon–2.30 p.m. &
6.00 p.m.–11.30 p.m.
*Roast lunch *Veg *Open Air
*Book *AC AX BC DC

LA BRASSERIE (D)
272 Brompton Road
584 1668
☻ South Kensington
11.00 a.m.–midnight
*Breakfast *Open Air
*Book *AC AX BC DC

LA POPOTE (C)
3 Walton Street
589 9178
☻ Knightsbridge
1.00 p.m.–3.00 p.m. &
8.00 p.m.–11.30 p.m.
*Roast lunch *Veg *Open Air
*Book *AX BC DC

MES AMIS (D)
31 Basil Street
584 4484
☻ Knightsbridge
12.15 p.m.–3.00 p.m. &
7.15 p.m.–11.00 p.m.
*Open Air *Book *AC AX BC
DC

QUEENIES (C)
338 King's Road
352 9669
☻ Sloane Square
12.30 p.m.–2.30 p.m. &
7.00 p.m.–11.00 p.m.
*Roast lunch *Veg *Book
*AC AX BC DC

INDIAN

SHAHEEN OF KNIGHTSBRIDGE (B)
225 Brompton Road
581 5329
☻ Knightsbridge

Noon–11.30 p.m.
*Veg *T/A *Book *AC AX
BC DC

TANDOORI ASHOKA (B)
181 Fulham Road
352 3301
✪ South Kensington
Noon–2.30 p.m. &
6.00 p.m.–11.30 p.m.
*Veg *T/A *AC BC DC

TANDOORI OF CHELSEA
(C)
153 Fulham Road
589 7617
✪ South Kensington
12.30 p.m.–3.00 p.m. &
6.30 p.m.–11.30 p.m.
*Veg *T/A *Book *AC AX
BC DC

INTERNATIONAL

AVOIRDUPOIS (D)
334 King's Road
352 4071
✪ Sloane Square
Noon–3.00 p.m. &
7.15 p.m.–10.45 p.m.
*Brunch *Roast lunch
*Veg *Book *AC AX BC DC

BASIL STREET HOTEL
Basil Street
581 3311
✪ Knightsbridge
8.00 a.m.–10.00 a.m.
*Breakfast
– THE RESTAURANT (C)
12.30 p.m.–2.15 p.m. &
7.00 p.m.–9.30 p.m.

Piano music in the evening
*Roast lunch *Book
*AC AX BC DC

BISTRO VINO (B)
303 Brompton Road
589 7898
✪ South Kensington
Noon–3.00 p.m. &
6.00 p.m.–11.45 p.m.
*Veg

BLUSHES (B)
52 King's Road
589 6640
✪ Sloane Square
Noon–10.30 p.m.
Wine Bar/brasserie
*Veg *Open Air *Book
*AC AX BC DC

BOUZY ROUGE (A)
221 King's Road
351 1607
✪ Sloane Square
7.00 p.m.–11.00 p.m.
Wine Bar
*Veg *T/A *Open Air
*AC AX BC DC

CHELSEA POT (A)
356 King's Road
351 3605
✪ Sloane Square
Noon–11.30 p.m.
*Tea *Veg

DRAYCOTT'S (B)
114 Draycott Avenue
584 5359
✪ South Kensington
11.30 a.m.–2.00 p.m. &
7.00 p.m.–10.30 p.m.

Wine bar – no food served in
the evening
*Brunch *Veg *AC AX BC
DC

FOXTROT OSCAR (C)
79 Royal Hospital Road
352 7179
☻ Sloane Square
11.30 a.m.–2.30 p.m. &
7.30 p.m.–10.30 p.m.
*Brunch *Roast lunch *Veg
*Book *AC BC

HUFF'S (A)
Chelsea Farmers Market,
125 Sydney Street
352 5600
☻ South Kensington
10.30 a.m.–5.30 p.m.
*Breakfast *Tea *Not licensed
*Veg *T/A *Open Air

THE PHEASANTRY CAFÉ
(C)
152 King's Road
351 3084
☻ Sloane Square
Noon–11.00 p.m.
*Tea *Veg *Open Air *AC AX
DC

PIER 31 (D)
31 Cheyne Walk
352 5006
☻ Sloane Square
Noon–2.30 p.m. &
7.00 p.m.–11.30 p.m.
Japanese/French/Italian menu
Jazz piano in the evening
*Veg *Open Air *Book
*AC AX BC DC

ROWLEY'S (B)
38 Beauchamp Place
589 4856
☻ Knightsbridge
Noon–2.30 p.m. &
6.00 p.m.–11.00 p.m.
*AC AX BC DC

ITALIAN

DON LUIGI (C)
316 King's Road
352 0025
☻ Sloane Square
12.30 p.m.–3.00 p.m. &
6.30 p.m.–11.45 p.m.
Piano music in the evening
*Veg *AC AX BC DC

MERIDIANA (D)
169 Fulham Road
589 8815
☻ South Kensington
Noon–3.00 p.m. &
7.00 p.m.–11.30 p.m.
Piano music
*Veg *Open air *Book
*AC AX BC DC

PICASSO (A)
127 King's Road
352 4921
☻ Sloane Square
9.00 a.m.–11.00 p.m.
Café
*Breakfast *T/A *Open Air

PIZZA POMODORO (A)
51 Beauchamp Place
584 3491
☻ Knightsbridge
Noon–1.00 a.m.

Pizza and pasta and live
country music
*Veg *T/A *Book

PONTENUOVO (D)
126 Fulham Road
370 6656
✪ South Kensington
Noon–4.00 p.m. &
7.30 p.m.–11.30 p.m.
*Open Air *Book *AC AX BC
DC

THIRTEEN AND A HALF
(C)
13 Beauchamp Place
584 0798
✪ Knightsbridge
7.00 p.m.–10.30 p.m.
*Veg *Book *AC AX BC DC

TOSCANINI (C)
330 King's Road
351 3634
✪ Sloane Square
7.00 p.m.–11.30 p.m.
*Veg *Open Air *Book *AC
BC

TOTO'S (D)
Lennox Gardens Mews,
Walton Street
589 0075
✪ Knightsbridge
12.30 p.m.–3.30 p.m. &
7.30 p.m.–11.30 p.m.
*Open Air *Book *AC AX BC

PORTUGUESE

CARAVELA (B)
39 Beauchamp Place
584 2163
✪ Knightsbridge

7.00 p.m.–midnight
Portuguese/French menu and
fado singing
*Book *AC AX BC DC

O FADO (C)
50 Beauchamp Place
589 3002
✪ Knightsbridge
7.00 p.m.–midnight
Live music
*Book *AC AX BC DC

RUSSIAN

BORSHTCH 'N' CHEERS(C)
273 King's Road
352 5786
✪ Sloane Square
6.30 p.m.–midnight
Guitar music
*Veg *AX DC

BORSHTCH N'TEARS (C)
46 Beauchamp Place
584 9911
✪ Knightsbridge
6.00 p.m.–midnight
Guitar music
*Veg *Book *AC AX BC DC

SW4

ENGLISH

CHANGING TIMES (B)
22 North Street
720 9559
✪ Clapham Common
1.00 p.m.–3.00 p.m.
*Roast lunch *Veg *Book
*AC AX BC DC

INDIAN

GOLDEN CURRY (B)
131 Clapham High Street
720 9558
⊖ Clapham Common
Noon–midnight
*Veg *T/A *Book *AC AX
BC DC

MAHARANI (B)
117 Clapham High Street
622 2530
⊖ Clapham Common
Noon–12.30 a.m.
*Veg *T/A *Book
*AC AX BC DC

NEW AGRA (B)
10 Clapham Common
Southside
622 4470/720 5149
⊖ Clapham Common
Noon–midnight
*Veg *T/A *Book *AC AX
BC DC

SHAH IN SHAH (B)
126 Clapham High Street
622 0452
⊖ Clapham Common
1.00 p.m.–midnight
*Veg *T/A *Book *AC AX
BC DC

STANDARD (A)
172 Clapham High Street
622 0926
⊖ Clapham Common
Noon–midnight
*Veg *T/A *AC AX BC DC

INTERNATIONAL

METRO (A)
9 Clapham Common
Southside
627 0632
⊖ Clapham Common
12.30 p.m.–2.00 p.m. &
7.00 p.m.–10.30 p.m.
*Roast lunch *Veg *Open air

ORMES WINE BAR (A)
67 Abbeville Road
673 2568
⊖ Clapham Common
Noon–2.30 p.m. &
7.00 p.m.–10.30 p.m.
*Roast lunch *Veg *Open Air
*AC AX BC DC

TEA TIME (A)
21 The Pavement
622 4944
⊖ Clapham Common
10.00 a.m.–7.00 p.m.
Coffee shop/tea room
*Breakfast *Tea *Not licensed

SW5

AFRICAN

BALOGUN'S (C)
241 Old Brompton Road
373 8217
⊖ Earls Court
Noon–3.00 p.m. &
6.00 p.m.–midnight
*Veg *Open Air *AC AX BC
DC

AMERICAN

HUBY'S   (A)
159 Old Brompton Road
373 1926
⊖ Gloucester Road
11.30 a.m.–midnight
Burgers/pizzas etc.
*Veg *T/A *Open Air *Book

CHINESE

CRYSTAL PALACE   (B)
10 Hogarth Place
373 0754
⊖ Earls Court
Noon–2.30 p.m. &
6.00 p.m.–11.30 p.m.
*Veg *T/A *Book *AC AX
BC DC

HONG KONG   (C)
15 Kenway Road
370 5920
⊖ Earls Court
Noon–midnight
*T/A at 14 Hogarth Road
*Veg *AC AX BC DC

NEW LOTUS GARDEN (C)
257 Old Brompton Road
370 4450
⊖ Earls Court
1.00 p.m.–12.30 a.m.
*Veg *T/A *Book *AC AX
BC DC

TIGER LEE   (E)
251 Old Brompton Road
370 2323
⊖ Earls Court
6.00 p.m.–11.00 p.m.
*Book *AX BC DC

ENGLISH

BOSWELL'S   (C)
239 Old Brompton Road
373 3502
⊖ Earls Court
Noon–2.30 p.m. &
6.00 p.m.–11.00 p.m.
*Roast lunch *Veg *Open Air
*Book *AC AX BC DC

THE HOT POT   (A)
6 Kenway Road
373 1256
⊖ Earls Court
Noon–10.00 p.m.
Café
*Veg *T/A *AX BC DC

READS   (C)
152 Old Brompton Road
373 2445
⊖ Gloucester Road
Noon–3.00 p.m.
*Roast lunch *Open Air
*Book *AC AX BC DC

FAR EASTERN

THE PHILBEACH HOTEL
30–31 Philbeach Gardens
373 1244
⊖ Earls Court
9.00 a.m.–11.00 a.m.
*Breakfast
– THE GAZEBO   (B)
7.00 p.m.–11.00 p.m.
Thai cuisine
*Open Air *Book *AC AX
BC DC

FRENCH

TWENTIES (B)
232 Old Brompton Road
370 2788
⊖ Earls Court
Noon–3.00 p.m. &
8.00 p.m.–midnight
Cabaret act at 3.00 p.m.
*Veg *Book *AC AX BC

INDIAN

AKASH TANDOORI (B)
275 Old Brompton Road
373 7561
⊖ Earls Court
Noon–midnight
*Veg *T/A *Book *AC AX
BC DC

INDIA PALACE TANDOORI
(B)
8 Kenway Road
373 1256
⊖ Earls Court
Noon–2.30 p.m. &
5.30 p.m.–11.00 p.m.
*Veg *T/A *AX BC DC

THE NARAINE (B)
10 Kenway Road
370 3853
⊖ Earls Court
Noon–3.00 p.m. &
6.00 p.m.–midnight
*Veg *T/A *Book *AC BC
DC

NOORJAHAN (B)
2a Bina Gardens
373 6522
⊖ Gloucester Road

Noon–2.30 p.m. &
6.00 p.m.–11.30 p.m.
*Veg *T/A *AC AX BC DC

INTERNATIONAL

BISTRO BENITO (B)
166 Earls Court Road
373 6646
⊖ Earls Court
Noon–2.30 p.m. &
6.45 p.m.–11.00 p.m.
Italian/European menu
*Veg *Book *AC AX BC DC

THE POT (A)
5a Hogarth Place
370 4371
⊖ Earls Court
Noon–midnight
*Roast lunch *Veg *T/A
*AC AX BC

SPATS WINE BAR (A)
237 Earls Court Road
370 6899
⊖ Earls Court
7.00 p.m.–10.30 p.m.
*Veg *Open Air

ITALIAN

PONTEVECCHIO (D)
256 Old Brompton Road
373 9082
⊖ Earls Court
12.30 p.m.–2.30 p.m. &
7.30 p.m.–11.30 p.m.
*Veg *AC AX BC DC

SW6

AMERICAN

TOOTSIES (B)
177 New King's Road
736 4023
✪ Parsons Green
Noon–11.30 p.m.
*Veg *T/A *Open Air

FRENCH

PIGEON (B)
606 Fulham Road
736 4618
✪ Parsons Green
Noon–2.30 p.m. &
6.00 p.m.–11.00 p.m.
*Roast lunch *Veg *BC

TRENCHERMAN (B)
271 New King's Road
736 4988
✪ Parsons Green
12.30 p.m.–3.00 p.m.
*Roast lunch *Book *AX
BC DC

INDIAN

KABANA (C)
541 King's Road
731 0039
✪ Fulham Broadway
Noon–3.00 p.m. &
6.00 p.m.–midnight
*Veg *T/A *AC AX BC DC

MOTHER INDIA (B)
86c Lillie Road
385 1922
✪ West Kensington

Noon–midnight
*Veg *T/A *Book *AC AX
BC DC

UDDINS MANZIL
TANDOORI (B)
194 Wandsworth Bridge Road
736 3584
✪ Fulham Broadway
Noon–2.30 p.m. &
6.00 p.m.–11.30 p.m.
*Veg *T/A *AC AX BC

INTERNATIONAL

CROCODILE TEARS (B)
660 Fulham Road
731 1537
✪ Parsons Green
Noon–2.30 p.m. &
7.00 p.m.–10.00 p.m.
Restaurant and Wine Bar
*Roast lunch *Veg *Open Air
*Book *AC BC

ITALIAN

LITTLE ITALY (B)
175 New King's Road
731 6404
✪ Parsons Green
Noon–midnight
Home-made pasta and burgers
*Veg *Open Air

PERFECT PIZZA (A)
51 Fulham Broadway
381 2042
✪ Fulham Broadway
11.30 a.m.–midnight
Delivery service
*Veg *T/A

PIZZA MIA (A)
189 New King's Road
736 1145
☻ Parsons Green
Noon–midnight
Delivery service
*Veg *T/A *Open Air

PIZZA THE ACTION (A)
678 Fulham Road
736 2716
☻ Parsons Green
Noon–midnight
*Veg *T/A *Open Air
*AC AX BC DC

VILLA ESTENSE (B)
642 King's Road
731 4248
☻ Fulham Broadway
12.30 p.m.–2.45 p.m.
Pasta and pizza
*Veg *T/A *Book *AX BC

VEGETARIAN

THE WINDMILL (A)
486 Fulham Road
385 1570
☻ Fulham Broadway
7.00 p.m.–11.00 p.m.
*Not licensed *T/A

SW7

AMERICAN

**THE CHICAGO RIB
SHACK** (B)
1 Raphael Street
581 5595
☻ Knightsbridge

Noon–10.30 p.m.
*Book

**TEXAS LONE STAR
SALOON** (B)
154 Gloucester Road
370 5625
☻ Gloucester Road
Noon–11.30 p.m.
Mexican food

CHINESE

PAPER TIGER (C)
10 Exhibition Road
584 3737
☻ South Kensington
Noon–2.30 p.m. &
7.00 p.m.–midnight
*Veg *T/A *Book *AC AX
BC DC

ENGLISH

REMBRANDT HOTEL
22 Thurloe Place
589 8100
☻ South Kensington
3.00 p.m.–5.00 p.m.
*Tea
– THE CARVERY (C)
12.30 p.m.–2.30 p.m. &
6.00 p.m.–9.30 p.m.
*Roast lunch *Book *AC AX
BC

SCANDIES WINE BAR (B)
4 Kynance Place
589 3659
☻ Gloucester Road
12.30 p.m.–2.00 p.m. &
7.00 p.m.–10.30 p.m.
*Roast lunch *Veg *Book

FRENCH

LA CHANTERELLE (C)
119 Old Brompton Road
373 5522
● Gloucester Road
12.15 p.m.–2.30 p.m. &
7.15 p.m.–11.00 p.m.
French/English cuisine
*Roast lunch *Open Air
*Book *AC AX BC DC

LE ROUTIER (B)
19 Exhibition Road
584 8359
● South Kensington
Noon–2.30 p.m.
Brasserie-style
*Book *AC AX BC DC

INDIAN

ALADDIN (B)
28 Thurloe Street
589 0790
● South Kensington
Noon–midnight
*Veg *T/A *Book *AC AX
BC DC

**THE BOMBAY
BRASSERIE** (C)
140 Gloucester Road
370 4040
● Gloucester Road
12.30 p.m.–2.30 p.m. &
7.00 p.m.–10.30 p.m.
Piano music at lunchtime
*Veg *Open Air *Book
*AC AX BC DC

**KHYBER PASS
TANDOORI** (B)
21 Bute Street
589 7311
● South Kensington
Noon–2.30 p.m. &
6.00 p.m.–11.30 p.m.
*Veg *T/A *AC AX BC DC

MAJLIS (B)
32 Gloucester Road
584 3476
● Gloucester Road
Noon–3.00 p.m. &
6.00 p.m.–11.30 p.m.
*Veg *T/A *Book *AC AX
BC DC

MEMORIES OF INDIA (B)
18 Gloucester Road
589 6450
● Gloucester Road
Noon–2.30 p.m. &
5.30 p.m.–11.30 p.m.
*Veg *T/A *Open Air *Book
*AC AX BC DC

INTERNATIONAL

**THE BEGGARS
BANQUET** (A)
15 Harrington Gardens
373 2303
● Gloucester Road
1.00 p.m.–3.00 p.m.
*Roast lunch *Book

BLAKES HOTEL
33 Roland Gardens
370 6701
● Gloucester Road
*Breakfast *Tea

– THE RESTAURANT (E)
7.30 p.m.–11.30 p.m.
*Book *AC AX BC DC

ITALIAN

BELLAVISTA (B)
132 Cromwell Road
373 0200
✪ Gloucester Road
Noon–2.30 p.m. &
5.30 p.m.–11.30 p.m.
*Veg *Open Air *Book
*AC AX BC DC

MASTERS (C)
190 Queen's Gate
581 5666
✪ High Street Kensington
12.30 p.m.–3.00 p.m.
*Roast lunch *Book
*AC AX BC DC

PIZZA EXPRESS (A)
15 Gloucester Road
584 9078
✪ Gloucester Road
11.30 a.m.–midnight
*Veg *T/A

THE SOUTH KEN PASTA
BAR (A)
60 Old Brompton Road
584 4028
✪ South Kensington
Noon–3.00 p.m. &
6.00 p.m.–11.45 p.m.
*Veg *Book

POLISH

DAQUISE (A)
20 Thurloe Street
589 6117

✪ South Kensington
10.00 a.m.–11.30 p.m.
Polish/Russian menu

SW9

ENGLISH

TWENTY TRINITY
GARDENS (B)
20 Trinity Gardens
733 8838
✪ Brixton
12.30 p.m.–2.30 p.m. &
7.00 p.m.–10.30 p.m.
English/French cuisine
*Roast lunch *Veg *Open Air
*Book *BC

INDIAN

OVAL TANDOORI (C)
64a Brixton Road
582 1415
✪ Oval
Noon–midnight
*Veg *T/A *Book *AC AX
BC DC

PARADISE (B)
414–416 Coldharbour Lane
326 1047
✪ Brixton
Noon–3.00 p.m. &
6.00 p.m.–midnight
*Veg *T/A *Book *AC AX
BC DC

ROYAL TANDOORI (B)
66 Brixton Road
735 6012
✪ Oval

Noon–3.00 p.m. &
6.00 p.m.–midnight
*Veg *T/A *Book *AC AX
BC DC

SW10

AMERICAN

THE AMERICAN (A)
335 Fulham Road
352 7555
✪ South Kensington
Noon–12.30 a.m.
*T/A *Open Air
*AC AX BC

PARSONS (B)
311 Fulham Road
352 0651
✪ South Kensington
Noon–12.30 a.m.
*Veg *AC BC

TOOTSIES (A)
140 Fulham Road
370 2794
✪ South Kensington
9.00 a.m.–11.30 p.m.
*Breakfast *Veg *T/A

UP ALL NIGHT (B)
325 Fulham Road
352 1996
✪ South Kensington
Noon–6.00 a.m.
*T/A *AC AX BC

CHINESE

GOLDEN DUCK (C)
6 Hollywood Road
352 3500

✪ Earls Court
1.00 p.m.–3.00 p.m. &
7.00 p.m.–11.30 p.m.
*Veg *T/A *Book *AC AX
BC DC

RED PEPPER (C)
7 Park Walk
352 3546
✪ South Kensington
12.30 p.m.–3.00 p.m. &
7.00 p.m.–11.30 p.m.
*Veg *Book *AC AX BC DC

ENGLISH

CHELSEA WHARF (C)
15 Lots Road
351 0861
Noon–3.00 p.m. &
7.00 p.m.–11.00 p.m.
Piano music
*Brunch *Roast lunch
*Open Air *Book *AC AX BC

CLOWNS (B)
356 Fulham Road
352 1023
✪ Fulham Broadway
Noon–2.30 p.m.
Magician
*Roast lunch *Book *AC BC

HUNGRY HORSE (C)
196 Fulham Road
352 7757
✪ South Kensington
12.30 p.m.–3.00 p.m. &
7.00 p.m.–11.00 p.m.
*Roast lunch *Open Air
*Book *AC AX BC DC

JAKES (C)
14 Hollywood Road
352 8692
⊖ Earls Court
12.30 p.m.–2.30 p.m.
English/French cuisine
*Roast lunch *Veg *Open Air
*Book *AC AX BC DC

FAR EASTERN

BUSABONG (B)
331 Fulham Road
352 4742
⊖ South Kensington
12.30 p.m.–10.30 p.m.
Thai cuisine
*Veg *T/A *AC AX BC DC

FISH

LA CROISETTE (D)
168 Ifield Road
373 3694
⊖ Earls Court
1.00 p.m.–2.30 p.m. &
7.30 p.m.–10.00 p.m.
*Book *AX

FRENCH

ROY'S (C)
206 Fulham Road
352 6828
⊖ South Kensington
1.30 p.m.–3.00 p.m. &
7.30 p.m.–11.00 p.m.
French/English menu
Occasional cabaret acts
*Roast lunch *Veg *Book
*AC AX BC

SEPTEMBER (C)
457 Fulham Road
352 0206
⊖ Fulham Broadway
7.00 p.m.–11.00 p.m.
French/English menu
*Veg *AC AX BC DC

INDIAN

NAYAB (B)
9 Park Walk
352 2137
⊖ South Kensington
Noon–3.00 p.m. &
6.00 p.m.–midnight
*Veg *T/A *Book *AC AX
BC DC

INTERNATIONAL

AMBROSIANA
CRÊPERIE (B)
194 Fulham Road
351 0070
⊖ South Kensington
Noon–midnight
*Veg *Book

BISTRO VINO (B)
2 Hollywood Road
352 6439
⊖ Earls Court
7.00 p.m.–11.30 p.m.

ITALIAN

CHELSEA PASTA BAR (B)
313 Fulham Road
352 6912
⊖ South Kensington
Noon–midnight
*Veg

FLAVIO (B)
1a Langton Street
352 7414
◉ Fulham Broadway
Noon–2.45 p.m. &
7.00 p.m.–11.45 p.m.
*Roast lunch *Veg
*AC AX BC DC

LA FAMIGLIA (D)
7 Langton Street
351 0761
◉ Fulham Broadway
12.30 p.m.–2.30 p.m. &
7.30 p.m.–11.30 p.m.
*Open Air *Book *AC AX BC
DC

LA NASSA (C)
438 King's Road
351 4118
◉ Fulham Broadway
12.30 p.m.–2.30 p.m. &
7.30 p.m.–11.30 p.m.
*Open Air *Book *AC AX BC
DC

LEONARDO'S (B)
397 King's Road
352 4146
12.30 p.m.–2.30 p.m.
*Roast lunch *Veg *Book
*AC AX BC DC

PIZZA EXPRESS (A)
363 Fulham Road
352 5300
◉ South Kensington
11.30 a.m.–midnight
*Veg *T/A

SPANISH

EL BODEGAN (C)
9 Park Walk
352 1330
◉ South Kensington
12.30 p.m.–3.00 p.m. &
7.00 p.m.–midnight
*Open Air *Book *AC AX
BC DC

SW11

AMERICAN

THE INEBRIATED
NEWT (B)
172 Northcote Road
223 1637
◉ Clapham South
Noon–2.45 p.m. &
7.30 p.m.–11.00 p.m.
*Veg *T/A *Book *AC BC

LE GRAND CAFÉ (B)
25 Battersea Rise
228 7984
BR Clapham Junction
Noon–3.00 p.m. &
6.00 p.m.–11.00 p.m.
*Veg *Open Air *AC BC

CHINESE

JASMIN (C)
50 Battersea Rise
228 0336
◉ Clapham Common
Noon–3.00 p.m. &
6.00 p.m.–midnight
*Veg *T/A *Book *AC AX
BC DC

ENGLISH

NO NAME PLACE (C)
143 St John's Hill
228 3043
BR Clapham Junction
12.30 p.m.–2.45 p.m. &
7.30 p.m.–10.30 p.m.
English/French cuisine
*Roast lunch *Veg *Book
*AC AX BC DC

POLLYANNA'S (C)
2 Battersea Rise
228 0316
✺ Clapham South
Noon–3.00 p.m. &
7.00 p.m.–midnight
English/French cuisine
*Roast lunch *Veg *Open Air
*Book *AC AX BC DC

FRENCH

LA BOUFFE (B)
13 Battersea Rise
228 3384
BR Clapham Junction
11.00 a.m.–2.00 p.m. &
7.30 p.m.–10.30 p.m.
*Brunch *Book *AC BC

INDIAN

AKASH INDIAN
TANDOORI (B)
70 Northcote Road
228 6434
BR Clapham Junction
Noon–3.00 p.m. &
6.00 p.m.–midnight
*Veg *T/A *AC AX BC DC

INTERNATIONAL

ARMSTRONG'S WINE
BAR (B)
183 Lavender Hill
228 2660
✺ Clapham Common
11.00 a.m.–11.00 p.m.
Lunch: noon–3.00 p.m.
Dinner: 8.00 p.m.–11.00 p.m.
*Tea *Veg *Open Air *Book
*AC AX BC DC

BATTERSEA ARTS
CENTRE (A)
Old Town Hall
Lavender Hill
223 6557/223 8413
BR Clapham Junction
Noon–2.30 p.m. &
5.30 p.m.–9.00 p.m.
*Roast lunch *Not licensed
*Veg *AC BC

JUST WILLIAM'S WINE
BAR (B)
6 Battersea Rise
228 9980
✺ Clapham South
7.00 p.m.–10.00 p.m.
*Veg *Open Air *AC AX BC
DC

ITALIAN

ANTIPASTO E PASTA (B)
511 Battersea Park Road
223 9765
BR Clapham Junction
Noon–midnight
*Veg

LA PREFERITA (B)
163 Lavender Hill
223 1046
✆ Clapham Common
Noon–2.30 p.m. &
7.30 p.m.–11.30 p.m.
*Open Air *Book *AC AX BC
DC

SW12

INDIAN

LAHORI NAN KEBAB (A)
47 Balham Hill
673 7820
✆ Clapham South
Noon–midnight
*Not licensed *Veg *T/A

SW13

AMERICAN

MACARTHURS (A)
147 Church Road
748 3630
BR Barnes
Noon–11.30 p.m.
*Veg *T/A *Open Air *AC
BC

CHINESE

WEI HAI WEI (B)
7 The Broadway,
White Hart Lane
876 1165
BR Barnes Bridge

Noon–2.30 p.m. &
6.00 p.m.–11.30 p.m.
*Veg *T/A

FRENCH

BLOOMERS BRASSERIE (B)
94 Church Road
748 0359
BR Barnes
12.30 p.m.–3.00 p.m.
October–May *only*
Piano music and open fire
*Roast lunch *Veg *Book
*AC AX BC DC

INDIAN

GATE OF INDIA (B)
68 Church Road
748 6793
BR Barnes Bridge
Noon–3.00 p.m. &
6.00 p.m.–midnight
*Veg *T/A *Book *AC AX
BC DC

MONZIL (B)
88 Church Road
748 3809
BR Barnes Bridge
Noon–3.00 p.m. &
6.00 p.m.–midnight
*Veg *T/A *Book *AC AX
BC DC

INTERNATIONAL

THE OLD RANGOON (B)
201 Castelnau
741 9655
✆ Hammersmith

Noon–midnight
*Tea *Veg *Open Air *Book
*AC AX BC DC

ITALIAN

ROSE　　　　　　　　　　(C)
5 White Hart Lane
876 3335
BR Barnes Bridge
12.30 p.m.–3.30 p.m. &
7.00 p.m.–11.00 p.m.
*Roast lunch *Veg *Open Air
*Book *AC AX BC DC

SW14

AMERICAN

MACARTHURS　　　　　(A)
248 Upper Richmond Road
West
876 4445
BR Mortlake
Noon–11.30 p.m.
*Veg *T/A *AC BC

CHINESE

Mr LU　　　　　　　　　(B)
374 Upper Richmond
Road West
876 2531
BR Mortlake
Noon–2.00 p.m.
*T/A *Book *AC AX BC DC

ITALIAN

CARLO DOMINGO'S　　(C)
201 Upper Richmond Road
West
876 8147

BR Mortlake
Noon–3.00 p.m. &
6.00 p.m.–midnight
Italian and French cuisine
*Veg *Book *AC AX BC DC

PIZZA EXPRESS　　　　(A)
305 Upper Richmond Road
West
878 6833
BR Mortlake
11.30 a.m.–midnight
*Veg *T/A

SW15

ENGLISH

GAVIN'S BISTRO　　　　(B)
5 Lacy Road
785 9151
⊖ East Putney
12.30 p.m.–3.00 p.m.
*Roast lunch *Veg *Book

HENRIETTA'S　　　　　(B)
162 Lower Richmond Road
788 3844
⊖ Putney Bridge
1.00 p.m.–3.00 p.m.
English/French menu
*Roast lunch *Veg *Open Air
*Book *AX BC

FRENCH

MOSSOP'S　　　　　　　(B)
136 Upper Richmond Road
789 7043
⊖ East Putney

Noon–3.00 p.m. &
7.00 p.m.–11.45 p.m.
French/English cuisine
*Roast lunch *Open Air *BC

MIDDLE EASTERN

BUZKASH   (B)
4 Chelverton Road
788 0599
✪ Putney
6.00 p.m.–10.30 p.m.
Afghan cuisine
*Veg *T/A *Book *AC AX
BC DC

SCANDINAVIAN

ANNIA'S   (C)
349–351 Upper Richmond
Road
876 4456
✪ East Putney/Putney Bridge
12.30 p.m.–2.30 p.m. &
7.00 p.m.–11.30 p.m.
Swedish cooking
Barbecues in summer
*Veg *T/A *Open Air *Book
*AC AX BC DC

SW16

AMERICAN

HOLLYWOOD   (A)
394 Streatham High Road
769 3686
BR Streatham
8.30 p.m.–1.00 a.m.
Cocktail bar and 'basket food'

ITALIAN

LA BALERA   (C)
66 Streatham High Road
769 2646/0669
BR Streatham Hill
Noon–1.00 a.m.
Dance band music in evening
*Book *AC AX BC DC

PIZZA EXPRESS   (A)
14 High Parade,
Streatham High Road
677 3646
BR Streatham
11.30 a.m.–midnight
*Veg *T/A

VEGETARIAN

WHOLEMEAL
VEGETARIAN CAFÉ   (A)
1 Shrubbery Road
769 2423
BR Streatham Hill
Noon–10.00 p.m.
*T/A

SW17

FRENCH

HOULTS WINE BAR   (B)
20 Bellevue Road
672 6760
✪ Tooting Bec
Noon–3.00 p.m. &
7.00 p.m.–11.00 p.m.
Violin music in evening
*Veg *Open Air *Book
*AC AX BC DC

INDIAN

KOLAM (B)
58 Upper Tooting Road
672 5328
⊖ Tooting Bec
Noon–3.00 p.m. &
6.00 p.m.–11.00 p.m.
*Veg *T/A *Book *AC AX
BC DC

SREE KRISHNA (B)
192–194 Tooting High Street
672 4250
⊖ Tooting Broadway
Noon–3.00 p.m. &
6.00 p.m.–11.00 p.m.
*Veg *T/A

INTERNATIONAL

HARVEY'S (C)
2 Bellevue Road
672 0011
BR Wandsworth Common
12.30 p.m.–2.30 p.m.
*Roast lunch *Open Air
*AC AX BC DC

SW18

AMERICAN

JEEPERS (B)
350 York Road
870 5491
BR Wandsworth Town
Noon–3.00 p.m. &
7.00 p.m.–midnight
Mexican food/jazz at lunch/
piano music in evening
*Veg *T/A *Book *AC AX
BC DC

INDIAN

SONCHITA (B)
13 West Hill
874 9774
⊖ East Putney
Noon–3.00 p.m. &
6.00 p.m.–midnight
*Veg *T/A *Book *AC AX
BC DC

INTERNATIONAL

FRENCH'S WINE BAR (B)
55 East Hill
874 2808
BR Wandsworth
7.00 p.m.–11.15 p.m.
*Veg *T/A *Open Air *AC
BC

THE PATRIOTIC (B)
Fitzhugh Estate,
Trinity Road
870 6567
⊖ Tooting Bec
Noon–2.30 p.m. &
7.00 p.m.–10.30 p.m.
Wine Bar
*Open Air *Book

SW19

AMERICAN

TOOTSIES (A)
48 High Street
946 4135
⊖ Wimbledon
11.00 a.m.–11.30 p.m.
*Veg *T/A *Open Air

ENGLISH

YESTERDAY (B)
12 Leopold Road
946 4300
✪ Wimbledon
12.30 p.m.–2.15 p.m.
*Roast lunch *Open Air
*Book *AC BC

INDIAN

AHMED TANDOORI (B)
2 The Broadway
946 6214
✪ Wimbledon
Noon–3.00 p.m. &
6.00 p.m.–midnight
*Veg *T/A *AC AX BC DC

THE GOLDEN TANDOORI
(B)
57 Hartfield Road
542 0240
✪ Wimbledon
Noon–3.00 p.m. &
6.00 p.m.–midnight
*Veg *T/A *AC AX BC DC

RAJDOOT TANDOORI (B)
72 High Street
946 0238
✪ Wimbledon
12.30 p.m.–2.00 p.m. &
6.00 p.m.–11.30 p.m.
*T/A *Book *AC AX BC DC

ITALIAN

PIZZA EXPRESS (A)
84 High Street
946 6027
✪ Wimbledon
11.30 a.m.–midnight
*Veg *T/A

SAN LORENZO
FUORIPORTA (C)
38 Worple Road Mews
946 8463
✪ Wimbledon
Noon–2.30 p.m. &
7.30 p.m.–9.30 p.m.
*Open air *Book *AC AX BC
DC

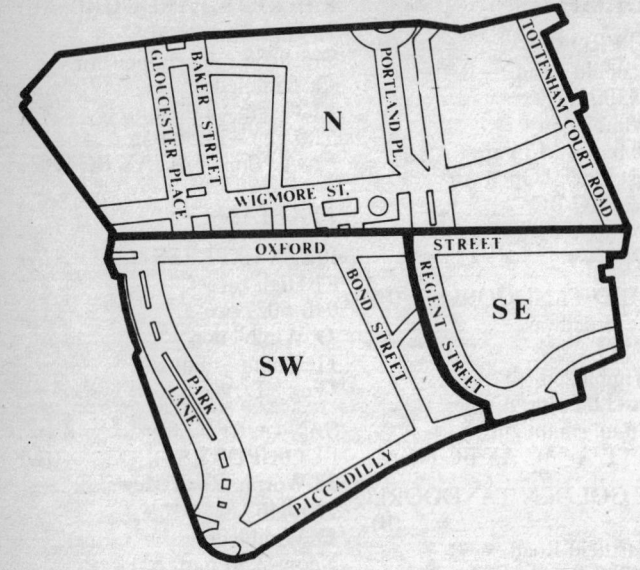

There are so many restaurants in the postal zone of W1 that, in this section only, the area has been divided into three:

W1 – North   =   W1 to the north of Oxford Street
W1 – South West   =   W1 to the west of Regent Street
W1 – South East   =   W1 to the east of Regent Street

W1–NORTH

AMERICAN

COCONUT GROVE   (B)
3–5 Barrett Street
486 5269

⊖ Bond Street
Noon–4.00 p.m. &
5.30 p.m.–10.30 p.m.
*Brunch *Veg *Open Air
*AC AX BC DC

JOHN G'S (A)
45 Crawford Street
724 1739
☉ Baker Street
9.30 a.m.–11.30 p.m.
*Brunch

ENGLISH

THE CUMBERLAND
HOTEL
Marble Arch
262 1234
☉ Marble Arch
– THE CARVERY (C)
Noon–3.00 p.m. &
6.00 p.m.–10.00 p.m.
*Roast lunch *AC AX BC DC

FLANAGANS (C)
100 Baker Street
935 0287
☉ Baker Street
Noon–2.30 p.m. &
6.00 p.m.–10.30 p.m.
Music in the evening
*Roast lunch *Veg
*AC AX BC DC

FISH

ANTOINE'S (C)
40 Charlotte Street
636 2817
☉ Goodge Street
Noon–2.30 p.m. &
6.00 p.m.–10.30 p.m.
*Book *AC AX BC DC

FRENCH

CAFÉ CRÊPERIE (A)
26 James Street
935 8480

☉ Bond Street
9.00 a.m.–midnight
*Breakfast *Veg *Open Air

CHEZ GERARD (C)
8 Charlotte Street
636 4975
☉ Tottenham Court Road
12.30 p.m.–2.30 p.m. &
6.30 p.m.–11.00 p.m.
*Book *AC BC

CHURCHILL HOTEL
30 Portman Square
486 5800
☉ Marble Arch
3.30 p.m.–5.30 p.m.
*Tea
– No 10 RESTAURANT (E)
Noon–3.00 p.m. &
6.00 p.m.–11.00 p.m.
*AC AX BC DC

THE MONTCALM
HOTEL
Great Cumberland Place
402 5121
☉ Marble Arch
– THE MONTCALM (E)
7.00 p.m.–10.30 p.m.
*AC AX BC DC

GREEK

APPOLONIA (B)
17a Percy Street
636 4140
☉ Tottenham Court Road
Noon–3.00 p.m. &
6.00 p.m.–midnight
*Veg *T/A *Open Air *Book
*AC AX BC DC

CHEZ ZORBA (B)
11 Charlotte Street
631 0895
● Goodge Street
Noon–3.00 p.m. &
5.30 p.m.–3.00 a.m.
*Book *AC AX BC DC

COSMAS TAVERNA (B)
29 Goodge Street
636 1877
● Goodge Street
5.00 p.m.–midnight
*T/A *AC AX BC DC

GRECIAN GRILL (C)
27 Percy Street
636 8913
● Tottenham Court Road
Noon–3.00 p.m. &
9.00 p.m.–9.00 a.m.
*Veg *AC AX BC DC

INDIAN

THE AGRA (B)
135 Whitfield Street
387 4828
● Warren Street
Noon–3.00 p.m. &
6.00 p.m.–11.30 p.m.
*Veg *T/A *AC AX BC DC

DIWAN-E-KHAS (B)
110 Whitfield Street
388 1321
● Warren Street
Noon–3.00 p.m. &
6.00 p.m.–midnight
*Veg *T/A *AC AX BC DC

THE GAYLORD (C)
79 Mortimer Street
580 3615

● Oxford Circus
Noon–3.00 p.m. &
6.00 p.m.–11.00 p.m.
*Veg *T/A *Book *AC AX
BC DC

THE GURKHA (B)
23 Warren Street
388 1640
● Warren Street
Noon–3.00 p.m. &
6.00 p.m.–midnight
Nepalese
*Veg *T/A *Book *AC AX
BC DC

KHYBER (B)
15 Seymour Place
723 1899
● Marble Arch
Noon–11.30 p.m.
*Veg T/A *AC AX BC DC

LAL QILA (C)
117 Tottenham Court Road
387 4570
● Warren Street
Noon–3.00 p.m. &
6.00 p.m.–11.30 p.m.
*Veg *T/A *AC AX BC DC

MAHAGOPAL (A)
160 New Cavendish Street
580 5607
● Oxford Circus
7.00 p.m.–11.30 p.m.
*Veg *T/A *AC AX BC DC

NATRAJ (A)
93 Charlotte Street
637 0050
● Goodge Street

Noon–3.00 p.m. &
6.00 p.m.–midnight
Nepalese
*Veg *T/A *Book *AC AX
BC DC

NEW GREAT INDIA (B)
22a Seymour Place
723 5166
✪ Marble Arch
Noon–midnight
*Veg *T/A *AC AX BC DC

ROMNA TANDOORI (B)
132 Seymour Place
723 7387
✪ Marylebone
Noon–midnight
*Veg *T/A *AC AX BC DC

WOODLANDS (B)
77 Marylebone Lane
486 3862
✪ Baker Street/Bond Street
Noon–3.00 p.m. &
6.00 p.m.–11.00 p.m.
South Indian vegetarian
*Veg *T/A *AC AX BC DC

INTERNATIONAL

ELYSÉE (D)
13 Percy Street
636 4804
✪ Tottenham Court Road
8.00 p.m.–4.00 a.m.
Mainly Greek food with
cabaret and dancing
*Open Air *Book *AC AX BC
DC

THE PORTMAN INTER-
CONTINENTAL
22 Portman Square
486 5844
✪ Marble Arch
– THE BAKERY (A)
11.00 a.m.–11.00 p.m.
*Tea
– TRUFFLES (C)
11.30 a.m.–4.00 p.m.
Jazz music
*Brunch *Roast lunch *Veg
*Book *AC AX BC DC

THE SELFRIDGE HOTEL
Orchard Street
408 2080
✪ Marble Arch/Bond Street
– LOUNGE (A)
10.00 a.m.–11.00 p.m.
Snacks served all day
3.00 p.m.–5.00 p.m.
*Tea
– FLETCHERS (D)
7.00 p.m.–10.15 p.m.
Piano music
*Book *AC AX BC DC

ITALIAN

SPAGHETTI HOUSE (B)
15–17 Goodge Street
636 6582
✪ Goodge Street
5.30 p.m.–10.00 p.m.
*Veg *Open Air *Book

TRATTORIA BERNIGRA (B)
69 Tottenham Court Road
580 0950
✪ Goodge Street
10.30 a.m.–11.30 p.m.
*Tea *Veg *T/A

JEWISH

PICNIC (B)
108 Seymour Place
723 7924
⊖ Edgware Road
Noon–2.30 p.m.
Café
*Not licensed *Veg *T/A

REUBENS
20a Baker Street
⊖ Bond Street
– SNACK BAR (A)
486 7079
11.00 a.m.–10.00 p.m.
*T/A
– RESTAURANT (B)
935 5945
Noon–10.00 p.m.
Kosher
*T/A *Book *AC AX BC DC

MIDDLE EASTERN

CARAVAN SERAI (B)
50 Paddington Street
935 1208
⊖ Baker Street
6.00 p.m.–11.00 p.m.
Afghan cuisine
*Veg *T/A *Book *AC AX
BC DC

TURKISH

TOPKAPI (B)
25 Marylebone High Street
486 1872
⊖ Bond Street/Baker Street
Noon–11.30 p.m.
*T/A *Book *AC AX BC DC

W1–SOUTH WEST

AMERICAN

THE AMERICAN HAMBURGER RESTAURANT (B)
455 Oxford Street
629 1602
⊖ Bond Street
Noon–midnight
*AC AX BC DC

CHICAGO PIZZA PIE FACTORY (B)
17 Hanover Square
629 2669
⊖ Oxford Circus
Noon–10.30 p.m.
*Veg

HARD ROCK CAFÉ (B)
150 Old Park Lane
629 0382
⊖ Hyde Park Corner
Noon–12.30 a.m.
*Veg *T/A *Open Air

WOLFE'S (B)
34 Park Lane
499 6897
⊖ Hyde Park Corner
11.30 a.m.–midnight
*T/A *AC AX DC

CHINESE

CHUNGS (B)
28 Duke Street
935 8992
⊖ Bond Street

Noon–3.00 p.m. &
6.00 p.m.–11.00 p.m.
*Veg *AC AX BC DC

MR KAI OF MAYFAIR (E)
65 South Audley Street
493 8988
☻ Green Park/Bond Street
Noon–3.00 p.m. &
7.00 p.m.–11.00 p.m.
Peking cuisine
*Veg *Book *AC AX BC DC

ENGLISH

THE DORCHESTER
HOTEL
55 Park Lane
629 8888
☻ Hyde Park Corner
– THE PROMENADE (A)
9.00 a.m.–11.00 p.m.
Snacks served all day
*Breakfast *Tea
– THE DORCHESTER
GRILL (D)
12.30 p.m.–2.30 p.m. &
7.00 p.m.–10.30 p.m.
*Roast lunch *Veg *Book
*AC AX BC DC

LONDON HILTON
HOTEL
Park Lane
493 8000
☻ Hyde Park Corner
7.00 a.m.–10.30 a.m.
*Breakfast

– THE BRITISH
HARVEST (C)
Noon–2.45 p.m. &
7.00 p.m.–10.45 p.m.
*Roast lunch *Book
*AC AX BC DC

RICHOUX (B)
172 Piccadilly
493 2204
☻ Green Park/Piccadilly
Circus
and
41a South Audley Street
629 5228
☻ Green Park/Hyde Park
Corner
10.00 a.m.–11.00 p.m.
*Breakfast *Tea *AC AX
BC DC

TIDDY DOL'S (D)
2 Hertford Street
499 2357
☻ Green Park
6.00 p.m.–1.00 a.m.
Folk music and disco dancing
*Veg *AC AX BC DC

FISH

SCOTTS (E)
20 Mount Street
629 5248
☻ Green Park/Bond Street
7.00 p.m.–9.00 p.m.
*Book *AC AX BC DC

VENDÔME (D)
20 Dover Street
629 5417
☻ Green Park

12.30 p.m.–2.30 p.m. &
7.00 p.m.–10.20 p.m.
*AC AX BC DC

FRENCH

ATHENAEUM HOTEL
116 Piccadilly
499 3464
❺ Hyde Park Corner
7.30 a.m.–10.30 a.m.
*Breakfast
3.00 p.m.–5.30 p.m.
*Tea
– THE RESTAURANT　　(D)
12.30 p.m.–2.30 p.m. &
7.00 p.m.–10.00 p.m.
*AC AX BC DC
– THE WINDSOR LOUNGE
　　　　　　　　　　　(B)
open 24 hours
Snacks and light meals
*AC AX BC DC

HOTEL BRISTOL
Berkeley Street
493 8282
❺ Green Park
– LOUIS D'OR
RESTAURANT　　　　(D)
12.30 p.m.–2.00 p.m. &
7.00 p.m.–11.00 p.m.
*AC AX BC DC

BROWN'S HOTEL
21–24 Dover Street or
55–60 Albemarle Street
493 6020
❺ Green Park
3.00 p.m.–6.00 p.m.
*Tea

– L'APERITIF
RESTAURANT　　　　(E)
499 6122
12.15 p.m.–2.30 p.m. &
6.30 p.m.–9.30 p.m.
*Book *AC AX BC DC

CLARIDGE'S HOTEL
Brook Street
629 8860
❺ Bond Street
7.30 a.m.–10.00 a.m.
*Breakfast
– CAUSERIE　　　　　(D)
Noon–3.00 p.m. &
6.00 p.m.–11.00 p.m.
Buffet lunches
*Book *AC AX BC DC
– THE RESTAURANT　　(F)
12.30 p.m.–3.00 p.m. &
7.00 p.m.–11.00 p.m.
*Veg *Book *AC AX BC DC

THE CONNAUGHT
HOTEL
Carlos Place
499 7070
❺ Bond Street
7.30 a.m.–10.00 a.m.
*Breakfast
3.30 p.m.–5.30 p.m.
*Tea
– THE RESTAURANT　　(F)
492 0668
12.30 p.m.–2.30 p.m. &
6.30 p.m.–10.30 p.m.
*Book *AC

THE CRÊPERIE　　　　(A)
56a South Molton Street
629 4794
❺ Bond Street

10.30 a.m.–8.00 p.m.
*Veg *Open Air

L'ARTISTE MUSCLÉ (B)
1 Shepherd Market
493 6150
⊖ Green Park
7.00 p.m.–10.30 p.m.
Wine Bar
*Veg *Open Air *AC AX BC

LONDON MARRIOTT
HOTEL
10 Grosvenor Square
493 1232
⊖ Bond Street
– DIPLOMAT
RESTAURANT (E)
Noon–2.00 p.m. &
7.00 p.m.–10.00 p.m.
Music at lunchtime
*Book *AC AX BC DC

MAYFAIR HOTEL
Stratton Street
629 7777
⊖ Green Park
– LE CHÂTEAUBRIAND (D)
12.30 p.m.–2.30 p.m. &
7.00 p.m.–10.30 p.m.
Piano music
*Brunch *Veg *Book
*AC AX BC DC

RELAIS DES AMIS (D)
17b Curzon Street
499 7595
⊖ Green Park/Hyde Park
Corner
12.15 p.m.–3.00 p.m. &
7.15 p.m.–11.00 p.m.
French/European cuisine
*Open Air *Book *AC AX
BC DC

THE RITZ HOTEL
Piccadilly
493 8181
⊖ Green Park
7.30 a.m.–10.30 a.m.
*Breakfast
4.00 p.m.–6.30 p.m.
*Tea and cabaret
– LOUIS XVI RESTAURANT
(F)
12.30 p.m.–2.00 p.m. &
7.30 p.m.–10.30 p.m.
*Veg *Book *AC AX BC DC

INDIAN

TANDOORI OF MAYFAIR
(D)
37a Curzon Street
629 0600
⊖ Green Park
12.30 p.m.–11.30 p.m.
*Veg *T/A *Book *AC AX
BC DC

INTERNATIONAL

DOWN'S WINE BAR (B)
5–6 Down Street
491 3810
⊖ Green Park
Noon–2.30 p.m. &
7.00 p.m.–11.30 p.m.
*Open Air

THE INN ON THE PARK
HOTEL
Hamilton Place
499 0888
⊖ Hyde Park Corner
– THE FOUR SEASONS (D)
Noon–3.00 p.m. &
7.00 p.m.–11.00 p.m.

French-inspired cuisine and
piano music at lunchtime
*AC AX BC DC
– LANES RESTAURANT (D)
Noon–3.00 p.m. &
7.00 p.m.–11.00 p.m.
*AC AX BC DC
– THE LOUNGE (B)
9.00 a.m.–2.00 a.m.
Food served all day
*Breakfast *Roast lunch *Tea
*Veg *AC AX BC DC

THE INTER-
CONTINENTAL HOTEL
1 Hamilton Place
409 3131
⊖ Hyde Park Corner
7.00 a.m.–10.00 a.m.
*Breakfast
3.30 p.m.–5.30 p.m.
*Tea
– THE COFFEE HOUSE (D)
Noon–3.00 p.m. &
7.00 p.m.–11.30 p.m.
Food served all day
*AC AX BC DC
– LE SOUFFLE (E)
Noon–3.30 p.m. &
7.00 p.m.–11.00 p.m.
French cuisine at dinner
*Brunch *Veg *Book
*AC AX BC DC

THE PARK LANE HOTEL
Piccadilly
499 6321
⊖ Green Park/Hyde Park
Corner
3.00 p.m.–6.00 p.m.
*Tea

– BRACEWELLS (D)
12.30 p.m.–2.30 p.m. &
7.00 p.m.–10.30 p.m.
*Roast lunch *Veg *Book
*AC AX BC DC
– THE GARDEN ROOM (B)
Noon–3.00 p.m. &
6.00 p.m.–10.00 p.m.
Snacks and light meals
*Veg *AC AX BC DC

ROCKAFELLA'S (B)
3 New Burlington Street
434 1892
⊖ Oxford Circus
9.00 p.m.–3.30 a.m.
Jazz most Sundays
*Veg *T/A *AX

TRADER VIC (E)
London Hilton Hotel,
22 Park Lane
493 7586
⊖ Hyde Park Corner
Noon–2.00 p.m. &
7.00 p.m.–11.30 p.m.
*AC AX BC DC

THE WESTBURY HOTEL
New Bond Street
629 7755
⊖ Green Park
7.30 a.m.–10.30 a.m.
*Breakfast
3.00 p.m.–5.30 p.m.
*Tea
– THE WESTBURY (D)
12.30 p.m.–2.30 p.m. &
7.00 p.m.–10.00 p.m.
*Book *AC AX BC DC

ITALIAN

LA FONTANA DE TREVI (B)
28 Maddox Street
629 0191
✪ Oxford Circus
Noon–3.00 p.m. &
6.00 p.m.–11.30 p.m.
*Book *AC AX BC DC

JAPANESE

IKEDA (F)
30 Brook Street
629 2730
✪ Bond Street
7.00 p.m.–10.00 p.m.
*Veg *T/A *Book *AC AX
BC DC

SAKURA (D)
9 Hanover Street
629 2961
✪ Oxford Circus
Noon–2.30 p.m. &
6.30 p.m.–9.30 p.m.
*Veg *Book *AC AX BC DC

SHOGUN (E)
Adams Row
493 1877
✪ Bond Street
6.00 p.m.–11.00 p.m.
*Book *AC AX BC DC

MIDDLE EASTERN

FAKHRELDINE (C)
85 Piccadilly
493 3424
✪ Green Park
Noon–midnight
Lebanese
*Veg *Book *AC AX BC DC

SPANISH

MARTINEZ (C)
25 Swallow Street
734 5066
✪ Piccadilly Circus
12.30 p.m.–3.00 p.m. &
6.30 p.m.–midnight
Flamenco floor-show
*AC AX BC DC

W1–SOUTH EAST

AMERICAN

MAXWELL'S (B)
25 Coventry Street
839 1374
✪ Piccadilly Circus
Noon–12.30 a.m.
*Veg *Book *AC BC

SURPRISE (B)
12 Great Marlborough Street
434 2666
✪ Oxford Circus
Noon–3.00 p.m.
American or English brunch
*Brunch *Roast lunch *Veg
*Book *AC AX BC DC

CHINESE

CHUEN CHENG KU (B)
17 Wardour Street
437 1398
✪ Piccadilly Circus
11.00 a.m.–midnight
Cantonese
*Veg *T/A *AC AX BC DC

DRAGON GATE (B)
7 Gerrard Street
734 5154
☻ Leicester Square
Noon–11.00 p.m.
Szechuan
*T/A *AX BC DC

DUMPLING INN (B)
15a Gerrard Street
437 2567
☻ Leicester Square
Noon–2.30 p.m. &
6.30 p.m.–11.00 p.m.
Pekingese and Cantonese
*Veg *T/A *Book *AC AX
BC DC

FAR EAST (B)
13 Gerrard Street
437 6148
☻ Leicester Square
7.00 p.m.–4.00 a.m.

FOOK LAM MOON (B)
10 Gerrard Street
437 5712
☻ Leicester Square
Noon–10.30 p.m.
Live music
*Veg *T/A *AC AX BC DC

GALLANT (C)
5 Macclesfield Street
437 2930
☻ Piccadilly Circus
Noon–11.30 p.m.
Cantonese
*AC AX BC DC

**GALLERY
RENDEZVOUS** (B)
53 Beak Street
734 0445

☻ Piccadilly Circus
Noon–2.30 p.m. &
6.00 p.m.–11.00 p.m.
Pekingese
*Book *AX BC DC

JADE GARDEN (A)
15 Wardour Street
439 7851
☻ Piccadilly Circus
11.30 a.m.–11.00 p.m.
*Veg *T/A *AC AX BC DC

KOWLOON (A)
21 Gerrard Street
437 1694
☻ Leicester Square
Noon–midnight
*Veg *T/A *Book *AC AX
BC DC

LEE HO FOOK (B)
15 Gerrard Street
734 9578
☻ Leicester Square
Noon–10.30 p.m.

LEY-ON (B)
56 Wardour Street
437 6465
☻ Piccadilly Circus
11.30 a.m.–11.00 p.m.
Cantonese
*T/A *AC AX BC DC

LIDO (B)
41 Gerrard Street
437 4431
☻ Leicester Square
4.00 p.m.–4.00 a.m.
Cantonese
*Veg *T/A *AC AX BC DC

LOK HO FOOK (B)
4 Gerrard Street
437 2001
⊖ Leicester Square
11.30 a.m.–1.00 a.m.
Cantonese
*Veg *Book *AC AX BC DC

LOON FUNG (B)
37 Gerrard Street
437 5429
⊖ Leicester Square
10.30 a.m.–11.30 p.m.
Cantonese
*Veg *T/A *Book *AC AX
BC DC

LOON WAH (B)
2 Macclesfield Street
734 5161
⊖ Piccadilly Circus
Noon–4.30 a.m.
Cantonese
*Veg *BC

THE MAYFLOWER (B)
68–70 Shaftesbury Avenue
734 9207
⊖ Piccadilly Circus
Noon–3.45 a.m.
*Veg *T/A *Book *AC AX
BC DC

NEW WORLD (B)
1 Gerrard Place
734 0677
⊖ Leicester Square
11.00 a.m.–11.45 p.m.
*Veg *T/A *Book *AC AX
BC DC

SHING ON (B)
58 Shaftesbury Avenue
437 6847

⊖ Piccadilly Circus
Noon–11.30 p.m.
Cantonese
*Veg *T/A *Book *AC AX
BC DC

TAI KA LOK (B)
18 Gerrard Street
437 2354
⊖ Leicester Square
Noon–11.30 p.m.
Cantonese
*Veg *T/A

WONG KEI (A)
41–43 Wardour Street
437 8408
⊖ Piccadilly Circus
Noon–11.30 p.m.
*Veg *T/A

YUNGS (B)
23 Wardour Street
437 4986
⊖ Piccadilly Circus
6.00 p.m.–2.00 a.m.
Cantonese
*T/A *AC AX BC DC

ENGLISH

THE REGENT PALACE
HOTEL
12 Sherwood Street
734 7000
⊖ Piccadilly Circus
– THE CARVERY (B)
12.30 p.m.–2.30 p.m. &
6.00 p.m.–9.00 p.m.
*Roast lunch *Veg
*AC AX BC DC

STARS　　　　　　　　　(C)
11 Soho Square
437 9535
✪ Tottenham Court Road
6.00 p.m.–11.00 p.m.
*Book *AC AX BC DC

FAR EASTERN

CHIANG MAI　　　　　　(B)
48 Frith Street
437 7444
✪ Tottenham Court Road
Noon–3.00 p.m. &
6.00 p.m.–10.30 p.m.
Thai
*Veg *Book *AC AX BC DC

THE EQUATORIAL　　　(B)
37 Old Compton Street
437 6112
✪ Leicester Square
Noon–11.15 p.m.
Singaporean
*Veg *T/A *Book *AC AX
BC DC

MELATI　　　　　　　　(C)
21 Great Windmill Street
437 2745
✪ Piccadilly Circus
Noon–11.30 p.m.
Malaysian/Singaporean
*Veg *T/A *Book *AC AX
BC DC

SINGAPORE MANDARIN
RESTAURANT　　　　　(B)
16 Old Compton Street
437 6517
✪ Leicester Square
6.00 p.m.–11.00 p.m.

Chinese/Malaysian/
Singaporean
*Veg *T/A *AX BC DC

FISH

WHEELER'S　　　　　　(C)
19 Old Compton Street
437 2706
✪ Leicester Square
12.30 p.m.–2.30 p.m. &
6.30 p.m.–10.00 p.m.
*Book *AC AX BC DC

FRENCH

LE BISTINGO　　　　　(B)
57 Old Compton Street
437 0784
✪ Piccadilly Circus
Noon–2.30 p.m. &
7.00 p.m.–11.00 p.m.
*AC AX BC DC

MAXINE'S DES
CHAMPS　　　　　　　(D)
ELYSÉES
21 Coventry Street
839 1069
✪ Piccadilly Circus
12.30 p.m.–3.00 p.m. &
5.30 p.m.–11.30 p.m.
*Veg *Book *AC AX BC DC

INDIAN

ASIA TANDOORI　　　(B)
44 Frith Street
437 8261
✪ Piccadilly Circus
Noon–3.00 p.m. &
5.30 p.m.–11.00 p.m.
*T/A *AX BC DC

KASHMIR (A)
5 Old Compton Street
734 1057
● Leicester Square
Noon–midnight
*Veg *T/A *Book *AC AX
BC DC

MAHARAJA TANDOORI (B)
14 Denman Street
437 4478
● Piccadilly Circus
Noon–midnight
*Veg *T/A *AC AX BC DC

MAHARANI (B)
77 Berwick Street
437 8568
● Oxford Circus
Noon–midnight
*Veg *T/A *AC AX BC DC

THE RED FORT (C)
77 Dean Street
437 2525
● Tottenham Court Road
Noon–3.00 p.m. &
6.00 p.m.–11.00 p.m.
*Veg *T/A *Book *AC AX
BC DC

THE REGENT
TANDOORI (B)
10 Denman Street
434 1134
● Piccadilly Circus
Noon–11.30 p.m.
Also serve steak and roasts
*Roast lunch *Veg *T/A
*Book *AC AX BC DC

VEERASWAMY (C)
99–101 Regent Street
734 1401

● Piccadilly Circus
Noon–2.30 p.m. &
7.00 p.m.–10.30 p.m.
*Veg *T/A *Book *AC AX
BC DC

INTERNATIONAL

CAFÉ ROYAL
68 Regent Street
437 9090
● Piccadilly Circus
– THE GRILL ROOM (E)
12.30 p.m.–2.15 p.m. &
7.00 p.m.–10.15 p.m.
English lunch/French dinner
*Roast lunch *Book
*AC AX BC DC
– THE NICOLS (A)
11.00 a.m.–7.00 p.m.
Snacks and light meals
*Tea *AC AX BC DC

THE INTERNATIONAL
VILLAGE at THE
TROCADERO
Piccadilly Circus
439 8476
● Piccadilly Circus
10.00 a.m.–midnight
*Breakfast *Tea
English, French and Italian
cafés, bars and buffets.
The main restaurants are:
– THE BRIGHTON
BELLE (C)
(enter from Rupert Street)
Noon–2.30 p.m.
& 7.00 p.m.–11.00 p.m.
English
*Book *AC AX BC DC

– CAFÉ MONTMARTRE (C)
Noon–2.30 p.m. &
7.00 p.m.–11.00 p.m.
French
*Book *AC AX BC DC

– VILLA VENEZIA   (C)
Noon–2.30 p.m. &
7.00 p.m.–11.00 p.m.
Italian
*Book *AC AX BC DC

NEW PICCADILLY CAFÉ (A)
8 Denman Street
437 8530
⊖ Piccadilly Circus
11.30 a.m.–10.30 p.m.
*Roast lunch *Not licensed

ITALIAN

BAR ITALIA   (A)
22 Frith Street
437 4520
⊖ Tottenham Court Road
7.00 a.m.–9.00 p.m.
Café – no hot food
*Breakfast *Not licensed

ESTORIL DA LUIGI
E ROBERTA   (D)
3 Denman Street
437 8700
⊖ Piccadilly Circus
Noon–2.30 p.m.
& 6.00 p.m.–10.00 p.m.
*AC AX BC DC

KETTNERS   (B)
29 Romilly Street
437 6437
⊖ Leicester Square
Noon–midnight
Mainly pizzas
*Veg *T/A *AC AX BC DC

LA TERRAZZA   (D)
19 Romilly Street
734 3334
⊖ Leicester Square
Noon–2.00 p.m. &
6.00 p.m.–11.00 p.m.
*Book *AC AX BC DC

LEONI'S QUO VADIS   (C)
26–29 Dean Street
437 4809
⊖ Leicester Square
11.30 p.m.–6.30 a.m.
*Breakfast
7.00 p.m.–10.30 p.m.
*Veg *Book *AC AX BC DC

PASTA FINO   (A)
27 Frith Street
439 8900
⊖ Leicester Square
6.00 p.m.–10.30 p.m.
*Veg *T/A *AC BC

PIZZA EXPRESS   (A)
10 Dean Street
437 9595
⊖ Tottenham Court Road
11.30 a.m.–midnight
Live jazz from 9.00 p.m.
*Veg *T/A *AX DC
and
29 Wardour Street
437 7215
⊖ Piccadilly Circus
11.30 a.m.–midnight
*Veg *T/A

TOPO GIGIO   (B)
46 Brewer Street
437 8516
⊖ Piccadilly Circus
Noon–11.30 p.m.
*Veg *AC AX BC DC

TRATTORIA
CAPPUCCETTO (B)
17 Moor Street
437 2527
☻ Leicester Square
Noon–3.00 p.m. &
6.00 p.m.–11.30 p.m.
*Veg *AC AX BC DC

JAPANESE

FUJI (D)
36 Brewer Street
734 0957
☻ Piccadilly Circus
6.00 p.m.–10.15 p.m.
*T/A *Book *AC AX BC DC

HOKKAI (C)
61 Brewer Street
734 5826
☻ Piccadilly Circus
6.00 p.m.–10.30 p.m.
*Book *AC AX BC DC

JEWISH

PHIL RABIN'S (A)
39 Great Windmill Street
437 8429
☻ Piccadilly Circus
11.00 a.m.–11.00 p.m.
*T/A

MIDDLE EASTERN

THE OLIVE TREE (B)
11 Wardour Street
734 0808
☻ Piccadilly Circus
Noon–10.30 p.m.
Lebanese
*Veg *T/A *AC AX BC

SWISS

THE SWISS CENTRE
1 Wardour Street
734 1291
☻ Leicester Square
*AC AX BC DC
– CHESA (D)
Noon–2.30 p.m. &
6.00 p.m.–11.00 p.m.
Full à la carte
*Book
– IMBISS (A)
Noon–11.00 p.m.
Coffee shop
*Tea *T/A
– LOCANDA (C)
Noon–11.00 p.m.
Fondue
– RENDEZVOUS (B)
Noon–11.00 p.m.
Snacks and light meals
*Veg
– TAVERNE (C)
Noon–11.00 p.m.
Cheese and meat specialities

W2

AMERICAN

MARSHALLS (B)
54 Porchester Road
221 5161
☻ Royal Oak
11.00 a.m.–3.00 p.m. &
7.00 p.m.–11.30 p.m.
Restaurant/Wine Bar with
music
*Veg *Book

AUSTRIAN

THE TIROLER HUT   (C)
27 Westbourne Grove
727 3981
✪ Bayswater
6.30 p.m.–11.30 p.m.
Austrian/German cuisine
*Veg *Book *AC AX BC DC

CHINESE

GREEN JADE   (B)
29–31 Porchester Road
229 7221
✪ Royal Oak
Noon–11.30 p.m.
*Veg *T/A *Book *AC AX
BC

HUNG TOA   (C)
54 Queensway
727 6017
✪ Bayswater
Noon–11.00 p.m.
*Veg *T/A

KAM TUNG   (B)
59 Queensway
229 6065
✪ Bayswater
Noon–11.45 p.m.
*Veg *T/A *AX

MANDARIN   (B)
33 Craven Road
723 8744
✪ Paddington/Lancaster Gate
Noon–2.30 p.m. &
6.00 p.m.–midnight
Pekingese
*Veg *T/A *Book *AX BC
DC

**THE MANDARIN
KITCHEN**   (B)
14 Queensway
727 9012
✪ Queensway
Noon–11.30 p.m.
*Veg *Book *AX BC DC

NEW LEE HO FOOK   (B)
48 Queensway
229 8624
✪ Bayswater
Noon–11.30 p.m.
*Veg *T/A *Book *AX

PENANG   (B)
41 Hereford Road
229 2982
✪ Bayswater
12.30 p.m.–11.00 p.m.
*Veg *T/A *AC BC DC

**YUNG'S NOODLE
RESTAURANT**   (B)
51 Queensway
727 5753
✪ Bayswater
11.00 a.m.–10.30 p.m.
*Not licensed *Veg *T/A

ENGLISH

HOT OFF THE PRESS   (B)
99 Queensway
727 0259
✪ Bayswater
8.00 a.m.–10.30 p.m.
*Roast lunch *Veg *BC

FAR EASTERN

BALI   (C)
101 Edgware Road
262 9100

✆ Marble Arch
Noon–11.30 p.m.
Indonesian/Malaysian
*Veg *T/A *Book *AC AX
BC DC

BUNGA RAYA (B)
107 Westbourne Grove
229 6180
✆ Bayswater
Noon–2.45 p.m. &
6.00 p.m.–11.30 p.m.
Malaysian
*Veg *AC AX BC DC

KEIO LONDON HOTEL
168 Sussex Gardens
402 9142
✆ Paddington
– RASA SAYANG WEST (B)
Noon–11.00 p.m.
Malaysian/Singaporean
*Veg *T/A *Book

SATAY HOUSE (B)
13 Sale Place
723 6763
✆ Edgware Road/Paddington
Noon–3.00 p.m. &
6.00 p.m.–11.00 p.m.
Malaysian
*Veg *T/A *Book

FRENCH

DOWNSTAIRS
CRÊPERIE (B)
86 Queensway
221 2455
✆ Bayswater
Noon–midnight
Also serve steaks etc.
*T/A *Book

LA BRASSERIE (C)
68 Queensway
727 4037
✆ Bayswater
Noon–3.00 p.m. &
6.00 p.m.–11.30 p.m.
*Book

LE BISTINGO (B)
117 Queensway
727 0743
✆ Bayswater
Noon–3.00 p.m. &
6.00 p.m.–11.00 p.m.
*Veg *AC AX BC DC

MAXINE'S DES CHAMPS
ELYSÉES (C)
125 Edgware Road
258 1801
✆ Edgware Road/Marble
Arch
Noon–midnight
*Veg *Book *AC AX BC DC

GERMAN

JAGERHÜTTE (C)
42 Queensway
229 7941
✆ Bayswater
11.00 a.m.–11.30 p.m.
German/Continental cuisine
Live music in the evening
*Book

GREEK

EL GOUCHO (C)
84 Queensway
229 4320
✆ Bayswater
Noon–1.30 a.m.
*T/A *AC AX BC DC

HALEPI (C)
18 Leinster Terrace
723 4097
✪ Lancaster Gate/Bayswater
Noon–1.00 a.m.
*Veg *Book *AC AX BC DC

HOMA (B)
106 Queensway
229 8470
✪ Bayswater
Noon–1.00 a.m.
Greek/Persian food and music
*Veg *T/A *AC AX BC DC

ROMANTICA (C)
12 Moscow Road
727 7112
✪ Bayswater
Noon–3.00 p.m. &
6.00 p.m.–midnight
Greek/Turkish cuisine
*Veg *AC AX BC DC

SANTORINI (B)
10 Moscow Road
229 1951
✪ Bayswater
Noon–3.00 p.m. &
6.00 p.m.–midnight
*Book *AC AX BC DC

SEMIRAMIS (B)
4 Hereford Road
727 4272
✪ Notting Hill Gate
7.00 p.m.–midnight
*Veg

HUNGARIAN

MIGNON (C)
2 Queensway
229 0093

✪ Queensway
11.00 a.m.–3.00 p.m. &
6.00 p.m.–midnight
*Veg *Book *AC AX BC DC

INDIAN

AL KHAYAM (B)
27–29 Westbourne Grove
727 5154
✪ Bayswater
Noon–midnight
*Veg *T/A *Book *AC AX
BC DC

BABA BHELPOORI
HOUSE (A)
118 Westbourne Grove
221 7502
✪ Bayswater
Noon–10.00 p.m.
Vegetarian food only
*Not licensed *Veg *T/A

BOMBAY PALACE (C)
50 Connaught Street
723 8855
✪ Marble Arch
Noon–3.00 p.m. &
6.00 p.m.–11.30 p.m.
*Veg *T/A *Book *AC AX
BC DC

DEEDAR (B)
12a Bathurst Street
262 5603
✪ Lancaster Gate
Noon–3.00 p.m. &
6.00 p.m.–11.30 p.m.
*Veg *T/A *AC AX BC DC

DIWANA BHELPOORI
HOUSE (B)
50 Westbourne Grove
221 0721
✜ Bayswater
Noon–3.00 p.m. &
6.00 p.m.–10.45 p.m.
Vegetarian food only
*Not licensed *Veg *T/A
*AC AX BC DC

KHAN'S (A)
13–15 Westbourne Grove
727 5420
✜ Bayswater
Noon–3.00 p.m. &
6.00 p.m.–midnight
*Veg *T/A *Book *AC AX
BC DC

KHYBER (B)
56 Westbourne Grove
727 4385
✜ Bayswater
Noon–midnight
*Veg *T/A *Book *AC AX
BC DC

MAHARAJAH (A)
50 Queensway
727 1135
✜ Bayswater
Noon–midnight
*Veg *Book *AC AX BC DC

MEHRAN (A)
115 Westbourne Grove
727 8938
✜ Bayswater
4.00 p.m.–2.00 a.m.
*Veg *T/A *Book *AC BC

NEW BENGAL (A)
189 Queensway
229 1640
✜ Bayswater/Royal Oak
Noon–11.30 p.m.
*Veg *T/A *AC AX BC DC

STANDARD (B)
23 Westbourne Grove
727 4818
✜ Bayswater
Noon–3.00 p.m. &
6.00 p.m.–midnight
*Veg *T/A *Book *AC AX
BC DC

VOGUE (C)
59 Edgware Road
723 1344
✜ Marble Arch
Noon–11.30 p.m.
*Veg *T/A *AC AX BC DC

INTERNATIONAL

ABBEYS (B)
109 Praed Street
723 2364
✜ Paddington/Edgware Road
Noon–2.00 p.m. &
7.30 p.m.–10.30 p.m.
English/Italian snacks
*Open Air *Book

BISTRO 75 (B)
75 Westbourne Grove
229 3771
✜ Bayswater
10.00 a.m.–midnight
Mexican/Italian/French
*Breakfast *Veg *AC AX BC

HOSPITALITY INN
HOTEL
104 Bayswater Road
262 4461
☻ Queensway
7.15 a.m.–10.00 a.m.
*Breakfast
– THE RESTAURANT   (C)
Noon–2.30 p.m. &
6.00 p.m.–10.15 p.m.
*Veg *Book *AC AX BC DC

MAISON BOUQUILLON (A)
45 Moscow Road
229 2107
☻ Bayswater
8.00 a.m.–8.00 p.m.
Coffee shop serving snacks
*Tea

NEW BOURN   (A)
111 Westbourne Grove
229 5861
☻ Bayswater
9.00 a.m.–9.00 p.m.
Café
*Breakfast *Roast lunch *Tea
*T/A *Open Air

THE SERPENTINE   (C)
Hyde Park
723 8784
☻ Lancaster Gate
Noon–3.30 p.m. &
7.00 p.m.–10.30 p.m.
*Veg *Open Air

ITALIAN

PIZZA EXPRESS   (A)
26 Porchester Road
229 7784
☻ Royal Oak

Noon–midnight
*Veg *T/A

TRAT WEST   (C)
143 Edgware Road
723 8203
☻ Edgware Road
Noon–2.30 p.m. &
6.00 p.m.–11.00 p.m.
*Book *AC AX BC DC

MIDDLE EASTERN

AL AMIR   (C)
112–114 Edgware Road
402 0087
☻ Edgware Road/Marble
Arch
Noon–midnight
Lebanese
*Veg *T/A *Book *AC AX
BC DC

AL OMARAA   (B)
27 Queensway
229 9898
☻ Bayswater
Noon–1.00 a.m.
Lebanese
*Veg *T/A *Book

IRAN AND THE
CONTINENT   (B)
44 Westbourne Grove
229 0416
☻ Bayswater
Noon–4.00 p.m.
Iranian
*Not licensed *Book *AC

THE LEBANESE
RESTAURANT   (C)
60 Edgware Road
723 9130

⊖ Marble Arch
Noon–midnight
Lebanese
*Veg *T/A *Book *AC AX
BC DC

MAROUSH (C)
21 Edgware Road
723 0773
⊖ Marble Arch
Noon–4.00 a.m.
Lebanese – mainly vegetarian
*Veg *T/A *AC AX BC DC

ZEINA ABU HAMMAD (B)
102 Queensway
727 0830
⊖ Bayswater/Queensway
11.00 a.m.–4.00 a.m.
Arabic/Oriental
*Veg *T/A *Book *AX

TURKISH

BODRUM (B)
26 Leinster Terrace
723 9346
⊖ Queensway
Noon–midnight
*Veg *T/A *Book *AC AX
BC DC

W4

AMERICAN

CASA MEXICANA (B)
30 Chiswick High Road
994 1941
⊖ Stamford Brook
6.00 p.m.–midnight

Mexican food and guitarist
*Veg *T/A *Book *AC AX
BC DC

MACARTHURS (A)
50 Turnham Green Terrace
994 3000
⊖ Turnham Green
Noon–11.30 p.m.
*Veg *T/A *AC BC

GERMAN

OLD HEIDELBERG
PÂTISSERIE (A)
270 Chiswick High Road
994 6621
⊖ Turnham Green
2.30 p.m.–5.30 p.m.
*Tea (only) *AC BC DC

INDIAN

CHISWICK TANDOORI (B)
532 Chiswick High Road
994 6266
⊖ Chiswick Park/
Gunnersbury
Noon–2.30 p.m. &
6.00 p.m.–11.30 p.m.
*Veg *T/A *AC AX BC DC

GANGES TANDOORI (B)
466 Chiswick High Road
994 1439/5823
⊖ Chiswick Park
Noon–2.45 p.m. &
6.00 p.m.–11.45 p.m.
*Veg *T/A *Book *AC AX
BC DC

INTERNATIONAL

PICKWICKS WINE BAR   (A)
13 Devonshire Road
747 1824
✆ Turnham Green
7.00 p.m.–10.30 p.m.
*Veg *T/A *Open Air
*AX BC DC

SOUTHEYS WINE BAR   (B)
144 Chiswick High Road
747 1946
✆ Turnham Green
Noon–3.00 p.m. &
7.00 p.m.–11.30 p.m.
*Veg *Open Air *AC AX BC
DC

TARTS CAFÉ   (B)
148 Chiswick High Road
747 1869
✆ Turnham Green
Noon–11.30 p.m.
*Tea *Veg *T/A *AC BC

ITALIAN

PIZZA EXPRESS   (A)
252 Chiswick High Road
747 0193
✆ Turnham Green
Noon–midnight
*Veg *T/A

W5

INDIAN

MONTY'S   (B)
224 South Ealing Road
560 2619

✆ South Ealing
Noon–3.00 p.m. &
6.00 p.m.–11.45 p.m.
*Veg *T/A *AC AX BC DC

INTERNATIONAL

BRENTHAM WINE BAR   (A)
124 Pitshanger Lane
998 6810
✆ Ealing Broadway
Noon–2.00 p.m. &
7.00 p.m.–10.30 p.m.
Guitar music in the evening
*Brunch *Veg *Open Air
*AC BC

ITALIAN

GINO'S   (B)
70 The Mall
567 5237
✆ Ealing Broadway
Noon–3.00 p.m. &
7.00 p.m.–11.30 p.m.

W6

AMERICAN

NEWTONS   (B)
98–100 Shepherd's Bush
Road
603 1931
✆ Shepherd's Bush/
Hammersmith
Noon–3.00 p.m. &
7.30 p.m.–11.00 p.m.
*T/A *Book *AC AX BC DC

ENGLISH

NOVOTEL LONDON HOTEL
1 Shortlands
741 1555
☠ Hammersmith
6.30 a.m.–9.30 a.m.
*Breakfast
1.30 p.m.–6.30 p.m.
*Tea
– THE GRILL (B)
Noon–2.30 p.m. &
6.30 p.m.–midnight
*Roast lunch *AC AX BC DC

INDIAN

ANARKALI (C)
303 King Street
748 1760
☠ Stamford Brook
Noon–2.45 p.m. &
6.00 p.m.–11.45 p.m.
*Veg *T/A *AC AX BC DC

BOMBAY INN (B)
177 King Street
748 1156
☠ Hammersmith
Noon–2.30 p.m. &
6.00 p.m.–midnight
*Veg *T/A *AC AX BC DC

LIGHT OF NEPAL (B)
268 King Street
748 3586
☠ Stamford Brook
Noon–2.30 p.m. &
6.00 p.m.–11.45 p.m.
Nepalese
*Veg *T/A *Open Air
*AC AX BC DC

INTERNATIONAL

P.J.'S WINE BAR (A)
138–140 King Street
748 9334
☠ Hammersmith
7.00 p.m.–10.30 p.m.
*Veg *AX BC DC

SUNDANCE STUDIOS (A)
Galena House,
Galena Road
741 8536
☠ Hammersmith
11.00 a.m.–3.00 p.m.
part of health club
*Veg

ITALIAN

DA GIANBRUNO (B)
6 Hammersmith Broadway
748 9393
☠ Hammersmith
Noon–3.00 p.m. &
6.00 p.m.–11.30 p.m.
*Veg *AC AX BC DC

POLISH

LOWICZANKA (B)
Polish Centre,
238 King Street
741 3225
☠ Stamford Brook
Noon–4.00 p.m. &
6.00 p.m.–10.00 p.m.
Piano music at lunchtime
*Veg *Book *AX DC

W8

AMERICAN

CASSIDY'S (B)
6 Holland Street
937 3367
✆ High Street Kensington
Noon–12.30 a.m.
*Tea *Veg *T/A *Open Air

HENRY J. BEAN'S (B)
54 Abingdon Road
937 3339
✆ High Street Kensington
Noon–10.30 p.m.
*Tea *Veg *Open Air

CHINESE

FU TONG (D)
29 Kensington High Street
937 1293
✆ High Street Kensington
Noon–11.30 p.m.
*Veg *T/A *Book *AC AX
BC DC

I CHING (C)
40 Earls Court Road
937 0409
✆ High Street Kensington
Noon–11.00 p.m.
Pekingese/Szechuan
*Veg *T/A *Book *AC AX
BC DC

JUNK TWO (C)
2–4 Thackeray Street
937 8508
✆ High Street Kensington
6.30 p.m.–11.30 p.m.

Pekingese/Cantonese
*Veg *T/A *Book *AC AX
BC DC

MANDARIN (B)
197c Kensington High Street
937 1551
✆ High Street Kensington
Noon–11.30 p.m.
*Veg *T/A *AC AX BC DC

SAILING JUNK (C)
59 Marloes Road
937 2589
✆ Earls Court
6.30 p.m.–11.30 p.m.
Cantonese/Pekingese
*Veg *AC AX BC DC

THE SINGING BAMBOO (C)
1st floor,
35 Marloes Road
373 3410
✆ Earls Court
6.00 p.m.–midnight
*Veg *T/A *AC AX BC DC

ENGLISH

JIMMIE'S WINE BAR (A)
Kensington Palace Barracks,
Kensington Church Street
937 9988
✆ High Street Kensington
Noon–2.00 p.m. &
7.00 p.m.–10.30 p.m.
Live music in the evening
*Roast lunch *Veg *T/A
*Open Air

KENSINGTON CLOSE
HOTEL
Wright's Lane
937 8170

✪ High Street Kensington
*Tea
– THE CARVERY (B)
11.30 a.m.–1.30 p.m.
*Roast lunch *Veg *Open Air
*Book *AC AX BC DC

MAGGIE JONES (C)
6 Old Court Place
937 6462
✪ High Street Kensington
12.45 p.m.–2.45 p.m. &
6.30 p.m.–10.30 p.m.
*Roast lunch *Book
*AC AX BC DC

FAR EASTERN

SIAM (C)
12 St Alban's Grove
937 8765
✪ Gloucester Road
Noon–2.30 p.m. &
6.00 p.m.–10.30 p.m.
Thai
*Veg *T/A *Book *AC AX
BC DC

THAI RESTAURANT (B)
209 Kensington High Street
937 2260
✪ High Street Kensington
Noon–3.00 p.m. &
6.00 p.m.–10.30 p.m.
Thai
*Veg *T/A *AC AX BC DC

FISH

THE ALCOVE (D)
17 Kensington High Street
937 1443
✪ High Street Kensington

Noon–2.30 p.m. &
7.00 p.m.–10.15 p.m.
*AC AX BC DC

FRENCH

THE ARK (C)
35 Kensington High Street
937 4294
✪ High Street Kensington
7.00 p.m.–11.00 p.m.
*Book *AC BC DC
and
THE ARK (B)
122 Palace Gardens Terrace
229 4024
✪ Notting Hill Gate
6.30 p.m.–11.30 p.m.
*Veg *Open Air *Book
*AC AX BC

LONDON TARA HOTEL
Scarsdale Place
937 7211
✪ High Street Kensington
– THE BRASSERIE (B)
7.00 a.m.–10.30 a.m. &
noon–10.45 p.m.
*Breakfast *Tea *Book
*AC AX BC DC

MANOUCHE (C)
10 Phillimore Gardens
937 4542
✪ High Street Kensington
Noon–2.30 p.m. &
6.00 p.m.–11.00 p.m.
*Veg *AC AX BC DC

MICHEL'S (D)
343 Kensington High Street
603 3613
✪ High Street Kensington

Noon–2.30 p.m. &
7.00 p.m.–10.30 p.m.
*Veg *Open Air *Book
*AC AX BC DC

THE ROOF GARDENS (C)
99 Kensington High Street
937 8923
⊖ High Street Kensington
12.30 p.m.–3.00 p.m.
*Roast lunch *Open Air *Book
*AC AX BC DC

TYCOON (D)
42 Kensington High Street
937 9795
⊖ High Street Kensington
6.00 p.m.–11.30 p.m.
Piano music
*Book *AC AX BC DC

INDIAN

KENSINGTON
TANDOORI (B)
1 Abingdon Road
937 6182
⊖ High Street Kensington
Noon–midnight
*Veg *T/A *Book *AC AX
BC DC

MALABAR (C)
27 Uxbridge Street
727 8800
⊖ Notting Hill Gate
1.00 p.m.–3.00 p.m. &
6.00 p.m.–11.00 p.m.
*Veg *T/A *Book *AC BC

INTERNATIONAL

BENEDICT'S WINE BAR (A)
106 Kensington High Street
937 7580
⊖ High Street Kensington
Noon–3.00 p.m. &
6.00 p.m.–10.30 p.m.
*Veg *AC AX BC DC

ITALIAN

AL GALLO D'ORO (E)
353 Kensington High Street
603 6951
⊖ High Street Kensington
Noon–3.00 p.m. &
7.00 p.m.–11.30 p.m.
*Veg *AC AX BC DC

PALMS (B)
3–5 Campden Hill Road
938 1830
⊖ High Street Kensington
Noon–midnight
*Tea *Veg *Open Air

PIZZA EXPRESS (A)
35 Earls Court Road
937 0761
⊖ High Street Kensington
Noon–midnight
*Veg *T/A

TOPO D'ORO (C)
39 Uxbridge Street
727 5813
⊖ Notting Hill Gate
Noon–2.30 p.m. &
6.00 p.m.–11.00 p.m.
*AC AX BC DC

TRATTOO (C)
2 Abingdon Road
937 4448

⊖ High Street Kensington
Noon–3.00 p.m. &
7.00 p.m.–11.00 p.m.
*Veg *Book *AC AX BC DC

MIDDLE EASTERN

AL-BASHA PALACE   (C)
222 Kensington High Street
937 1030
⊖ High Street Kensington
Noon–midnight
Lebanese
*Veg *T/A *Open Air *Book
*AC AX BC DC

BYBLOS   (B)
262 Kensington High Street
603 4422
⊖ High Street Kensington
Noon–midnight
Lebanese
*Veg *T/A *AC AX BC DC

PHOENICIA   (C)
11 Abingdon Road
937 0120
⊖ High Street Kensington
Noon–midnight
Lebanese
*Veg *T/A *Book *AC AX
BC DC

SOFREH KHANEH   (A)
188 Campden Hill Road
221 6741
⊖ Notting Hill Gate
9.30 a.m.–10.30 p.m.
Iranian
*Not licensed *Veg *T/A

W9

CHINESE

PANGS   (C)
215 Sutherland Avenue
289 2562
⊖ Maida Vale
Noon–2.45 p.m. &
6.30 p.m.–10.45 p.m.
*Veg *T/A *AC AX BC DC

INTERNATIONAL

RAOUL'S   (A)
13 Clifton Road
289 7313
⊖ Maida Vale
9.00 a.m.–6.00 p.m.
Snacks and light meals
*Breakfast *Tea *Not licensed

W10

INDIAN

BONGO   (B)
148 Ladbroke Grove
969 1611
⊖ Ladbroke Grove
5.30 p.m.–midnight
*Veg *Book *AC AX BC DC

W11

AMERICAN

TOOTSIES   (A)
120 Holland Park Avenue
229 8567

⊖ Holland Park
and
115 Notting Hill Gate
727 6562
⊖ Notting Hill Gate
Noon–11.30 p.m.
*Veg *T/A

ENGLISH

JULIE'S BAR   (B)
137 Portland Road
727 7985
⊖ Holland Park
Noon–10.30 p.m.
Light meals
*Tea

JULIE'S RESTAURANT   (C)
135 Portland Road
229 8331
⊖ Holland Park
12.30 p.m.–2.15 p.m. &
7.45 p.m.–10.30 p.m.
English/French cuisine
*Roast lunch *Veg *Open Air
*Book *AC AX BC DC

FRENCH

LA RÉSIDENCE   (C)
148 Holland Park Avenue
221 6090
⊖ Holland Park
12.30 p.m.–2.30 p.m. &
6.30 p.m.–10.30 p.m.
*Book *AC AX BC

LEITH'S   (E)
92 Kensington Park Road
229 4481
⊖ Notting Hill Gate
7.30 p.m.–11.30 p.m.
*Veg *Book *AC AX BC DC

MONSIEUR THOMPSON'S
                                      (C)
29 Kensington Park Road
727 9957
⊖ Notting Hill Gate
12.30 p.m.–2.30 p.m.
*Veg *AC AX BC DC

GREEK

CLEOPATRA TAVERNA (C)
148 Notting Hill Gate
727 4046
⊖ Notting Hill Gate
7.00 p.m.–1.00 a.m.
*Veg *AC AX BC DC

INDIAN

LALBAG TANDOORI   (A)
188 Westbourne Grove
727 7558
⊖ Notting Hill Gate
Noon–3.00 p.m. &
6.00 p.m.–midnight
*Veg *T/A *Book *AC AX
BC DC

INTERNATIONAL

HOLLANDS WINE BAR   (A)
6 Portland Road
229 3130
⊖ Holland Park
12.15 p.m.–2.15 p.m. &
7.00 p.m.–10.30 p.m.
*Brunch *Veg *Open Air
*Book *AC BC

KENSINGTON HILTON
HOTEL
179 Holland Park Avenue
603 3355

✪ Shepherd's Bush
6.30 a.m.–10.45 a.m.
*Breakfast
– THE RESTAURANT   (C)
12.45 p.m.–2.45 p.m. &
5.30 p.m.–10.45 p.m.
American jazz brunch
*Brunch *Roast lunch *Book
*AC AX BC DC

OBELISK   (B)
294 Westbourne Grove
229 1877
✪ Notting Hill Gate
12.30 p.m.–11.00 p.m.
*Veg *Open Air *AC BC

TARTS RESTAURANT   (B)
2a Kensington Park Road
229 6731
✪ Notting Hill Gate
Noon–11.00 p.m.
*Tea *Veg *T/A *AC BC

ITALIAN

BERTORELLI   (B)
17 Notting Hill Gate
727 7604
✪ Notting Hill Gate
Noon–3.00 p.m. &
6.00 p.m.–11.30 p.m.
*Veg *Book *AC AX BC DC

PIZZA EXPRESS   (A)
137 Notting Hill Gate
229 6000
✪ Notting Hill Gate
Noon–midnight
*Veg *T/A

JAPANESE

HIROKO OF KENSINGTON
                                        (D)
179 Holland Park Avenue
603 5003
✪ Shepherd's Bush
Noon–2.00 p.m. &
6.00 p.m.–9.30 p.m.
*Veg *Book *AC AX BC DC

W12

AMERICAN

THE HAT SHOP   (B)
11 Goldhawk Road
740 6437
✪ Goldhawk Road
Noon–11.00 p.m.
*Veg *T/A *Book

INDIAN

AJANTA TANDOORI   (B)
12 Goldhawk Road
743 5191
✪ Goldhawk Road
Noon–2.30 p.m. &
6.00 p.m.–11.45 p.m.
*Veg *T/A *AC AX BC

RAJPUT   (B)
144 Goldhawk Road
740 9036
✪ Goldhawk Road
Noon–3.00 p.m. &
6.00 p.m.–midnight
*Veg *T/A *Book *AC AX
BC DC

SHIREEN TANDOORI   (B)
270 Uxbridge Road
743 6857
⊖ Shepherd's Bush
11.00 a.m.–3.00 p.m. &
6.00 p.m.–11.30 p.m.
*Veg *T/A *AC AX BC DC

W13

CHINESE

MAXIM   (B)
155 Northfield Avenue
567 1719
⊖ Northfields
6.30 p.m.–midnight
*Veg *T/A *Book *AC AX
BC DC

FAR EASTERN

SINAR MATAHARI   (B)
146 The Broadway
840 4450
⊖ Ealing Broadway
1.00 p.m.–2.30 p.m. &
6.00 p.m.–10.30 p.m.
Indonesian
*Veg *T/A *AX

W14

CHINESE

MAMA SAN   (C)
11 Russell Gardens
602 0312
⊖ Shepherd's Bush

12.30 p.m.–2.30 p.m. &
6.30 p.m.–11.00 p.m.
*Veg *T/A *Book

ENGLISH

OLIVER'S   (B)
10 Russell Gardens
603 7645
⊖ Shepherd's Bush
Noon–4.15 p.m. &
6.00 p.m.–10.00 p.m.
English/International
*Roast lunch *Not licensed
*Veg *Open Air

INDIAN

HUNZA   (A)
73 Hammersmith Road
603 3629
⊖ Hammersmith
Noon–3.00 p.m. &
6.00 p.m.–midnight
*Veg *T/A *AC AX BC DC

MIDDLE EASTERN

YUS   (B)
7 Hammersmith Road
603 3980
⊖ Hammersmith
Noon–2.00 a.m.
Iranian
*T/A *Book *AX

WC1

CHINESE

CHUNG'S   (B)
15–17 Brunswick Centre
278 4945

◉ Russell Square
Noon–11.00 p.m.
*Veg

MR KAI OF RUSSELL
SQUARE (D)
50 Woburn Place
580 1188
◉ Russell Square
Noon–2.00 p.m. &
7.00 p.m.–11.15 p.m.
*Veg *Book *AC AX BC DC

ENGLISH

KENILWORTH HOTEL
97 Great Russell Street
636 3283
◉ Tottenham Court Road
– THE RESTAURANT (B)
12.30 p.m.–2.30 p.m. &
6.00 p.m.–10.00 p.m.
*Roast lunch *Book
*AC AX BC DC

KINGSLEY HOTEL
Bloomsbury Way
242 5881
◉ Tottenham Court Road
– THE CARVERY (C)
Noon–2.00 p.m. &
6.30 p.m.–9.00 p.m.
*Roast lunch *AC AX BC DC

THE RUSSELL HOTEL
Russell Square
837 6470
◉ Russell Square
8.00 a.m.–10.00 a.m.
*Breakfast
3.30 p.m.–6.00 p.m.
*Tea

– THE CARVERY (B)
Noon–2.30 p.m. &
6.00 p.m.–9.30 p.m.
*Roast lunch *AC AX BC DC

INDIAN

SHARUNA (B)
107 Great Russell Street
636 5922
◉ Tottenham Court Road
Noon–10.00 p.m.
*Veg *T/A *AC AX BC DC

TAGORE (B)
8 Brunswick Centre
837 9397
◉ Russell Square
Noon–3.00 p.m. &
6.00 p.m.–11.00 p.m.
*Veg *T/A *Book *AC AX
BC DC

INTERNATIONAL

MY OLD DUTCH (B)
131 High Holborn
242 5200
◉ Holborn
Noon–midnight
Pancakes
*Veg

OODLES (A)
42 New Oxford Street
580 9521/3762
◉ Tottenham Court Road
Noon–8.00 p.m.
*Veg *T/A *AC BC

ITALIAN

PIZZA EXPRESS (A)
30 Coptic Street
636 3232
♦ Tottenham Court Road
Noon–midnight
*Veg *T/A

WC2

AMERICAN

CAFÉ PACIFICO (B)
5 Langley Street
379 7728
♦ Covent Garden
7.00 p.m.–10.45 p.m.
Mexican
*Veg *AC BC

GODFATHERS (A)
146 Charing Cross Road
240 6908
♦ Tottenham Court Road
11.30 a.m.–12.30 a.m.
Pizzas
*Veg *T/A *AC AX BC DC

JOE ALLEN (C)
13 Exeter Street
836 0651
♦ Covent Garden
Noon–11.30 p.m.
*Brunch *Veg *Book

L. S. GRUNT'S (B)
12 Maiden Lane
379 7722
♦ Covent Garden
Noon–10.00 p.m.
Pizzas
*Veg *AC BC

MAXWELL'S (B)
16–17 Russell Street
836 0303
♦ Covent Garden
Noon–midnight
*Book *AC BC

PEPPERMINT PARK (B)
13 Upper St Martin's Lane
836 5234
♦ Leicester Square
12.30 p.m.–midnight
*Brunch *Tea *Veg *Book
*AC AX BC DC

ROCK GARDEN (B)
6 The Piazza
240 3961
♦ Covent Garden
10.00 a.m.–midnight
Live music in the basement
*Veg *T/A *Open air *BC

**TONY ROMA'S A PLACE
FOR RIBS** (B)
46–47 St Martin's Lane
379 3330
♦ Leicester Square
Noon–1.00 a.m.
Jazz piano in the evening
*Veg *T/A *Book *AC AX
BC

CHINESE

CANTON (A)
11 Newport Place
437 6220
♦ Leicester Square
open 24 hours
*Veg *AX BC DC

DIAMOND (B)
23 Lisle Street
437 2517
☻ Leicester Square
Noon–2.30 a.m.
*Veg *T/A

DYNASTY (B)
10 Charing Cross Road
240 2796
☻ Leicester Square
Noon–2.30 p.m. &
5.30 p.m.–11.30 p.m.
*Veg *T/A *AC AX BC DC

FUNG SHING (C)
15 Lisle Street
437 1539
☻ Leicester Square
Noon–midnight
*Veg *T/A *AC AX BC DC

HAPPY GARDEN (C)
47 Charing Cross Road
437 7472
☻ Leicester Square
Noon–midnight
*Veg *AX DC

JOY KING LAU (B)
3 Leicester Street
437 1132
☻ Leicester Square
11.00 a.m.–10.30 p.m.
Cantonese
*Veg *T/A *Book *AC AX
BC DC

SHU SHAN (C)
36 Cranbourn Street
836 7501
☻ Leicester Square

Noon–11.00 p.m.
Szechuan
*Veg *Book *AC AX BC DC

ENGLISH

BATES (C)
11 Henrietta Street
240 7600
☻ Covent Garden
Noon–3.00 p.m. &
5.30 p.m.–10.30 p.m.
*Veg *Book *AC AX BC DC

CHARING CROSS HOTEL
Strand
839 7282
☻ Charing Cross
8.00 a.m.–10.45 a.m.
*Breakfast
3.30 p.m.–6.00 p.m.
*Tea
– BETJEMAN CARVERY (C)
Noon–10.30 p.m.
*Roast lunch *AC AX BC DC

DRURY LANE HOTEL
10 Drury Lane
836 6666
☻ Covent Garden
– MAUDIE'S (C)
12.30 p.m.–2.00 p.m. &
6.30 p.m.–10.00 p.m.
English/French cuisine
*Book *AC AX BC DC

LYONS CORNER HOUSE
(A)
450 Strand
930 9381
☻ Charing Cross
8.00 a.m.–8.00 p.m.

Snacks and light meals
*Breakfast *Tea *AC AX
BC DC

PORTERS (B)
17 Henrietta Street
836 6466
⊖ Covent Garden
Noon–3.00 p.m. &
5.00 p.m.–10.30 p.m.
*Roast lunch *Veg *AC BC

THE SAVOY HOTEL
Strand
836 4343
⊖ Charing Cross/
Embankment
8.00 a.m.–10.30 a.m.
*Breakfast
3.30 p.m.–5.45 p.m.
*Tea
– THE RESTAURANT (E)
12.30 p.m.–2.30 p.m. &
7.00 p.m.–10.30 p.m.
English/French cuisine
*Roast lunch *Veg *Book
*AC AX BC DC

THE STRAND PALACE
HOTEL
Strand
836 8080
⊖ Covent Garden
– THE CARVERY (C)
Noon–2.30 p.m. &
6.00 p.m.–9.00 p.m.
*Roast lunch *Veg *AC AX
BC DC

THE TUDOR ROOMS (D)
80–81 St Martin's Lane
240 3978
⊖ Leicester Square

7.30 p.m.–2.00 a.m.
Medieval banquet with
entertainment and dancing
*Veg *Book *AC AX BC DC

THE WALDORF HOTEL
Aldwych
836 2400
⊖ Covent Garden
3.30 p.m.–6.30 p.m.
*Tea and music in Palm Court
– PALM COURT (C)
Noon–2.30 p.m. &
6.00 p.m.–10.00 p.m.
*Brunch *Veg *AC AX
BC DC
– THE WALDORF (D)
6.00 p.m.–10.00 p.m.
English/French cuisine
*Book *AC AX BC DC

FAR EASTERN

NEW RASA SAYANG (B)
3 Leicester Place
437 4556
⊖ Leicester Square
Noon–10.15 p.m.
South-east Asian
*Veg *Book *AX BC DC

FISH

FRÈRE JACQUES (C)
38 Long Acre
836 7823
⊖ Covent Garden
Noon–2.30 p.m. &
7.00 p.m.–midnight
*Book *AC AX BC DC

MANZI'S (C)
1 Leicester Street
734 0224

⊖ Leicester Square
5.30 p.m.–11.30 p.m.
*Book *AC AX BC DC

PAYTON PLAICE (B)
96 Charing Cross Road
379 3277
⊖ Leicester Suare
11.45 a.m.–10.30 p.m.
*Veg *Book

FRENCH

CAFÉ PELICAN (C)
45 St Martin's Lane
379 0309
⊖ Leicester Square
11.00 a.m.–12.30 a.m.
Lunch: 12.30 p.m.–2.30 p.m.
Dinner: 6.00 p.m.–12.30 a.m.
Café/restaurant
*Breakfast *Brunch *Veg
*AC AX BC DC

THE CRÊPERIE (A)
Unit 21, The Market
836 2137
⊖ Covent Garden
10.00 a.m.–11.30 p.m.
*Breakfast *Veg *T/A
*Open Air

HOWARD HOTEL
Temple Place
836 3555
⊖ Charing Cross
– QUAI D'OR (D)
12.15 p.m.–2.30 p.m. &
7.00 p.m.–11.00 p.m.
*Roast lunch *Book
*AC AX BC DC

INDIAN

ALDWYCH TANDOORI (B)
2–4 Lancaster Place
240 2717
⊖ Charing Cross
Noon–2.45 p.m. &
5.30 p.m.–midnight
*Veg *T/A *AC AX BC DC

GANDHI (B)
31 Villiers Street
930 7663
⊖ Embankment
Noon–11.00 p.m.
*Veg *T/A *Book *AC AX
BC DC

THE GRAND INDIAN (B)
6 New Row
240 0785
⊖ Leicester Square
Noon–3.00 p.m. &
5.30 p.m.–11.30 p.m.
*Veg *T/A *Book *AC AX
BC DC

THE INDIA CLUB (B)
143 Strand
836 0650
⊖ Covent Garden
Noon–2.30 p.m. &
6.00 p.m.–8.00 p.m.
*Veg *T/A

LAST DAYS OF THE
RAJ (C)
22 Drury Lane
836 1628
⊖ Covent Garden
7.00 p.m.–11.30 p.m.
*Veg *T/A *Book *AC AX
BC DC

STRAND TANDOORI (B)
45 Bedford Street
240 1333
⊖ Leicester Square
Noon–3.00 p.m. &
6.00 p.m.–11.00 p.m.
*Veg *T/A *AC AX BC DC

TASTE OF INDIA (C)
25 Catherine Street
836 2538
⊖ Covent Garden
Noon–2.30 p.m. &
5.30 p.m.–11.30 p.m.
*Veg *T/A *Book *AC AX
BC DC

INTERNATIONAL

BLAKE'S WINE AND FOOD
BAR (A)
34 Wellington Street
836 5298
⊖ Covent Garden
Noon–10.00 p.m.
*Veg *AC AX BC DC

EDEN (A)
Unit 5, The Market
836 0272
⊖ Covent Garden
9.00 a.m.–11.00 p.m.
Self-service
*T/A *Open Air

FARMHOUSE TABLE (B)
190 Shaftesbury Avenue
836 1149
⊖ Tottenham Court Road
Noon–10.30 p.m.
*Roast lunch *Book
*AC AX BC DC

R. S. HISPANIOLA (D)
Victoria Embankment
839 3011
⊖ Embankment
Noon–2.30 p.m. &
7.00 p.m.–9.30 p.m.
Restaurant ship on the Thames
*Roast lunch *Veg

HOBSON'S WINE BAR (B)
20 Upper St Martin's Lane
836 5849
⊖ Leicester Square
7.00 p.m.–10.30 p.m.

TUTTONS (C)
11–12 Russell Street
836 1167
⊖ Covent Garden
9.00 a.m.–10.00 a.m.
*Breakfast
Noon–11.30 p.m.
*Veg *Open Air *AC AX
BC DC

ISRAELI

GABY'S CONTINENTAL
BAR (B)
30 Charing Cross Road
836 4233
⊖ Leicester Square
Noon–10.00 p.m.
*Not licensed *Veg

JERUSALEM (A)
150 Shaftesbury Avenue
836 7145
⊖ Leicester Square
Noon–11.00 p.m.
*Veg *T/A

ITALIAN

COVENT GARDEN PASTA BAR (B)
30 Henrietta Street
836 8396
⊖ Covent Garden
12.30 p.m.–10.30 p.m.
*Veg

GIARDINO'S (B)
32 Long Acre
836 8529
⊖ Covent Garden
Noon–11.30 p.m.
Restaurant/antipasta bar
*Tea *Veg *AC AX BC DC

TRATTORIA ITALIANO BIAGIO (C)
15 Villiers Street
839 3633
⊖ Embankment
11.30 a.m.–12.15 a.m.
*Veg *Book *AC AX BC DC

JAPANESE

HOUSE OF AZAMI (C)
13–15 West Street
240 0634
⊖ Leicester Square
6.00 p.m.–10.30 p.m.
*Book *AC AX BC DC

VEGETARIAN

BUNJIE'S COFFEE HOUSE (A)
27 Litchfield Street
240 1796
⊖ Leicester Square

5.00 p.m.–11.00 p.m.
Self-service and folk music
*Not licensed

OUT OF TOWN RICHMOND

CHINESE

KEW RENDEZVOUS (C)
110 Kew Road
948 4343
⊖ Kew Gardens
Noon–2.30 p.m. &
6.00 p.m.–11.30 p.m.
*Veg *T/A *Book *AC AX BC DC

RED LION (B)
18 Red Lion Street
940 2371
⊖ Richmond
Noon–2.30 p.m. &
6.00 p.m.–midnight
Pekingese
*Veg *T/A *Book *AC AX BC DC

RICHMOND RENDEZVOUS (B)
1 Wakefield Road
940 6869
⊖ Richmond
Noon–2.30 p.m. &
6.00 p.m.–11.30 p.m.
Pekingese
*Veg *T/A *Book *AC AX BC DC

ENGLISH

COLIN'S WINE BAR (B)
135 Kew Road
940 5552
✆ Richmond
11.00 a.m.–2.30 p.m. &
7.00 p.m.–10.30 p.m.
*Roast lunch *Book
*AC AX BC DC

MRS BEETON'S (A)
58 Hill Rise
940 9561
10.00 a.m.–5.00 p.m.
*Roast lunch *Tea
*Not licensed *Veg *Book

OSCAR'S (B)
149 Kew Road
940 8298
✆ Richmond
12.30 p.m.–2.30 p.m.
English/French cuisine
*Roast lunch *Open Air
*Book *AC AX BC DC

INDIAN

HAWELI (B)
15–17 Hill Rise
940 3002
✆ Richmond
12.30 p.m.–4.00 p.m. &
6.30 p.m.–11.00 p.m.
*Veg *T/A *Book *AC AX
BC DC

INTERNATIONAL

PISSARRO'S WINE BAR (B)
1–3 Kew Green
940 3987

✆ Kew Gardens/Richmond
Noon–2.00 p.m.
& 7.00 p.m.–10.30 p.m.
*Roast lunch *Veg

ITALIAN

CAFFE MAMMA (B)
24 Hill Street
940 1625
✆ Richmond
Noon–midnight
Mainly pasta
*Veg *T/A *Open Air *AC
BC DC

RUSSIAN

BALALAIKA (B)
10 Red Lion Street
948 2366
✆ Richmond
Noon–2.00 p.m.
Ukrainian/Slavic
*Veg *AC AX BC DC

WHOLEFOOD

RICHMOND HARVEST (A)
5 Dome Buildings,
The Quadrant
940 1138
✆ Richmond
11.30 a.m.–11.00 p.m.
*Veg *Book

BREAKFAST AND/OR BRUNCH

This is a list of restaurants serving breakfast and/or brunch. The opening time is given in brackets.
See main text for details.

E1

ENGLISH
G & T Restaurant (7.30 a.m.)
The Tower Hotel
– The Picnic Basket
(7.00 a.m.)

EC1

ENGLISH
Barbican City Hotel
(7.00 a.m.)

EC2

ENGLISH
The Great Eastern Hotel
(8.00 a.m.)

INTERNATIONAL
Chubbies (8.00 a.m.)

N1

INTERNATIONAL
Serendipity (noon)

N4

VEGETARIAN
Seasons (10.00 a.m.)

N10

ITALIAN
Guideberry (11.00 a.m.)

NW1

FRENCH
Le Bistroquet (9.00 a.m.)
Pratts (9.00 a.m.)

INTERNATIONAL
Harewood Hotel (7.30 a.m.)

NW3

ENGLISH
Farquharsons (10.00 a.m.)

FRENCH
Dome (9.00 a.m.)

INTERNATIONAL
Hampstead Pâtisserie & Tea
Rooms (9.30 a.m.)
Rumbold's Tea Rooms
(10.00 a.m.)

VEGETARIAN
Zorba The Buddha Rajneesh
(8.00 a.m.)

SE10

INTERNATIONAL
Meantime (noon)

SW1

ENGLISH
Grandma Lee's (7.00 a.m.)
Holiday Inn (7.00 a.m.)
Sheraton Park Tower Hotel
(8.00 a.m.)

– The Restaurant (noon)
Upper Crust In Belgravia
(10.00 a.m.)

FRENCH
La Brasserie At Dolphin
Square (7.30 a.m.)
Le Caprice (noon)

INTERNATIONAL
Belgravia Sheraton Hotel
(8.00 a.m.)
The Cavendish Hotel
– The Cavendish (12.30 p.m.)
Hyde Park Hotel (7.30 a.m.)

SW3

FRENCH
Brasserie St Quentin
(10.00 a.m.)
Capital Hotel (7.00 a.m.)
La Brasserie (11.00 a.m.)

INTERNATIONAL
Avoirdupois (noon)
Basil Street Hotel (8.00 a.m.)
Draycott's (11.30 a.m.)
Foxtrot Oscar (11.30 a.m.)
Huff's (10.30 a.m.)

ITALIAN
Picasso (9.00 a.m.)

SW4

INTERNATIONAL
Tea Time (10.00 a.m.)

SW5

FAR EASTERN
The Philbeach Hotel
(9.00 a.m.)

SW7

INTERNATIONAL
Blakes Hotel (7.30 a.m.)

SW10

AMERICAN
Tootsies (9.00 a.m.)

ENGLISH
Chelsea Wharf (noon)

SW11

FRENCH
La Bouffe (11.00 a.m.)

W1 – NORTH

AMERICAN
Coconut Grove (noon)
John G's (9.30 a.m.)

FRENCH
Café Crêperie (9.00 a.m.)

INTERNATIONAL
The Portman Inter-
Continental
– Truffles (11.30 a.m.)

W1 – SOUTH WEST

ENGLISH
The Dorchester Hotel
– The Promenade (9.00 a.m.)
London Hilton Hotel
(7.00 a.m.)
Richoux (10.00 a.m.)

FRENCH
Athenaeum Hotel (7.30 a.m.)
Claridge's Hotel (7.30 a.m.)
The Connaught Hotel
(7.30 a.m.)

Mayfair Hotel
– Le Châteaubriand
(12.30 p.m.)
The Ritz Hotel (7.30 a.m.)

INTERNATIONAL
The Inn On The Park Hotel
– The Lounge (9.00 a.m.)
The Inter-Continental Hotel
(7.00 a.m.)
– Le Souffle (noon)
The Westbury Hotel
(7.30 a.m.)

W1 – SOUTH EAST

AMERICAN
Surprise (noon)

INTERNATIONAL
The International Village at
The Trocadero (10.00 a.m.)

ITALIAN
Bar Italia (7.00 a.m.)

W2

INTERNATIONAL
Bistro 75 (10.00 a.m.)
Hospitality Inn Hotel
(7.15 a.m.)
New Bourn (9.00 a.m.)

W5

INTERNATIONAL
Brentham Wine Bar (noon)

W6

ENGLISH
Novotel London Hotel
(6.30 a.m.)

W8

FRENCH
London Tara Hotel
– The Brasserie (7.00 a.m.)

W9

INTERNATIONAL
Raoul's (9.00 a.m.)

W11

INTERNATIONAL
Hollands Wine Bar
(12.15 p.m.)
Kensington Hilton Hotel
(6.30 a.m.)
– The Restaurant (12.45 p.m.)

WC1

ENGLISH
The Russell Hotel (8.00 a.m.)

WC2

AMERICAN
Joe Allen (noon)
Peppermint Park (12.30 p.m.)

ENGLISH
Charing Cross Hotel
(8.00 a.m.)
Lyons Corner House
(8.00 a.m.)
The Savoy Hotel (8.00 a.m.)
The Waldorf Hotel
– Palm Court (noon)

FRENCH
Café Pelican (11.00 a.m.)
The Crêperie (10.00 a.m.)

TRADITIONAL SUNDAY LUNCH

This is a list of restaurants
serving roast lunch.
See main text for details.

E1

ENGLISH
Dickens Inn By The Tower
– Pickwick Room
The Tower Hotel
– The Carvery

E2

AMERICAN
The Ringside

E11

ENGLISH
The Woodbine Wine Rooms

EC1

ENGLISH
Barbican City Hotel
– The Carvery
Café St Pierre
Rudland & Stubbs

EC2

ENGLISH
Barbican Centre
– The Cut Above
The Great Eastern Hotel
– City Gates Restaurant

N1

ENGLISH
Mr Bumble

INTERNATIONAL
Uppers Bistro

N6

ENGLISH
The Orangery

FRENCH
One Hampstead Lane

N9

INTERNATIONAL
Gatto Blu International

N14

FRENCH
L'Oiseau Noir

NW1

ENGLISH
Mustoe Bistro
My Fair Lady

FRENCH
Le Routier
Pratts

NW2

ENGLISH
Quincy's

NW3

AUSTRIAN
The Third Man

ENGLISH
Finches
Kenwood House
– The Coach House
– The Old Kitchen
Turpin's

FISH
La Gaffe

FRENCH
Bunny's
Fagin's Kitchen

INTERNATIONAL
Hill House

NW6

ENGLISH
Arches Wine Bar
Peter's

NW8

ENGLISH
Ladbroke Westmoreland Hotel
– Lord's Carver Restaurant

INTERNATIONAL
Oslo Court Restaurant

ITALIAN
Fontana Amorosa

SE10

FRENCH
Brandies

SE16

ENGLISH
Downtown

SE22

FRENCH
Le Moulin
The Pyramid

SE24

FRENCH
Bon Ton Roulet

SE26

ENGLISH
Delvino's

INTERNATIONAL
Mister Moon's

SW1

ENGLISH
Chimes
Goring Hotel
– The Restaurant
Grumbles
Holiday Inn
– Papillon
Hyde Park Hotel
– The Grill Room
St Ermin's Hotel
– The Carvery
Upper Crust in Belgravia

SW3

ENGLISH
Drakes
The English House
Nineteen
Reflections
Waltons

FRENCH
Dominic's
La Popote
Queenies

INTERNATIONAL
Avoirdupois
Basil Street Hotel
– The Restaurant
Foxtrot Oscar

SW4

ENGLISH
Changing Times

INTERNATIONAL
Metro
Ormes Wine Bar

SW5

ENGLISH
Boswell's
Reads

INTERNATIONAL
The Pot

SW6

FRENCH
Pigeon
Trencherman

INTERNATIONAL
Crocodile Tears

SW7

ENGLISH
Rembrandt Hotel
– The Carvery
Scandies Wine Bar

FRENCH
La Chanterelle

INTERNATIONAL
The Beggars Banquet

ITALIAN
Masters

SW9

ENGLISH
Twenty Trinity Gardens

SW10

ENGLISH
Chelsea Wharf
Clowns
Hungry Horse
Jakes

FRENCH
Roy's

ITALIAN
Flavio
Leonardo's

SW11

ENGLISH
No Name Place
Pollyanna's

INTERNATIONAL
Battersea Arts Centre

SW13

FRENCH
Bloomers Brasserie

ITALIAN
Rose

SW15

ENGLISH
Gavin's Bistro
Henrietta's

FRENCH
Mossop's

SW17

INTERNATIONAL
Harvey's

SW19

ENGLISH
Yesterday

W1 – NORTH

ENGLISH
The Cumberland Hotel
– The Carvery
Flanagans

INTERNATIONAL
The Portman Inter-
Continental
– Truffles

W1 – SOUTH WEST

ENGLISH
The Dorchester Hotel
– The Dorchester Grill
London Hilton Hotel
– The British Harvest

INTERNATIONAL
The Inn On The Park Hotel
– The Lounge
The Park Lane Hotel
– Bracewells

W1 – SOUTH EAST

AMERICAN
Surprise

ENGLISH
The Regent Palace Hotel
– The Carvery

INDIAN
The Regent Tandoori

INTERNATIONAL
Café Royal
– The Grill Room
New Piccadilly Café

W2

ENGLISH
Hot Off The Press

INTERNATIONAL
New Bourn

W6

ENGLISH
Novotel London Hotel
– The Grill

W8

ENGLISH
Jimmie's Wine Bar
Kensington Close Hotel
– The Carvery
Maggie Jones

FRENCH
The Roof Gardens

W11

ENGLISH
Julie's Restaurant

INTERNATIONAL
Kensington Hilton Hotel
– The Restaurant

W14

ENGLISH
Oliver's

WC1

ENGLISH
Kenilworth Hotel
– The Restaurant
Kingsley Hotel
– The Carvery
The Russell Hotel
– The Carvery

WC2

ENGLISH
Charing Cross Hotel
– Betjeman Carvery
Porters
The Savoy Hotel
– The Restaurant
The Strand Palace Hotel
– The Carvery

FRENCH
Howard Hotel

INTERNATIONAL
Farmhouse Table
R. S. Hispaniola

OUT OF TOWN – RICHMOND

ENGLISH
Colin's Wine Bar
Mrs Beeton's
Oscar's

INTERNATIONAL
Pissarro's Wine Bar

AFTERNOON TEA

This is a list of places serving
afternoon tea.
See main text for details.

E1

ENGLISH
The Tower Hotel
– The Picnic Basket

EC2

INTERNATIONAL
Barbican Centre
– The Waterside Café

N1

INTERNATIONAL
Serendipity

N6

ENGLISH
The Orangery

NW1

FRENCH
Le Bistroquet
Pratts

NW3

ENGLISH
Farquharsons
Kenwood House
– The Coach House
– The Old Kitchen

FRENCH
Dome

INTERNATIONAL
Hampstead Pâtisserie & Tea Rooms
Louis Pâtisserie
Rumbold's Tea Rooms

SE1

INTERNATIONAL
Royal Festival Hall
– Coffee Lounge

SW1

ENGLISH
Goring Hotel
Grandma Lee's
St Ermin's Hotel
Sheraton Park Tower Hotel
Upper Crust In Belgravia

FRENCH
Hyatt Carlton Tower Hotel
Royal Horseguards Hotel
– Coffee Corner

INTERNATIONAL
Belgravia Sheraton Hotel
Cadogan Hotel
The Cavendish Hotel
Hyde Park Hotel

SW3

AMERICAN
Henry J. Bean's

FRENCH
Brasserie St Quentin
Capital Hotel

INTERNATIONAL
Chelsea Pot
Huff's
The Pheasantry Café

SW4

INTERNATIONAL
Tea Time

SW7

ENGLISH
Rembrandt Hotel

INTERNATIONAL
Blakes Hotel

SW11

INTERNATIONAL
Armstrong's Wine Bar

SW13

INTERNATIONAL
The Old Rangoon

W1 – NORTH

FRENCH
Churchill Hotel

INTERNATIONAL
The Portman Inter-Continental
– The Bakery
The Selfridge Hotel
– Lounge

ITALIAN
Trattoria Bernigra

W1 – SOUTH WEST

ENGLISH
The Dorchester Hotel
– The Promenade
Richoux

FRENCH
Athenaeum Hotel
Brown's Hotel
The Connaught Hotel
The Ritz Hotel

INTERNATIONAL
The Inn On The Park Hotel
– The Lounge
The Inter-Continental Hotel
The Park Lane Hotel
The Westbury Hotel

W1 – SOUTH EAST

INTERNATIONAL
Café Royal
– The Nicols
The International Village at
The Trocadero

SWISS
The Swiss Centre
–Imbiss

W2

INTERNATIONAL
Maison Bouquillon
New Bourn

W4

GERMAN
Old Heidelberg Pâtisserie

INTERNATIONAL
Tarts Café

W6

ENGLISH
Novotel London Hotel

W8

AMERICAN
Cassidy's
Henry J. Bean's

ENGLISH
Kensington Close Hotel

FRENCH
London Tara Hotel
– The Brasserie

ITALIAN
Palms

W9

INTERNATIONAL
Raoul's

W11

ENGLISH
Julie's Bar

INTERNATIONAL
Tarts Restaurant

WC1

ENGLISH
The Russell Hotel

WC2

AMERICAN
Peppermint Park

ENGLISH
Charing Cross Hotel
Lyons Corner House

The Savoy Hotel
The Waldorf Hotel

ITALIAN
Giardino's

OUT OF TOWN – RICHMOND

ENGLISH
Mrs Beeton's

LATE NIGHT

This is a list of restaurants open after 11.30 p.m. The closing time is given in brackets.
See main text for details.

E1

ENGLISH
The Tower Hotel
– The Picnic Basket (midnight)

INDIAN
Clifton (1.00 a.m.)
India Grill (12.30 a.m.)
Sheba Tandoori (midnight)
Sita Tandoori (midnight)
Sunar Bangla (midnight)

E2

INTERNATIONAL
Venus Steak House (1.00 a.m.)

E4

INDIAN
Mumtaz Tandoori (midnight)

E7

INDIAN
Bala (12.30 a.m.)

E18

CHINESE
Dragon Inn (midnight)

INDIAN
Meghna Grill (midnight)

EC1

INDIAN
The Jamuna (midnight)

EC4

ENGLISH
City of London Tavern
(1.00 a.m.)

N1

INDIAN
Goan Restaurant (midnight)
Manzil Tandoori (midnight)
Parveen Tandoori (12.30 a.m.)
Sonar Gaon (midnight)

ITALIAN
Pizza Express (midnight)

TURKISH
Hodja Nasreddin (3.00 a.m.)
Sultan Ahmet (2.30 a.m.)
Sultan's Delight (1.00 a.m.)

N3

GREEK
Sparta Restaurant (midnight)

N6

CHINESE
New Dragon (midnight)

N7

INDIAN
Taj Mahal (12.30 a.m.)

N8

INDIAN
Jalaliah Restaurant (midnight)

INTERNATIONAL
Criterion Steak House
(2.00 a.m.)

N13

INDIAN
Dipali Restaurant (midnight)

NW10

AMERICAN
Mean Fiddler (1.00 a.m.)

INDIAN
Khas Tandoori (midnight)

NW11

INDIAN
Mogul Room (midnight)

SE1

INDIAN
Castle Tandoori (midnight)

SE3

INDIAN
Sopna Tandoori (midnight)

SE4

INDIAN
Indiana Tandoori (midnight)

SE5

ITALIAN
New La Belle Italia (midnight)

SE8

TURKISH
Marmara (12.30 a.m.)

SE10

CHINESE
Mr Chung (midnight)

FRENCH
Brandies (midnight)

INDIAN
Greenwich Tandoori
(midnight)

SE11

INDIAN
Gandhi's (11.45 p.m.)

SE13

INDIAN
Curry Garden (midnight)

SE22

INDIAN
Dulwich Tandoori (midnight)

SE23

INDIAN
Dewaniam (midnight)

SW1

AMERICAN
Hamburger Heaven (midnight)
Sloanes 208 (midnight)

CHINESE
Mr Chow (midnight)

ENGLISH
Sheraton Park Tower Hotel
– The Restaurant (midnight)

FRENCH
Le Caprice (midnight)
Maxine's des Champs Elysées
(midnight)

INDIAN
Pimlico Tandoori (midnight)
Yasmine (midnight)

ITALIAN
Pizza Express (midnight)
Pizza on the Park (midnight)
Villa dei Cesari (2.00 a.m.)

SW2

ITALIAN
Pizza Plus (midnight)

N14

INDIAN
Emperor of India (midnight)
Standard (midnight)

N16

CHINESE
Eleganza (midnight)

INTERNATIONAL
Crazy Horse (12.45 a.m.)

N19

**PORTUGUESE &
SPANISH**
La Parra (midnight)

N21

INDIAN
Raf of India (midnight)

N22

INDIAN
Eastern Eye (midnight)

NW1

GREEK
Andy's Kebab House
(midnight)
Ararat (midnight)

INDIAN
Light of India (midnight)
Rana of Camden (midnight)
Sagarmatha (midnight)
Tandoor Mahal (midnight)

INTERNATIONAL
Primrose (midnight)

MIDDLE EASTERN
Ali Baba (midnight)

NW2

INDIAN
Cricklewood Tandoori
(midnight)
Shama Tandoori (midnight)
Yeti Tandoori (midnight)

INTERNATIONAL
Martha's Vineyard (midnight)

NW3

AMERICAN
Maxwell's (midnight)

AUSTRIAN
The Third Man (midnight)

CHINESE
Gourmet Rendezvous
(midnight)
Weng Wah House (midnight)

ENGLISH
Farquharsons (midnight)
Finches (midnight)

GREEK
Skorpios (2.00 a.m.)

INDIAN
Beer & Curry (midnight)
Bullock Cart (midnight)
Raj of Hampstead (midnight)

INTERNATIONAL
The Milk Churn (midnight)
Parks (midnight)
Peppercorns (1.00 a.m.)

ITALIAN
Pizza Express (midnight)

NW4

INTERNATIONAL
Chaglayan Kebab House
(midnight)

NW6

INDIAN
Bangladesh Cuisine (midnight)
Kilburn Tandoori (midnight)
Raffles (midnight)

INTERNATIONAL
Jockey's Club (3.00 a.m.)

NW7

CHINESE
Tai Coon (midnight)

SW3

AMERICAN
Wolfe's (midnight)

CHINESE
Choy's (midnight)
Dumpling House (midnight)

ENGLISH
Nineteen (11.45 p.m.)

FRENCH
Astrix (midnight)
La Brasserie (midnight)

INTERNATIONAL
Bistro Vino (11.45 p.m.)

ITALIAN
Don Luigi (11.45 p.m.)
Pizza Pomodoro (1.00 a.m.)

PORTUGUESE
Caravela (midnight)
O Fado (midnight)

RUSSIAN
Borshtch 'n' Cheers (midnight)
Borshtch n'Tears (midnight)

SW4

INDIAN
Golden Curry (midnight)
Maharani (12.30 a.m.)
New Agra (midnight)
Shah In Shah (midnight)
Standard (midnight)

SW5

AFRICAN
Balogun's (midnight)

AMERICAN
Huby's (midnight)

CHINESE
Hong Kong (midnight)
New Lotus Garden
(12.30 a.m.)

FRENCH
Twenties (midnight)

INDIAN
Akash Tandoori (midnight)
The Naraine (midnight)

INTERNATIONAL
The Pot (midnight)

SW6

INDIAN
Kabana (midnight)
Mother India (midnight)

ITALIAN
Little Italy (midnight)
Perfect Pizza (midnight)
Pizza Mia (midnight)
Pizza the Action (midnight)

SW7

CHINESE
Paper Tiger (midnight)

INDIAN
Aladdin (midnight)

ITALIAN
Pizza Express (midnight)
The South Ken Pasta Bar
(midnight)

SW9

INDIAN
Oval Tandoori (midnight)
Paradise (midnight)
Royal Tandoori (midnight)

SW10

AMERICAN
The American (12.30 a.m.)
Parsons (12.30 a.m.)
Up All Night (6.00 a.m.)

INDIAN
Nayab (midnight)

INTERNATIONAL
Ambrosiana Crêperie
(midnight)

ITALIAN
Chelsea Pasta Bar (midnight)
Flavio (11.45 p.m.)
Pizza Express (midnight)

SPANISH
El Bodegan (midnight)

SW11

CHINESE
Jasmin (midnight)

ENGLISH
Pollyanna's (midnight)

INDIAN
Akash Indian Tandoori
(midnight)

ITALIAN
Antipasto e Pasta (midnight)

SW12

INDIAN
Lahori Nan Kebab (midnight)

SW13

INDIAN
Gate of India (midnight)
Monzil (midnight)

INTERNATIONAL
The Old Rangoon (midnight)

SW14

ITALIAN
Carlo Domingo's (midnight)
Pizza Express (midnight)

SW15

FRENCH
Mossop's (11.45 p.m.)

SW16

AMERICAN
Hollywood (1.00 a.m.)

ITALIAN
La Balera (1.00 a.m.)
Pizza Express (midnight)

SW18

AMERICAN
Jeepers (midnight)

INDIAN
Sonchita (midnight)

SW19

INDIAN
Ahmed Tandoori (midnight)

The Golden Tandoori
(midnight)

ITALIAN
Pizza Express (midnight)

W1 – NORTH

FRENCH
Café Crêperie (midnight)

GREEK
Appolonia (midnight)
Chez Zorba (3.00 a.m.)
Cosmas Taverna (midnight)
Grecian Grill (9.00 a.m.)

INDIAN
Diwan-e-Khas (midnight)
The Gurkha (midnight)
Natraj (midnight)
New Great India (midnight)
Romna Tandoori (midnight)

INTERNATIONAL
Elysée (4.00 a.m.)

W1 – SOUTH WEST

AMERICAN
The American Hamburger
Restaurant (midnight)
Hard Rock Café (12.30 a.m.)
Wolfe's (midnight)

ENGLISH
Tiddy Dol's (1.00 a.m.)

FRENCH
Athenaeum Hotel
– The Windsor Lounge (open
24 hours)

INTERNATIONAL
The Inn on the Park Hotel

– The Lounge (2.00 a.m.)
Rockafella's (3.30 a.m.)

MIDDLE EASTERN
Fakhreldine (midnight)

SPANISH
Martinez (midnight)

W1 – SOUTH EAST

AMERICAN
Maxwell's (12.30 a.m.)

CHINESE
Chuen Cheng Ku (midnight)
Far East (4.00 a.m.)
Kowloon (midnight)
Lido (4.00 a.m.)
Lok Ho Fook (1.00 a.m.)
Loon Wah (4.30 a.m.)
The Mayflower (3.45 a.m.)
New World (11.45 p.m.)
Yungs (2.00 a.m.)

INDIAN
Kashmir (midnight)
Maharaja Tandoori (midnight)
Maharani (midnight)

ITALIAN
Kettners (midnight)
Leoni's Quo Vadis (6.30 a.m.)
Pizza Express (midnight)

W2

CHINESE
Kam Tung (11.45 p.m.)
Mandarin (midnight)

FRENCH
Downstairs Crêperie
(midnight)
Maxine's des Champs Elysées
(midnight)

GREEK
El Goucho (1.30 a.m.)
Halepi (1.00 a.m.)
Homa (1.00 a.m.)
Romantica (midnight)
Santorini (midnight)
Semiramis (midnight)

HUNGARIAN
Mignon (midnight)

INDIAN
Al Khayam (midnight)
Khan's (midnight)
Khyber (midnight)
Maharajah (midnight)
Mehran (2.00 a.m.)
Standard (midnight)

INTERNATIONAL
Bistro 75 (midnight)

ITALIAN
Pizza Express (midnight)

MIDDLE EASTERN
Al Amir (midnight)
Al Omaraa (1.00 a.m.)
The Lebanese Restaurant
(midnight)
Maroush (4.00 a.m.)
Zeina Abu Hammad
(4.00 a.m.)

TURKISH
Bodrum (midnight)

W4

AMERICAN
Casa Mexicana (midnight)

INDIAN
Ganges Tandoori (11.45 p.m.)

ITALIAN
Pizza Express (midnight)

W5

INDIAN
Monty's (11.45 p.m.)

W6

ENGLISH
Novotel London Hotel
– The Grill (midnight)

INDIAN
Anarkali (11.45 p.m.)
Bombay Inn (midnight)
Light of Nepal (11.45 p.m.)

W8

AMERICAN
Cassidy's (12.30 a.m.)

CHINESE
The Singing Bamboo
(midnight)

INDIAN
Kensington Tandoori
(midnight)

ITALIAN
Palms (midnight)
Pizza Express (midnight)

MIDDLE EASTERN
Al-Basha Palace (midnight)
Byblos (midnight)
Phoenicia (midnight)

W10

INDIAN
Bongo (midnight)

W11

GREEK
Cleopatra Taverna (1.00 a.m.)

INDIAN
Lalbag Tandoori (midnight)

ITALIAN
Pizza Express (midnight)

W12

INDIAN
Ajanta Tandoori (11.45 p.m.)
Rajput (midnight)

W13

CHINESE
Maxim (midnight)

W14

INDIAN
Hunza (midnight)

MIDDLE EASTERN
Yus (2.00 a.m.)

WC1

INTERNATIONAL
My Old Dutch (midnight)

ITALIAN
Pizza Express (midnight)

WC2

AMERICAN
Godfathers (12.30 a.m.)
Maxwell's (midnight)
Peppermint Park (midnight)
Rock Garden (midnight)

Tony Roma's A Place For Ribs
(1.00 a.m.)

CHINESE
Canton (open 24 hours)
Diamond (2.30 a.m.)
Fung Shing (midnight)
Happy Garden (midnight)

FISH
Frère Jacques (midnight)

FRENCH
Café Pelican (12.30 a.m.)

INDIAN
Aldwych Tandoori (midnight)

ITALIAN
Trattoria Italiano Biagio
(12.15 a.m.)

OUT OF TOWN – RICHMOND

CHINESE
Red Lion (midnight)

ITALIAN
Caffe Mamma (midnight)

OPEN AIR EATING

These restaurants have tables
outside and are open for
lunch and dinner unless stated
otherwise e.g. (Lunch) = open
for lunch only.
See main text for details.

E11

ITALIAN
Papillon

E18

CHINESE
Ho Ho

EC1

ENGLISH
Café St Pierre (Lunch)
Rudland & Stubbs (Lunch)

EC2

INTERNATIONAL
Barbican Centre
– The Waterside Café (Lunch)

N1

ENGLISH
Mr Bumble (Lunch)

INTERNATIONAL
Varnams (Lunch)

N6

ENGLISH
The Orangery (Lunch)

FRENCH
One Hampstead Lane (Lunch)

ITALIAN
San Carlo

WHOLEFOOD
Earth Exchange

N8

GREEK
Arocaria (Dinner)

N15

VEGETARIAN
Deens (Dinner)

N16

INTERNATIONAL
Crazy Horse (Dinner)
Fox's Wine Bar

N19

PORTUGUESE &
SPANISH
La Parra

NW1

ENGLISH
Chalk & Cheese (Lunch)
The One Legged Goose

FRENCH
Le Bistroquet
Le Routier

GREEK
Ararat

INTERNATIONAL
Harewood Hotel
– Streetcars

NW2

ENGLISH
Quincy's (Lunch)

NW3

AMERICAN
Maxwell's

ENGLISH
Farquharsons

Kenwood House
– The Coach House (Lunch)
Turpin's (Lunch)

FISH
La Gaffe

INTERNATIONAL
Hill House
Peppercorns
Tinot's Wine Bar (Dinner)

ITALIAN
Ciao (Dinner)
La Baita

JEWISH
Fay Schneider

NW6

ENGLISH
Arches Wine Bar (Lunch)
Peter's (Lunch)

FRENCH
The Lantern

INTERNATIONAL
Hobnobs (Dinner)
No 77 Wine Bar (Dinner)

NW8

ENGLISH
Knights On The Park

INTERNATIONAL
Baracca
Oslo Court Restaurant
(Lunch)

ITALIAN
Fontana Amorosa (Lunch)
Rossetti

SE10

INTERNATIONAL
Bar du Musée

SE16

ENGLISH
Downtown (Lunch)

SE22

FRENCH
Le Moulin
The Pyramid (Lunch)

SE26

INTERNATIONAL
Mister Moon's (Lunch)

SW1

ENGLISH
Grumbles (Lunch)
Methuselah's (Lunch)
Upper Crust In Belgravia
(Lunch)

FISH
Carafe

INTERNATIONAL
The Wren At St James's
(Lunch)

SW3

AMERICAN
Henry J. Bean's
Wolfe's

FISH
Le Suquet

FRENCH
Brasserie des Amis
Café Bouchon
Dominic's
La Brasserie
La Popote
Mes Amis

INTERNATIONAL
Blushes
Bouzy Rouge (Dinner)
Huff's (Lunch)
The Pheasantry Café
Pier 31

ITALIAN
Meridiana
Picasso
Pontenuovo
Toscanini (Dinner)
Toto's

SW4

INTERNATIONAL
Metro
Ormes Wine Bar

SW5

AFRICAN
Balogun's

AMERICAN
Huby's

ENGLISH
Boswell's
Reads (Lunch)

FAR EASTERN
The Philbeach Hotel
– The Gazebo (Dinner)

INTERNATIONAL
Spats Wine Bar (Dinner)

SW6

AMERICAN
Tootsies

INTERNATIONAL
Crocodile Tears

ITALIAN
Little Italy
Pizza Mia
Pizza The Action

SW7

FRENCH
Là Chanterelle

INDIAN
The Bombay Brasserie
Memories Of India

ITALIAN
Bellavista

SW9

ENGLISH
Twenty Trinity Gardens

SW10

AMERICAN
The American

ENGLISH
Chelsea Wharf
Hungry Horse
Jakes (Lunch)

ITALIAN
La Famiglia
La Nassa

SPANISH
El Bodegan

SW11

AMERICAN
Le Grand Café

ENGLISH
Pollyanna's

INTERNATIONAL
Armstrong's Wine Bar
Just William's Wine Bar
(Dinner)

ITALIAN
La Preferita

SW13

AMERICAN
Macarthurs

INTERNATIONAL
The Old Rangoon

ITALIAN
Rose

SW15

ENGLISH
Henrietta's (Lunch)

FRENCH
Mossop's

SCANDINAVIAN
Annia's

SW17

FRENCH
Hoults Wine Bar

INTERNATIONAL
Harvey's (Lunch)

SW18

INTERNATIONAL
French's Wine Bar (Dinner)
The Patriotic

SW19

AMERICAN
Tootsies

ENGLISH
Yesterday (Lunch)

ITALIAN
San Lorenzo Fuoriporta

W1 – NORTH

AMERICAN
Coconut Grove

FRENCH
Café Crêperie

GREEK
Appolonia

INTERNATIONAL
Elysée (Dinner)

ITALIAN
Spaghetti House (Dinner)

W1 – SOUTH WEST

AMERICAN
Hard Rock Café

FRENCH
The Crêperie (Lunch)
L'Artiste Musclé (Dinner)
Relais Des Amis

INTERNATIONAL
Down's Wine Bar

W2

INTERNATIONAL
Abbeys
New Bourn
The Serpentine

W4

INTERNATIONAL
Pickwicks Wine Bar (Dinner)
Southeys Wine Bar

W5

INTERNATIONAL
Brentham Wine Bar

W6

INDIAN
Light of Nepal

W8

AMERICAN
Cassidy's
Henry J. Bean's

ENGLISH
Jimmie's Wine Bar
Kensington Close Hotel
– The Carvery (Lunch)

FRENCH
The Ark (Dinner)
Michel's
The Roof Gardens (Lunch)

ITALIAN
Palms

MIDDLE EASTERN
Al-Basha Palace

W11

ENGLISH
Julie's Restaurant

INTERNATIONAL
Hollands Wine Bar
Obelisk

W14

ENGLISH
Oliver's

WC2

AMERICAN
Rock Garden

FRENCH
The Crêperie

INTERNATIONAL
Eden
Tuttons

OUT OF TOWN – RICHMOND

ENGLISH
Oscar's (Lunch)

ITALIAN
Caffe Mamma

CUISINE INDEX

This is a list of types of cuisine and the postal zones under which they are listed in the main text.

AFGHAN

see Middle Eastern

AFRICAN

SW5

AMERICAN

E2, NW3, NW10, SW1, SW3, SW5, SW6, SW7, SW10, SW11, SW13, SW14, SW16, SW18, SW19, W1 (North), W1 (South West), W1 (South East), W2, W4, W6, W8, W11, W12, WC2.

AUSTRIAN

NW3, W2.

CHINESE

E14, E17, E18, EC2, N1, N6, N16, NW1, NW3, NW7, NW8, NW10, NW11, SE10, SE22, SW1, SW3, SW5, SW7, SW10, SW11, SW13, SW14, W1 (South West), W1 (South East), W2, W8, W9, W13, W14, WC1, WC2, Richmond.

ENGLISH

E1, E11, EC1, EC2, EC4, N1, N6, NW1, NW2, NW3, NW6, NW8, SE16, SE26, SW1, SW3, SW4, SW5, SW7, SW9, SW10, SW11, SW15, SW19, W1 (North), W1 (South West), W1 (South East), W2, W6, W8, W11, W14, WC1, WC2, Richmond.

FAR EASTERN

N8, SW5, SW10, W1 (South East), W2, W8, W13, WC2.

FISH

E1, NW3, SW1, SW3, SW10, W1 (North), W1 (South West), W1 (South East), W8, WC2.

FRENCH

N6, N14, NW1, NW3, NW5, NW6, NW8, SE3, SE10, SE22, SE24, SW1, SW3, SW5, SW6, SW7, SW10, SW11, SW13, SW15, SW17, W1 (North), W1 (South West), W1 (South East), W2, W8, W11, WC2.

GERMAN

W2, W4.

GREEK

N3, N8, NW1, NW3, SW1, W1 (North), W2, W11.

HUNGARIAN

W2.

INDIAN

E1, E4, E7, E18, EC1, EC4, N1, N7, N8, N10, N13, N14, N21, N22, NW1, NW2, NW3, NW6, NW8, NW10, NW11, SE1, SE3, SE4, SE10, SE11, SE13, SE22, SE23, SW1, SW3, SW4, SW5, SW6, SW7, SW9, SW10, SW11, SW12, SW13, SW17, SW18, SW19, W1 (North), W1 (South West), W1 (South East), W2, W4, W5, W6, W8, W10, W11, W12, W14, WC1, WC2, Richmond.

INDONESIAN

see Far Eastern

INTERNATIONAL

E2, EC2, N1, N8, N9, N16, NW1, NW2, NW3, NW4, NW6, NW8, SE1, SE5, SE9, SE10, SE21, SE26, SW1, SW3, SW4, SW5, SW6, SW7, SW10, SW11, SW13, SW17, SW18, W1 (North), W1 (South West), W1 (South East), W2, W4, W5, W6, W8, W9, W11, WC1, WC2, Richmond.

IRANIAN

see Middle Eastern

ISRAELI

WC2.

ITALIAN

E11, E17, N1, N6, N10, NW3, NW8, NW11, SE5, SW1, SW2, SW3, SW5, SW6, SW7, SW10, SW11, SW13, SW14, SW16, SW19, W1 (North), W1 (South West), W1 (South East), W2, W3, W5, W6, W8, W11, WC1, WC2, Richmond.

JAPANESE

NW3, NW4, W1 (South West), W1 (South East), W11, WC2.

JEWISH

E1, EC1, NW3, NW8, NW11, W1 (North), W1 (South East).

LEBANESE

see Middle Eastern

MALAYSIAN

see Far Eastern

MEXICAN

see American

MIDDLE EASTERN

NW1, SW15, W1 (North), W1 (South West), W1 (South East), W2, W8, W14.

PIZZA

see Italian or American

POLISH

SW7, W6.

PORTUGUESE & SPANISH

N19, NW8, SW3, SW10, W1 (South West).

RUSSIAN

SW3, Richmond.

SCANDINAVIAN

SW15.

SINGAPOREAN

see Far Eastern

SPANISH

see Portuguese & Spanish

STEAKS

see International

SWISS

W1 (South East).

THAI

see Far Eastern

TURKISH

N1, SE8, W1 (North), W2.

VEGETARIAN

N4, N15, NW3, SW6, SW16, WC2.

WEST INDIAN

N4.

WHOLEFOOD

N6, Richmond.

ENTERTAINMENT

This section is divided into three broad categories and split into sub-divisions within which the venues are listed alphabetically. The headings are:

MUSIC	CABARET & THEATRE
Brass & Military Bands	Cabaret
Classical Music	Theatre
Folk Music	NIGHTLIFE
Jazz	Casinos
Rock	Dinner & Dancing
Miscellaneous	Discos & Dance Halls

At the back of this section is a postal zone index where the information already listed is re-grouped by postal area.

In addition to the places listed on the next pages, there are a few notes to be added:

CINEMAS
These are not included because all may open on Sundays. See Press for further information and programme details.

THEATRES
Although there have been some exceptions in the past, West End theatres are not generally open on Sunday. The theatre section of this book covers the most regular fringe theatre etc.

CONCERTS
There are places which stage major concerts on Sundays but these are not held regularly and, therefore, are not

included here. See Press for announcements and information.

FESTIVALS
There are many fairs, festivals and special events throughout the year. Again, see Press for announcements and information.

MUSIC

BRASS & MILITARY BANDS

The parks listed here have band concerts during the summer. The performances usually last approximately 1½ hours and all are free.

Further information may be obtained during office hours Monday–Friday on the number given or (where indicated) the Department of the Environment (D.O.E.) on 212 3434 or the Greater London Council (G.L.C.) on 633 1707.

ALEXANDRA PARK, N22
444 7696
BR Alexandra Palace
End July–2nd week September:
3.00 p.m. in The Grove

BATTERSEA PARK, SW11
(G.L.C.)
BR Battersea Park
June–August:
3.00 p.m.

BURGESS PARK
Albany Road, SE5
(G.L.C.)
June–August:
3.00 p.m.

CUTTY SARK GARDENS
King William Walk, SE10
(G.L.C.)
BR Greenwich/Maze Hill
June–August:
3.00 p.m.

FINSBURY PARK, N4
(G.L.C.)
⊖ Finsbury Park
June–August:
3.00 p.m.

GREENWICH PARK, SE10
(D.O.E.)
BR Maze Hill
June–August:
3.00 p.m. and 6.00 p.m.

HOLLAND PARK, W8
(G.L.C.)
⊖ Holland Park/High Street Kensington
June–August:
3.00 p.m.

HYDE PARK, W2
(D.O.E.)
☉ Hyde Park Corner
June–August:
3.00 p.m. and 6.00 p.m.

KENSINGTON GARDENS,
W2
(D.O.E.)
☉ Queensway/High Street
Kensington
June–August:
3.00 p.m.

PARLIAMENT HILL, NW3
(G.L.C.)
☉ Hampstead
June–August:
3.00 p.m.

REGENT'S PARK, NW1
(D.O.E.)
☉ Baker Street/Regent's Park
June–August:
3.00 p.m. and 6.00 p.m.

ST JAMES'S PARK, SW1
(D.O.E.)
☉ St James's Park/ Green
Park
June–August:
3.00 p.m. and 6.00 p.m.

VICTORIA PARK, E9
(G.L.C.)
☉ Bethnal Green
June–August:
3.00 p.m.

WATERLOW PARK, N6
278 4444
☉ Archway/Highgate
June–September:
3.00 p.m.

CLASSICAL MUSIC

This is a list of the principal
and most regular venues for
classical music.

See Press for price and
programme details of these and
any other Sunday concerts.

BARBICAN HALL
Barbican Centre,
Silk Street, EC2
628 8795
Credit cards: 638 8891
Recorded information:
628 2295/9760
Telephone booking:
10.00 a.m.–8.00 p.m.
Box office open:
12.30 p.m.–8.00 p.m.
☉ Moorgate
Evening concerts
*Restaurant/bar/café

CONWAY HALL
Red Lion Square, WC1
242 8032
☉ Holborn
October–April:
Evening concerts

CRYSTAL PALACE
CONCERT BOWL
Crystal Palace Park, SE19
Further information from the
Royal Festival Hall (see below)
BR Crystal Palace
mid-June to mid-August:
Evening concerts

LAUDERDALE HOUSE
Waterlow Park, N6
348 8716

◒ Highgate/Archway
Afternoon concerts
*Café

NEW END THEATRE
27 New End, NW3
435 6053
◒ Hampstead
Lunchtime concerts

PURCELL ROOM
(see Royal Festival Hall)

QUEEN ELIZABETH
HALL
(see Royal Festival Hall)

ROYAL ALBERT HALL
Kensington Gore, SW7
589 8212
Credit cards: 589 9465
◒ South Kensington
Variety of evening concerts all
year and Promenade season
in summer
*Refreshments

ROYAL FESTIVAL HALL
Belvedere Road, SE1
928 3191
Credit cards: 928 8800
Recorded information:
928 3002
Box office open:
1.30 p.m.–9.00 p.m.
◒ Waterloo/Embankment
Afternoon and evening
concerts
*Restaurant/bar/café *Shop

WIGMORE HALL
36 Wigmore Street, W1
935 2141
◒ Bond Street/Oxford Circus

November–March:
Afternoon and evening
concerts
April–November:
'Coffee Concerts' at
11.30 a.m.

FOLK MUSIC

Most of the places listed here
are pubs with music at
lunchtime or in the evening as
indicated. At some, the
entertainment is free; at others,
you may be charged a pound
or two.

ARCHWAY TAVERN
1 Archway Road, N19
272 2840
◒ Archway
Lunchtime and evening
Free

BOSTON ARMS
178 Junction Road, N19
272 3411
◒ Tufnell Park
Country music
Evening
Charge

CAPITAL FOLK CLUB
at MARQUIS OF
ANGLESEA
39 Bow Street, WC2
Enquiries: 330 4122
◒ Covent Garden
Evening
Charge (reduced for members)
*Food & drink

CHESTNUT TREE, E17
(see Chestnuts Folk Club)

CHESTNUTS FOLK CLUB
at CHESTNUT TREE
757 Lea Bridge Road, E17
Enquiries: 803 1757
● Walthamstow Central
Evening
Charge (reduced for members)

CRYPT FOLK CLUB
at ST MARTIN-IN-THE-
FIELDS
Trafalgar Square, WC2
Enquiries: 836 0624
● Charing Cross/Leicester
Square
Evening
Charge (reduced for members)
*Snacks

FAVOURITE PUB
7 Queensland Road, N7
607 2036
● Holloway
Lunchtime and evening
Free

FROG AND FIRKIN
41 Tavistock Crescent, W11
727 9250
● Westbourne Park
Evening
Free
*Pub food

GEORGE AND DRAGON
183 Acton High Street, W3
992 1932
● Acton Town
Country & Western
Evening
Free
*Pub food

HOP POLES
17 King Street, W6
748 1411
● Hammersmith
Evening
Free

MARQUIS OF ANGLESEA,
WC2
(see Capital Folk Club)

MEAN FIDDLER
28a Harlesden High Street,
NW10
961 5490
● Willesden Junction
Lunchtime – Folk
Evening – Country & Western
Membership available
Charge
*Restaurant/bar/snacks

THE OLD SHIP
2 Sylvester Path, E8
986 1641
BR Hackney Central
Lunchtime and evening
Free
*Snacks

PRINCE OF WALES, SW19
(see Wimbledon Folk Club)

THE PROSPECT OF
WHITBY
57 Wapping Wall, E1
481 1317
● Wapping
Lunchtime and evening
Free

ST JOHN'S TAVERN
91 Junction Road, N19
272 1587

☻ Archway
Country Music
Evening
Free

ST MARTIN-IN-THE-
FIELDS, WC2
(see Crypt Folk Club)

SIR GEORGE ROBEY
240 Seven Sisters Road, N4
263 4581
☻ Finsbury Park
Lunchtime and evening
Free at lunchtime

THE SWAN
215 Clapham Road, SW9
274 1526
☻ Stockwell
Evening
Free

THE VICTORIA
203 Holloway Road, N7
607 1952
☻ Holloway Road
Lunchtime and evening
Free

THE WELLINGTON
98–102 Uxbridge Road, W12
743 4671
☻ Shepherd's Bush
Country & Western
Evening
Free
*Pub food

THE WHITE HORSE
80 Liverpool Road, N1
359 4554
☻ Angel

Lunchtime – Country
Evening – Folk
Free
*Snacks

WIMBLEDON FOLK
CLUB
at PRINCE OF WALES
The Broadway, SW19
Enquiries: 946 5041
☻ Wimbledon
Evening
Charge (reduced for members)

JAZZ

Most of the places listed here
are pubs with music at
lunchtime or in the evenings
as indicated. At some, the
entertainment is free; at others,
you may be charged a pound
or two.

BARBICAN CENTRE
Silk Street, EC2
628 8795
☻ Moorgate
Lunchtime
Free
*Restaurant/bar/café

THE BASIN
Portobello Dock,
Ladbroke Grove, W10
960 5456
☻ Ladbroke Grove
Lunchtime and evening
Membership available
Charge
*Restaurant

BASS CLEF
35 Coronet Street, N1
729 2476/2440
⊖ Old Street
Lunchtime – Big Band
Evening – Jazz
Membership available
Charge
*Restaurant/bar

BATTERSEA ARTS
CENTRE
Old Town Hall,
Lavender Hill, SW11
223 8413/6557
BR Clapham Junction
Lunchtime
Charge
*Restaurant

BRIDGE LANE THEATRE
Battersea Bridge Road, SW11
228 8828
BR Clapham Junction
Evening
Charge
*Food

THE BULL'S HEAD
373 Lonsdale Road, SW13
876 5241
⊖ Hammersmith
Lunchtime and evening
Charge
*Buffet lunch/restaurant

CHAT'S PALACE
42–44 Brooksby's Walk, E9
986 6714
⊖ Bethnal Green
Lunchtime
Membership available
Charge

THE FALCON
234 Royal College Street,
NW1
485 3834
⊖ Camden Town
Evening
Free

THE GRIFFIN
9–11 Villiers Street, WC2
839 3113
⊖ Charing Cross
Lunchtime
Free

HACKNEY LABOUR
CLUB
96 Dalston Lane, E8
Enquiries: 249 4326
BR Dalston Junction
Lunchtime
Membership available
Free

HALF MOON
93 Lower Richmond Road,
SW15
788 2387
⊖ Putney Bridge
Lunchtime
Charge
*Pub food

HALF MOON HOTEL
10 Half Moon Lane, SE24
274 2733
BR Herne Hill
Evening
Charge
*Food

100 CLUB
100 Oxford Street, W1
636 0933

⊖ Tottenham Court Road/
Oxford Circus
Evening
Membership available
Charge (reduced for members)
*Food

JEEPERS WINE BAR
350 York Road, SW18
870 5491
BR Wandsworth Town
Lunchtime
Free
*Restaurant

THE JOLLY GARDENERS
63 Lacy Road, SW15
788 7508
⊖ Putney Bridge
Lunchtime
Free

MARQUIS CORNWALLIS
31 Marchmont Street, WC1
837 6072
⊖ Russell Square
Lunchtime
Charge
*Pub food

THE MONARCH
49 Chalk Farm Road, NW1
485 2344
⊖ Chalk Farm
Lunchtime
Free
*Snacks

NEW MERLIN'S CAVE
Margery Street, WC1
837 2097
⊖ Angel

Lunchtime
Free
*Restaurant

THE PIED BULL
1 Liverpool Road, N1
837 3218
⊖ Angel
Lunchtime and evening
Free at lunchtime
*Restaurant

PIZZA EXPRESS
10 Dean Street, W1
437 9595
⊖ Tottenham Court Road
Evening
Charge
*Restaurant

THE PRINCE OF ORANGE
118 Lower Road, SE16
237 9181
⊖ Surrey Docks
Lunchtime and evening
Free
*Pub food

THE RED LION
33–39 Rosoman Street, EC1
837 4865
⊖ Farringdon/Angel
Lunchtime
Free
*Pub food

THREE COMPASSES
66 Cowcross Street, EC1
253 3368
⊖ Farringdon
Lunchtime
Free
*Food

THE TRAMSHED
51 Woolwich New Road, SE18
855 3371
BR Woolwich Arsenal
Lunchtime
Free
*Pub food

TUFNELL PARK TAVERN
162 Tufnell Park Road, N7
272 2078
⊖ Tufnell Park
Evening
Free
*Food

THE WASHINGTON
50 Englands Lane, NW3
722 6118
⊖ Belsize Park
Evening
Free

THE WELLINGTON
98–102 Uxbridge Road, W12
743 4671
⊖ Shepherd's Bush
Lunchtime
Free
*Pub food

ROCK

Most of the places listed here
are pubs with music at
lunchtime or in the evening as
indicated. At some, the
entertainment is free; at others,
you may be charged a pound
or two.

BULL AND GATE
389 Kentish Town Road,
NW5
485 5358
⊖ Kentish Town
Evening
Charge

FATHER RED CAP
319 Camberwell Road, SE5
703 9208
⊖ Elephant & Castle/Oval
Evening
Free

THE GREEN MAN
355 Bromley Road, SE6
698 3746
BR Beckenham Hill
Lunchtime and evening
Free
*Pub food

THE GREYHOUND
175 Fulham Palace Road, W6
385 0526
⊖ Hammersmith
Evening
Free
*Snacks

HALF MOON
93 Lower Richmond Road,
SW15
788 2387
⊖ Putney Bridge
Evening
Charge
*Pub food

THE KING'S HEAD
4 Fulham High Street, SW6
736 1413

⊖ Putney Bridge
Evening
Charge

LEO'S
490 Fulham Road, SW6
385 3942
⊖ Fulham Broadway
Evening
Free
*Pub food

MARQUEE
90 Wardour Street, W1
437 6603
⊖ Piccadilly Circus/
Tottenham Court Road
Evening
Membership available
Charge (reduced for members)
*Bars

OLD TIGER'S HEAD
351 Lee High Road, SE12
852 9708
BR Lee Green/Lewisham
Evening
Charge

PEGASUS
109 Green Lanes, N16
226 5930
⊖ Manor House
Evening
Charge

RUSKIN ARMS
386 High Street North, E12
472 0377
⊖ East Ham
Evening
Free

STEPTOES FREE HOUSE
102 Stoke Newington Church
Street, N16
254 2906
BR Stoke Newington
Evening
Free

TORRINGTON
4 Lodge Lane, N12
445 4710
⊖ Woodside Park
Evening
Charge

MISCELLANEOUS

Most of the places listed here
are pubs with music at
lunchtime or in the evening as
indicated. At some, the
entertainment is free; at others,
you may be charged a pound
or two.

ALBANY EMPIRE
Douglas Way, SE8
691 3333
⊖ New Cross
Various bands
Evening
Membership available
Charge (reduced for members)
*Food

CARNEY ARMS
317 Finchley Road, NW3
794 6058
⊖ Finchley Road
Popular music
Evening
Free

THE CRICKETERS
Kennington Oval, SE11
735 3059
⊖ Oval
Various bands
Lunchtime and evening
Free at lunchtime
*Food (lunch)

DINGWALLS
Camden Lock Place, NW1
267 4967
⊖ Camden Town
Various bands
Evening
Charge
*Food

DUBLIN CASTLE
94 Parkway, NW1
485 1773
⊖ Camden Town
Blues
Evening
Charge

FROG AND FIRKIN
41 Tavistock Crescent, W11
727 9250
⊖ Westbourne Park
Piano music
Lunchtime
Free
*Food

GEORGE CANNING
95 Effra Road, SW2
274 6329
⊖ Brixton
Soul music
Evening
Free
*Snacks

GOLDSMITHS TAVERN
316 New Cross Road, SE14
692 3648
⊖ New Cross
Rock/punk/jazz
Evening
Free

HARE AND HOUNDS
181 Upper Street, N1
226 2992
⊖ Highbury & Islington
Various bands
Evening
Charge

THE HOG'S GRUNT, NW2
(see The Production Village)

JEEPERS WINE BAR
350 York Road, SW18
870 5491
BR Wandsworth Town
Piano music
Evening
Free
*Restaurant

THE KING'S HEAD
115 Upper Street, N1
226 1916
⊖ Angel
Latin American/jazz/funk
Evening
Charge

LYCEUM
Wellington Street, WC2
836 3715
⊖ Charing Cross
Wide variety of concerts
Evening
Charge
*Snacks

THE MAGIC HOUR, NW2
(see The Production Village)

PHEASANT AND FIRKIN
166 Goswell Road, EC1
253 7429
⊖ Angel
Lunchtime – Piano music
Evening – Guitar music
Free
*Snacks

THE PLOUGH
90 Stockwell Road, SW9
274 3879
⊖ Stockwell
Rock and Blues
Evening
Free

PRINCESS LOUISE
208–209 High Holborn, WC1
405 8816
⊖ Holborn
Various bands
Evening
Free
*Snacks

THE PRODUCTION
VILLAGE
100 Cricklewood Lane, NW2
450 8969
⊖ Willesden Green/Golders
Green
All types of music/various
bands
Lunchtime and evening
Free
*Restaurant

ROCK GARDEN
6 The Piazza, WC2
240 3961
⊖ Covent Garden
All types of music/various
bands
Evening
Charge
*Restaurant

ROYAL ALBERT HALL
Kensington Gore, SW7
589 8212
⊖ South Kensington
Wide variety of concerts
Evening
Charge
*Refreshments

TWENTIES
232 Old Brompton Road, SW5
370 2788
⊖ Earls Court
Piano music
Evening
Free
*Restaurant

CABARET & THEATRE

CABARET

This is a list of places with cabaret acts on a regular basis.

You will generally have to pay to see these shows which are usually in the evening unless stated to the contrary.

BATTERSEA ARTS
CENTRE
Old Town Hall,
Lavender Hill, SW11
223 8413/6557

BR Clapham Junction
* Restaurant

BRABANT ROAD T.U.
CENTRE
2a Brabant Road, N22
Enquiries: 487 3440
⊖ Wood Green
*Licensed bar

COCKNEY CABARET &
MUSIC HALL
18 Charing Cross Road, WC2
836 2348
⊖ Leicester Square
Fixed-price dinner and show
*Restaurant

CRAZY LARRY'S
533 King's Road, SW10
(entrance in Lots Road)
352 3518
⊖ Sloane Square/Fulham
Broadway
*Snacks

THE KING'S HEAD
2 Crouch End Hill, N8
340 1028
⊖ Finsbury Park/Archway
*Food

THE MITRE
338 Tunnel Avenue, SE10
Enquiries: 833 1918
BR Greenwich
*Food

THE MONARCH
49 Chalk Farm Road, NW1
485 2344
⊖ Chalk Farm
Free
*Snacks

THE RED LION
33–39 Rosoman Street, EC1
837 4865
⊖ Farringdon/Angel
Lunchtime
Free
*Pub food

RITZ HOTEL
Piccadilly, W1
493 8181
⊖ Green Park
Tea and cabaret 5.00 p.m.

THE TRAMSHED
51 Woolwich New Road, SE18
855 3371
BR Woolwich Arsenal
*Pub food

TWENTIES
232 Old Brompton Road, SW5
370 2788
⊖ Earls Court
Lunch and cabaret
*Restaurant

THEATRE

The theatres listed here
include fringe shows, pub
theatre, puppets and children's
shows.

At some theatres it is necessary
to take out membership, for
which there is a nominal
charge, at least ½ hour before
the show starts. Membership
is often valid at other theatres.

Advance booking for many
fringe shows is available at:
FRINGE BOX OFFICE
Duke of York's Theatre,
St Martin's Lane, WC2
379 6002
Open Monday–Friday
10.00 a.m.–6.00 p.m.
Bookings may be made in
person or by credit card over
the telephone.

ARTS THEATRE, WC2
(see Unicorn Theatre For
Children)

BATTERSEA ARTS
CENTRE
Old Town Hall,
Lavender Hill, SW11
223 8413/6557
BR Clapham Junction
Afternoon and evening shows
*Restaurant

THE BEAR AND STAFF,
WC2
(see Café Theatre Upstairs)

BRIDGE LANE THEATRE
Battersea Bridge Road, SW11
228 8828
BR Clapham Junction
Evening
*Food

BUSH THEATRE
2 Goldhawk Road, W12
743 3388
⊖ Goldhawk Road/
Shepherd's Bush
Evening

CAFÉ THEATRE
UPSTAIRS
at THE BEAR AND STAFF
37 Charing Cross Road, WC2
240 0794
⊖ Leicester Square/Charing
Cross
Evening
*Snacks

COCKPIT THEATRE
Gateforth Street, NW8
402 5081
⊖ Marylebone/Edgware Road
Evening
*Coffee Bar

FINBOROUGH THEATRE
118 Finborough Road, SW10
373 3842
⊖ Earls Court
Evening

INSTITUTE OF
CONTEMPORARY ARTS
Nash House, The Mall, SW1
930 3647
Recorded information:
930 6393
⊖ Charing Cross
*Restaurant/bar

LITTLE ANGEL
MARIONETTE
THEATRE
14 Dagmar Passage, N1
226 1787
⊖ Angel/Highbury &
Islington
Afternoon shows

THE MAN IN THE MOON
392 King's Road, SW3
351 2876

⊖ Sloane Square
Evening and late shows

NEW END THEATRE
27 New End, NW3
435 6053
⊖ Hampstead
Evening

NEW INN THEATRE
62 St Mary's Road, W5
567 8352
⊖ South Ealing
Evening
*Refreshments

ODYSSEY THEATRE
at TUFNELL PARK
TAVERN
162 Tufnell Park Road, N7
272 1386
⊖ Tufnell Park
Evening
*Snacks

OLD RED LION
418 St John Street, EC1
837 7816
⊖ Angel
Evening
*Snacks

OVAL HOUSE
52–54 Kennington Oval, SE11
735 2786
⊖ Oval
Two theatres
Evening and late shows
*Café

PUPPET THEATRE
BARGE
moored at Camden Lock,
NW1
482 3830

⊖ Camden Town
Moored from October to
Easter; tours canals in summer
Noon and afternoon shows

THE QUESTORS
THEATRE
Mattock Lane, W5
567 5184
⊖ Ealing Broadway

RAVENSCOURT PARK
SUMMER THEATRE
Ravenscourt Avenue, W6
Enquiries: 741 3696
⊖ Hammersmith
June–September:
Afternoon
*Teas

RIVERSIDE STUDIOS
Crisp Road, W6
748 3354
⊖ Hammersmith
Evening
*Restaurant/bar

SIR RICHARD STEELE
97 Haverstock Hill, NW3
722 1003
⊖ Chalk Farm/Belsize Park
Evening

THEATRO TECHNIS
26 Crowndale Road, NW1
387 6617
⊖ Camden Town
Evening
*Refreshments

TUFNELL PARK TAVERN,
N7
(see Odyssey Theatre)

UNICORN THEATRE FOR
CHILDREN
at ARTS THEATRE
6 Great Newport Street, WC2
836 3334/2132
⊖ Leicester Square
Afternoon
*Restaurant

NIGHTLIFE

CASINOS

A declaration of your intention
to gamble must be completed
and signed 48 hours before
using the gaming facilities of a
casino.

The cost of membership varies
considerably – ring for details.

CASANOVA CASINO
52 Grosvenor Street, W1
629 1463
⊖ Bond Street/Green Park
2.00 p.m.–4.00 a.m.
*Restaurant

CHARLIE CHESTER
CASINO
12 Archer Street, W1
734 0255
⊖ Piccadilly Circus
2.00 p.m.–4.00 a.m.
*Restaurant

CLERMONT
44 Berkeley Square, W1
493 5587
⊖ Green Park
1.00 p.m.–4.00 a.m.
*Restaurant

GOLDEN HORSESHOE
CASINO
3–4 Archer Street, W1
437 5036
⊖ Piccadilly Circus
2.00 p.m.–4.00 a.m.
*Restaurant

GOLDEN NUGGET
22–32 Shaftesbury Avenue,
W1
734 6211
⊖ Piccadilly Circus
2.00 p.m.–4.00 a.m.
*Bar/snacks

INTERNATIONAL
SPORTING CLUB
45 Park Lane, W1
629 6666
⊖ Hyde Park Corner/Marble
Arch
Noon–4.00 a.m.
Casino and disco
*Restaurant/bars

DINNER & DANCING

Some of these places offer a
fixed-price evening of
entertainment and dancing;
some are restaurants with a
dance floor; and others have a
separate area for dancing e.g. a
basement disco.

The type of cuisine is given –
see 'Restaurants' for further
information.

BEEFEATER
Ivory House,
St Katharine's Dock, E1
408 1001

✪ Tower Hill
English

CITY OF LONDON TAVERN
Blackfriars Lane, EC4
408 1001
✪ Blackfriars
English

ELYSÉE
13 Percy Street, W1
636 4804
✪ Tottenham Court Road
International

LA BALERA
66 Streatham High Road, SW16
769 2646/0669
BR Streatham Hill
Italian

LA PARRA
114 Junction Road, N19
272 4009/0494
✪ Tufnell Park/Archway
Portuguese & Spanish

THE THIRD MAN
30 Englands Lane, NW3
586 8619
✪ Belsize Park
Austrian

TIDDY DOL'S
2 Hertford Street, W1
499 2357
✪ Green Park
English

THE TUDOR ROOMS
80–81 St Martin's Lane, WC2
240 3978

✪ Leicester Square
English

VILLA DEI CESARI
135 Grosvenor Road, SW1
834 9872
✪ Pimlico
Italian

DISCOS & DANCE HALLS

This list includes nightclubs, pub discos and places with dancing in the afternoon/early evening.

Membership may be optional or essential and you will be charged admission unless stated otherwise.

Some have rules about dress – check on this and membership details before going.

ALBANY EMPIRE
Douglas Way, SE8
691 3333
✪ New Cross
2.00 p.m.–4.30 p.m.
Hip Hop Club for under 18's
*Snacks

ALL NATIONS CLUB
4 Martello Street, E8
249 2168/254 2722
✪ Bethnal Green
9.00 p.m.–2.00 a.m.
*Food and drink

THE BELL
259 Pentonville Road, N1
837 5617

● King's Cross
7.30 p.m.–10.30 p.m.
Gay disco
*Pub food

BENJY'S
562a Mile End Road, E3
980 6427
● Mile End
9.00 p.m.–1.00 a.m.
Gay club
*Snacks

BENTLEY'S
23 Barking Road, E16
476 2001
BR Canning Town
9.00 p.m.–2.00 a.m.
*Snacks

BUSBY'S
157 Charing Cross Road,
WC2
734 6963
● Tottenham Court Road
8.00 p.m.–midnight
Jewish club
Disco for under 18's
*Snacks

CITY OF LONDON
TAVERN
Blackfriars Lane, EC4
408 1001
● Blackfriars
6.30 p.m.–1.00 a.m.
*Food

CRISPIN'S WINE BAR
46–47 The Mall, W5
567 8966
● Ealing Broadway
7.00 p.m.–10.30 p.m.
Free

DEURAGON ARMS
9 Shepherd's Lane, E9
985 4045
BR Hackney
8.00 p.m.–10.30 p.m.
Free
*Pub food

DINGLES DISCO
Fulham Broadway, SW6
385 0834
● Fulham Broadway
9.00 p.m.–1.00 a.m.
Disco and live bands
*Snacks

DOUGIES NIGHTCLUB
229 Lower Clapton Road, E5
985 9192
BR Clapton
8.30 p.m.–2.00 a.m.
Disco and occasional cabaret
*Restaurant/wine bar

ELTONS
2 Chesnut Road, N17
808 5048
● Seven Sisters
9.00 p.m.–1.00 a.m.
*Snacks/cocktails

EMPIRE BALLROOM
Leicester Square, WC2
437 1446
● Leicester Square/Piccadilly
Circus
8.00 p.m.–1.00 a.m.
Disco and live bands
*Snacks

THE FORUM
9 Highgate Road, NW5
267 3334
● Kentish Town

9.30 p.m.–1.00 a.m.
*Snacks

THE GREEN MAN
355 Bromley Road, SE6
698 3746
BR Beckenham Hill
8.00 p.m.–10.30 p.m.
Disco and live bands
Free
*Pub food

HENRY AFRICA'S
9 Young Street, W8
937 9493
⊖ High Street Kensington
10.30 p.m.–2.00 a.m.
Gay club

INTERNATIONAL
SPORTING CLUB, W1
(see Casinos)

JOCKEY'S CLUB
1 Broadhurst Gardens, NW6
328 0928
⊖ Finchley Road
9.00 p.m.–3.00 a.m.
*Restaurant

LA PARRA
114 Junction Road, N19
272 4009/0494
⊖ Tufnell Park/Archway
9.00 p.m.–3.00 a.m.
Free to restaurant patrons
*Restaurant

LES ELITES
253 Finchley Road, NW3
794 6628
⊖ Finchley Road
9.30 p.m.–2.00 a.m.
*Restaurant/cocktails

MAXIMUS
14 Leicester Square, WC2
734 4111
⊖ Leicester Square/Piccadilly
Circus
8.00 p.m.–2.00 a.m.
*Bars/snacks

NIGHTMOVES CLUB
RESTAURANT
142 Shoreditch High Street,
E1
739 7264
⊖ Old Street/Shoreditch
8.30 p.m.–1.00 a.m.
*Snacks

PURPLE PUSSYCAT
307 Finchley Road, NW3
Information: Day 207 3407
Evening 794 2801
⊖ Finchley Road
9.00 p.m.–3.00 a.m.
*Snacks

RAMARA'S NIGHT CLUB
243 Finchley Road, NW3
794 5207
⊖ Finchley Road
9.00 p.m.–1.00 a.m.
*Restaurant

ROXANNE'S
11 Harrington Gardens, SW7
370 0876
⊖ Gloucester Road
8.00 p.m.–1.00 a.m.
*Restaurant

SABRA
at SPATS
37 Oxford Street, W1
437 7945

☻ Tottenham Court Road
8.00 p.m.–2.00 a.m.
Gay club
*Snacks

SELINA'S
575 High Road, E11
539 0766
☻ Leytonstone
8.00 p.m.–10.30 p.m.
Gay disco

THE SHADY GROVE
7 Bruce Grove, N17
801 3786
☻ Seven Sisters
7.00 p.m.–1.00 a.m.
*Snacks

SPATS, W1
(see Sabra)

TABERNACLE
COMMUNITY CENTRE
Powis Square, W11
221 5172/229 0949
☻ Ladbroke Grove
4.00 p.m.–10.30 p.m.
*Snacks

TIPPLES .
502 Bethnal Green Road, E2
739 2536
☻ Bethnal Green
8.00 p.m.–10.30 p.m.
Free

POSTAL ZONE INDEX

This is a list of venues by postal zone. See main text for details.

The categories are:

MUSIC
Brass & Military Bands
Classical Music
Folk Music
Jazz
Rock
Miscellaneous

CABARET & THEATRE
Cabaret
Theatre

NIGHTLIFE
Casinos
Dinner & Dancing
Discos & Dance Halls

L = Lunchtime
E = Evening
A = Afternoon

E1

FOLK MUSIC
The Prospect of Whitby (L/E)

DINNER & DANCING
Beefeater (E)

DISCOS & DANCE HALLS
Nightmoves Club Restaurant
(E)

E2

DISCOS & DANCE HALLS
Tipples (E)

E3

DISCOS & DANCE HALLS
Benjy's (E)

E5

DISCOS & DANCE HALLS
Dougies Nightclub (E)

E8

FOLK MUSIC
The Old Ship (L/E)

JAZZ
Hackney Labour Club (L)

DISCOS & DANCE HALLS
All Nations Club (E)

E9

BRASS & MILITARY
BANDS
Victoria Park (A)

JAZZ
Chat's Palace (L)

DISCOS & DANCE HALLS
Deuragon Arms (E)

E11

DISCOS & DANCE HALLS
Selina's (E)

E12

ROCK
Ruskin Arms (E)

E16

DISCOS & DANCE HALLS
Bentley's (E)

E17

FOLK MUSIC
Chestnuts Folk Club (E)

EC1

JAZZ
The Red Lion (L)
Three Compasses (L)

MISCELLANEOUS
Pheasant and Firkin (L/E)

CABARET
The Red Lion (L)

THEATRE
The Old Red Lion (E)

EC2

CLASSICAL MUSIC
Barbican Hall (E)

JAZZ
Barbican Centre (L)

EC4

DINNER & DANCING
City of London Tavern (E)

DISCOS & DANCE HALLS
City of London Tavern (E)

N1

FOLK MUSIC
The White Horse (L/E)

JAZZ
Bass Clef (L/E)
The Pied Bull (L/E)

MISCELLANEOUS
Hare and Hounds (E)
The King's Head (E)

THEATRE
Little Angel Marionette
Theatre (A)

DISCOS & DANCE HALLS
The Bell (E)

N4

BRASS & MILITARY
BANDS
Finsbury Park (A)

FOLK MUSIC
Sir George Robey (L/E)

N6

BRASS & MILITARY
BANDS
Waterlow Park (A)

CLASSICAL MUSIC
Lauderdale House (A)

N7

FOLK MUSIC
Favourite Pub (L/E)
The Victoria (L/E)

JAZZ
Tufnell Park Tavern (E)

THEATRE
Odyssey Theatre (E)

N8

CABARET
The King's Head (E)

N12

ROCK
Torrington (E)

N16

ROCK
Pegasus (E)
Steptoes Free House (E)

N17

DISCOS & DANCE HALLS
Eltons (E)
The Shady Grove (E)

N19

FOLK MUSIC
Archway Tavern (L/E)
Boston Arms (E)
St John's Tavern (E)

DINNER & DANCING
La Parra (E)

DISCOS & DANCE HALLS
La Parra (E)

N22

BRASS & MILITARY
BANDS
Alexandra Park (A)

CABARET
Brabant Road T.U. Centre (E)

NW1

BRASS & MILITARY
BANDS
Regent's Park (A/E)

JAZZ
The Falcon (E)
The Monarch (L)

MISCELLANEOUS
Dingwalls (E)
Dublin Castle (E)

CABARET
The Monarch (E)

THEATRE
Puppet Theatre Barge (A)
Theatro Technis (E)

NW2

MISCELLANEOUS
The Production Village (L/E)

NW3

BRASS & MILITARY
BANDS
Parliament Hill (A)

CLASSICAL MUSIC
New End Theatre (L)

JAZZ
The Washington (E)

MISCELLANEOUS
Carney Arms (E)

THEATRE
New End Theatre (E)
Sir Richard Steele (E)

DINNER & DANCING
The Third Man (E)

DISCOS & DANCE HALLS
Les Elites (E)
Purple Pussycat (E)
Ramara's Night Club (E)

NW5

ROCK
Bull and Gate (E)

DISCOS & DANCE HALLS
The Forum (E)

NW6

DISCOS & DANCE HALLS
Jockey's Club (E)

NW8

THEATRE
Cockpit Theatre (E)

NW10

FOLK MUSIC
Mean Fiddler (L/E)

SE1

CLASSICAL MUSIC
Royal Festival Hall (A/E)

SE5

BRASS & MILITARY
BANDS
Burgess Park (A)

ROCK
Father Red Cap (E)

SE6

ROCK
The Green Man (L/E)

DISCOS & DANCE HALLS
The Green Man (E)

SE8

MISCELLANEOUS
Albany Empire (E)

DISCOS & DANCE HALLS
Albany Empire (A)

SE10

BRASS & MILITARY
BANDS
Cutty Sark Gardens (A)
Greenwich Park (A/E)

CABARET
The Mitre (E)

SE11

MISCELLANEOUS
The Cricketers (L/E)

THEATRE
Oval House (E)

SE12

ROCK
Old Tiger's Head (E)

SE14

MISCELLANEOUS
Goldsmiths Tavern (E)

SE16

JAZZ
The Prince of Orange (L/E)

SE18

JAZZ
The Tramshed (L)

CABARET
The Tramshed (E)

SE19

CLASSICAL MUSIC
Crystal Palace Concert Bowl
(E)

SE24

JAZZ
Half Moon Hotel (E)

SW1

BRASS & MILITARY
BANDS
St James's Park (A/E)

THEATRE
Institute of Contemporary Arts

DINNER & DANCING
Villa dei Cesari (E)

SW2

MISCELLANEOUS
George Canning (E)

SW3

THEATRE
The Man in the Moon (E)

SW5

MISCELLANEOUS
Twenties (E)

CABARET
Twenties (L)

SW6

ROCK
The King's Head (E)
Leo's (E)

DISCOS & DANCE HALLS
Dingles Disco (E)

SW7

CLASSICAL MUSIC
Royal Albert Hall (E)

MISCELLANEOUS
Royal Albert Hall (E)

DISCOS & DANCE HALLS
Roxanne's (E)

SW9

FOLK MUSIC
The Swan (E)

MISCELLANEOUS
The Plough (E)

SW10

CABARET
Crazy Larry's (E)

THEATRE
Finborough Theatre (E)

SW11

BRASS & MILITARY BANDS
Battersea Park (A)

JAZZ
Battersea Arts Centre (L)
Bridge Lane Theatre (E)

CABARET
Battersea Arts Centre (E)

THEATRE
Battersea Arts Centre (A/E)
Bridge Lane Theatre (E)

SW13

JAZZ
The Bull's Head (L/E)

SW15

JAZZ
Half Moon (L)
The Jolly Gardeners (L)

ROCK
Half Moon (E)

SW16

DINNER & DANCING
La Balera (E)

SW18

JAZZ
Jeepers Wine Bar (L)

MISCELLANEOUS
Jeepers Wine Bar (E)

SW19

FOLK MUSIC
Wimbledon Folk Club (E)

W1

CLASSICAL MUSIC
Wigmore Hall (A/E)

JAZZ
100 Club (E)
Pizza Express (E)

ROCK
Marquee (E)

CABARET
Ritz Hotel (A)

CASINOS
Casanova Casino (A/E)
Charlie Chester Casino (A/E)
Clermont (A/E)

Golden Horseshoe Casino (A/E)
Golden Nugget (A/E)
International Sporting Club (A/E)

DINNER & DANCING
Elysée (E)
Tiddy Dol's (E)

DISCOS & DANCE HALLS
International Sporting Club (E)
Sabra (E)

W2

BRASS & MILITARY BANDS
Hyde Park (A/E)
Kensington Gardens (A)

W3

FOLK MUSIC
George and Dragon (E)

W5

THEATRE
New Inn Theatre (E)
Questors Theatre (E)

DISCOS & DANCE HALLS
Crispin's Wine Bar (E)

W6

FOLK MUSIC
Hop Poles (E)

ROCK
The Greyhound (E)

THEATRE
Ravenscourt Park Summer
Theatre (A)
Riverside Studios (E)

W8

BRASS & MILITARY BANDS
Holland Park (A)

DISCOS & DANCE HALLS
Henry Africa's (E)

W10

JAZZ
The Basin (L/E)

W11

FOLK MUSIC
Frog and Firkin (E)

MISCELLANEOUS
Frog and Firkin (L)

DISCOS & DANCE HALLS
Tabernacle Community Centre (A/E)

W12

FOLK MUSIC
The Wellington (E)

JAZZ
The Wellington (L)

THEATRE
Bush Theatre (E)

WC1

CLASSICAL MUSIC
Conway Hall (E)

JAZZ
Marquis Cornwallis (L)
New Merlin's Cave (L)

MISCELLANEOUS
Princess Louise (E)

WC2

FOLK MUSIC
Capital Folk Club (E)
Crypt Folk Club (E)

JAZZ
The Griffin (L)

MISCELLANEOUS
Lyceum (E)
Rock Garden (E)

CABARET
Cockney Cabaret & Music
Hall (E)

THEATRE
Café Theatre Upstairs (E)
Unicorn Theatre for Children
(A)

DINNER & DANCING
Tudor Rooms (E)

DISCOS & DANCE HALLS
Busby's (E)
Empire Ballroom (E)
Maximus (E)

JAUNTS & EXCURSIONS

This section is divided into the following categories:

MUSEUMS   CANAL TRIPS
ART GALLERIES   RIVER TRIPS
HISTORIC BUILDINGS   WALKS
ANIMALS & BIRDS   Guided Walks
GARDENS &   Nature Trails
   NATURAL HISTORY   COACH TOURS
OTHER OUTINGS

With the exception of River Trips, the information is listed alphabetically.

At the back of this section is a postal zone index where the information already given is re-grouped by postal area. This is designed to help you make the best use of your time in a given area by indicating whether a place is open all day or only in the afternoon. In this way, you can decide, for example, to visit a museum in the morning and an art gallery in the afternoon with a break for lunch in between. Guided Walks and Coach Tours are not included in the postal zone index because they start from so many different points.

MUSEUMS

BADEN-POWELL HOUSE
Queen's Gate, SW7
584 7030
✪ South Kensington/
Gloucester Road

9.00 a.m.–6.00 p.m.
Free
Record of the life of Baden-Powell, founder of the Scout movement.

BEAR GARDENS MUSEUM
1 Bear Gardens, SE1
928 6342
⊖ Mansion House/London Bridge
10.30 a.m.–5.30 p.m.
Admission charge
Permanent exhibition of Elizabethan theatre.

BETHNAL GREEN MUSEUM OF CHILDHOOD
Cambridge Heath Road, E2
980 2415
⊖ Bethnal Green
2.30 p.m.–6.00 p.m.
Free
Specializes in toys, puppets and dolls' houses. Also fine examples of Spitalfields silk wedding dresses, silver, glass and ceramics.

BRITISH LIBRARY AND MUSEUM
Great Russell Street, WC1
636 1555
⊖ Tottenham Court Road
2.30 p.m.–6.00 p.m.
Free
Library contains Magna Carta, First Folio of works by Shakespeare and many books, manuscripts, stamps etc. Museum contains antiquities, prints and drawings from all ages and civilizations. Special exhibitions also held.
*Coffee shop

BROOMFIELD MUSEUM
Broomfield Park,
Palmers Green, N13
882 1354
⊖ Arnos Grove/Bounds Green
Easter–September:
10.00 a.m.–8.00 p.m.
October–Easter:
10.00 a.m.–5.00 p.m. or park closing time if earlier
Free
Local and natural history; paintings and pottery; and Victorian nursery with games and dolls.

CHURCH FARM HOUSE MUSEUM
Greyhound Hill, NW4
203 0130
⊖ Hendon Central
2.00 p.m.–5.30 p.m.
Free
Local history and rooms furnished in period.
Special exhibitions also held.

COMMONWEALTH INSTITUTE
Kensington High Street, W8
602 3252
Recorded information:
602 3257
⊖ High Street Kensington
2.00 p.m.–5.00 p.m.
Free
Range of exhibitions from Commonwealth countries showing their history, scenery, resources and way of life. Art gallery exhibits works by Commonwealth artists.

Special exhibitions also held.
*Coffee shop *Bookstall

EPPING FOREST MUSEUM
Queen Elizabeth's Hunting
Lodge,
Rangers Road, E4
529 6681
BR Chingford
2.00 p.m.–6.00 p.m.
Admission charge
Tudor building containing
local and natural history.

GEFFRYE MUSEUM
Kingsland Road, E2
739 8368
● Old Street
2.00 p.m.–5.00 p.m.
Free
18th Century almshouses with
rooms showing furniture and
decoration of English middle-
class homes since the 16th
Century.
*Coffee bar

GEOLOGICAL MUSEUM
Exhibition Road, SW7
589 3444
● South Kensington
2.30 p.m.–6.00 p.m.
Free
Physical and regional geology;
principles of geological
science; mineralogy; fossils;
and collection of gemstones.
*Book shop

GUNNERSBURY PARK MUSEUM
Gunnersbury Park, W3
992 1612

● Acton Town
March–October (BST end):
2.00 p.m.–6.00 p.m.
October (start
BST)–February:
2.00 p.m.–4.00 p.m.
Free
Carriages, dolls and dolls'
houses in 19th Century house.
Local archaeology, history and
topography.
*Tea pavilion

HERALD'S MUSEUM AT THE TOWER OF LONDON
Tower of London, EC3
709 0765
● Tower Hill
April–September (only):
2.00 p.m.–5.15 p.m.
Admission included in charge
to Tower of London
Shows the development and
application of heraldry on
wide range of materials – glass,
china, coins etc.

HERITAGE MOTOR MUSEUM
Syon Park,
Brentford, Middlesex
560 1378
● Gunnersbury
March–October:
10.00 a.m.–5.30 p.m.
November–February:
10.00 a.m.–4.00 p.m.
Admission charge
Historic British cars.
*Café in Syon Park

HORNIMAN MUSEUM
100 London Road, SE23
699 2339/1872
BR Forest Hill
2.00 p.m.–6.00 p.m.
Free
Ethnography and natural
history. Aquarium; arts and
crafts; world religions and
superstitions; and musical
instruments.
Special exhibitions also held.
*Tea room (April–September)

IMPERIAL WAR MUSEUM
Lambeth Road, SE1
735 8922
⊖ Lambeth North
2.00 p.m.–5.50 p.m.
Free
Extensive record of every
aspect of First and Second
World Wars. Equipment,
weapons, uniforms, medals etc.

JEWISH MUSEUM
Woburn House,
Upper Woburn Place, WC1
387 3081/388 4525
⊖ Russell Square/Euston
Square
10.30 a.m.–12.45 p.m.
Free
Antiquities used in Jewish
ceremony, ritual and worship.

KEW BRIDGE ENGINES
MUSEUM
Kew Bridge Road,
Brentford, Middlesex
(entrance in Green Dragon
Lane)
568 4757

11.00 a.m.–5.00 p.m.
Admission charge
19th Century pumping station
housing Victorian steam
engines, two of which can be
seen operating at 3.00 p.m. Also
working forge, models and
traction engines.
*Tea room *Bookstall

KODAK MUSEUM
Headstone Drive,
Harrow, Middlesex
863 0534
⊖ Harrow & Wealdstone
2.00 p.m.–6.00 p.m.
Free
History of photography –
books, apparatus and
exhibitions.

LONDON TOY AND
MODEL MUSEUM
21–23 Craven Hill, W2
262 9450/7905
⊖ Lancaster Gate/Paddington
11.00 a.m.–5.00 p.m.
Admission charge
Extensive collection of model
aeroplanes, cars, trains;
clockwork toys; dolls and
bears. Garden with railway,
roundabout and boating pond.
*Café *Shop

LONDON TRANSPORT
MUSEUM
Covent Garden Market, WC2
379 6344
⊖ Covent Garden
10.00 a.m.–5.15 p.m.
Admission charge

Vast collection of buses, trams and trains illustrating the development of metropolitan transport. Audio-visual shows and working models.
*Café *Shop

MUSEUM OF GARDEN HISTORY
St Mary-at-Lambeth,
Lambeth Road, SE1
373 4030
⊖ Westminster/Lambeth North
March–November (only):
10.30 a.m.–5.00 p.m.
Free
Shrubs, trees, flowers and books illustrate the history of gardens and gardening. Temporary exhibitions also held.
*Tea, coffee and biscuits

THE MUSEUM OF LONDON
London Wall, EC2
600 3699
⊖ St Paul's/Moorgate
2.00 p.m.–6.00 p.m.
Free
Everything exhibited is used to illustrate the history of London since pre-Roman times. Items include the Lord Mayor's coach, Selfridges lifts and reconstructed rooms and shops.
*Coffee shop

MUSEUM OF MANKIND
6 Burlington Gardens, W1
437 2224

⊖ Green Park/Piccadilly Circus
2.30 p.m.–6.00 p.m.
Free
Range of ethnograhic exhibitions illustrating the culture of various peoples.

THE MUSICAL MUSEUM
368 High Street,
Brentford, Middlesex
560 8108
⊖ Gunnersbury
April–October (only):
2.00 p.m.–5.00 p.m.
Admission charge
Large collection of musical instruments including pianos, violins, musical boxes and a Wurlitzer organ.

NATIONAL ARMY MUSEUM
Royal Hospital Road, SW3
730 0717
⊖ Sloane Square
2.00 p.m.–5.30 p.m.
Free
Chronological history of the British Army since 1485. Uniforms, maps, medals, manuscripts and Weapon Gallery.

NATIONAL MARITIME MUSEUM
Romney Road, SE10
858 4422
BR Maze Hill
Summer: 2.00 p.m.–5.30 p.m.
Winter: 2.00 p.m.–5.00 p.m.
Admission charge

Record of maritime history.
Models, paintings, uniforms,
instruments, charts and relics.
*Coffee shop

NATURAL HISTORY MUSEUM

Cromwell Road, SW7
589 6323
⊖ South Kensington
2.30 p.m.–6.00 p.m.
Free
Range of exhibitions showing
history and development of all
living things and their habitats.
*Café/snack bar

ROTUNDA MUSEUM OF ARTILLERY

Repository Road, SE18
858 5533 Ext. 385
BR Woolwich Arsenal
April–October:
1.00 p.m.–5.00 p.m.
November–March:
1.00 p.m.–4.00 p.m.
Free
Tent-shaped museum housing
original and replica items of
artillery.

ROYAL AIR FORCE MUSEUM

Hendon Aerodrome, NW9
205 2266
⊖ Colindale
2.00 p.m.–6.00 p.m.
Free
History of aviation including
uniforms, medals, instruments,
weapons and more than forty
aircraft. Exhibitions are held
in the Art Gallery.

– BATTLE OF BRITAIN MUSEUM

Admission charge
Audio-visual display and
collection of aircraft involved
in Battle of Britain in 1940.

– BOMBER COMMAND MUSEUM

Admission charge
Collection of items related to
all aspects and development
of bomber operations.
*Restaurant *Shop

ROYAL HOSPITAL MUSEUM

Royal Hospital Chelsea,
Royal Hospital Road, SW3
730 0161
⊖ Sloane Square
April–September (only):
10.00 a.m.–noon &
2.00 p.m.–4.00 p.m.
Free
Collection of items related to
the hospital's history – plans,
maps, uniforms etc.

ST BRIDE'S CRYPT MUSEUM

St Bride's Church,
Fleet Street, EC4
353 1301
⊖ Blackfriars
9.00 a.m.–5.00 p.m.
Free
Archaeological remains of
many previous churches since
6th Century and historical
record of print and printing.

SCIENCE MUSEUM
Exhibition Road, SW7
589 3456
⊖ South Kensington
2.30 p.m.–6.00 p.m.
Free
History, development and
application of sciences and
technology. Exhibits include
many working models,
dioramas, industrial and
domestic appliances.
*Book shop

VICTORIA AND ALBERT
MUSEUM
Cromwell Road, SW7
589 6371
⊖ South Kensington
2.30 p.m.–5.50 p.m.
Free
Extensive collections of fine
and applied arts from many
countries and periods
including furniture, textiles,
costume, prints and drawings.
Special exhibitions also held.
*Restaurant *Shop

WALLACE COLLECTION
Hertford House,
Manchester Square, W1
935 0687
⊖ Bond Street
2.00 p.m.–5.00 p.m.
Free
Collection includes paintings
of most European schools and
sculpture, furniture, ceramics,
armour etc.

WILLIAM MORRIS
GALLERY
Lloyd Park,
Forest Road, E17
527 5544
⊖ Walthamstow Central
First Sunday of each month:
10.00 a.m.–noon &
2.00 p.m.–5.00 p.m. or dusk if
earlier
Collection of wallpapers, arts
and crafts, textiles, carpets and
furniture in 18th Century
house where Morris grew up.

WIMBLEDON LAWN
TENNIS MUSEUM
The All England Club,
Church Road, SW19
946 6131
⊖ Wimbledon
2.00 p.m.–5.00 p.m.
Closed during Championships
Admission charge
History of tennis and lawn
tennis including equipment
and clothes.

ART GALLERIES

THE ART CENTRE
Syon Park,
Brentford, Middlesex
568 6021
⊖ Gunnersbury
Noon–5.00 p.m.
Free
Work of contemporary artists
for sale.
*Café in Syon Park

BANKSIDE GALLERY
48 Hopton Street, SE1
928 7521
✪ Blackfriars
2.00 p.m.–6.00 p.m.
Admission charge
Exhibitions from the U.K. and
abroad

BARBICAN CENTRE ART
GALLERY
Silk Street, Barbican, EC2
638 4141
✪ Moorgate
Noon–6.00 p.m.
Admission charge
Wide range of temporary
exhibitions
*Restaurant/café *Shop

BATTERSEA ARTS
CENTRE
Old Town Hall,
176 Lavender Hill, SW11
223 6557
BR Clapham Junction
11.00 a.m.–9.00 p.m.
Free
Exhibitions of contemporary
art.
*Restaurant

BLACK-ART GALLERY
225 Seven Sisters Road, N4
263 1918
✪ Finsbury Park
2.00 p.m.–7.00 p.m.
Free
Work by contemporary black
artists. Some items for sale.
*Shop

CAMDEN ARTS CENTRE
Arkwright Road, NW3
435 2643/5224
✪ Hampstead/Finchley Road
2.00 p.m.–6.00 p.m.
Free
Work by contemporary artists.

CANADA HOUSE
Trafalgar Square, SW1
629 9492
✪ Charing Cross
Noon–5.30 p.m.
Free
Work by Canadian artists.

CHALCOT GALLERY
50 Chalcot Road, NW1
722 6924/348 1919
✪ Chalk Farm
11.00 a.m.–5.30 p.m.
Free
Frequent exhibitions of fine
art. Some items for sale.

COURTAULD
INSTITUTE GALLERIES
Woburn Square, WC1
580 1015/636 2095
✪ Russell Square
2.00 p.m.–5.00 p.m.
Free
Many collections of Old
Master, Impressionist and Post-
Impressionist paintings and
drawings.

THE CRAFTS COUNCIL
12 Waterloo Place, SW1
930 4811
✪ Piccadilly Circus
2.00 p.m.–5.00 p.m.
Free

Exhibitions throughout the year of arts and crafts.
*Coffee bar *Bookstall

DULWICH PICTURE GALLERY
College Road, SE21
693 5254
BR West Dulwich/North Dulwich
2.00 p.m.–5.00 p.m.
Admission charge
Built by Sir John Soane and contains collection of Old Master paintings including works by Gainsborough, Hogarth, Murillo, Poussin, Rembrandt, Reynolds, Rubens and Van Dyck.

HAYWARD GALLERY
Belvedere Road, SE1
928 3144/5708
Recorded information:
261 0127
✪ Waterloo/Embankment
Noon–6.00 p.m.
Admission charge
Exhibitions of historical and contemporary art from the U.K. and abroad.
*Bookstall

INSTITUTE OF CONTEMPORARY ARTS
Nash House, The Mall, SW1
930 3647
Recorded information:
930 6393
✪ Charing Cross
Noon–8.00 p.m.

Admission charge for day pass
Three galleries exhibiting contemporary art.
*Restaurant/bar

LAUDERDALE HOUSE
Waterlow Park,
Highgate Hill, N6
348 8716
✪ Highgate/Archway
Noon–5.00 p.m.
Free
Exhibitions of contemporary art. Some items for sale. Antiques fair held twice a month.
*Café

LOGGIA GALLERY
15 Buckingham Gate, SW1
828 5963
✪ St James's Park/Victoria
2.00 p.m.–6.00 p.m.
Free
Contemporary painting and sculpture for sale.

THE NATIONAL GALLERY
Trafalgar Square, WC2
839 3321
Recorded information:
839 3526
✪ Charing Cross/Leicester Square
2.00 p.m.–6.00 p.m.
Free
National collection of European painting, including many Old Masters, from the 13th to the 19th Century. Special exhibitions also held.
*Restaurant *Shop

NATIONAL PORTRAIT
GALLERY
St Martin's Place, WC2
930 1552
✺ Charing Cross/Leicester
Square
2.00 p.m.–6.00 p.m.
Free
Chronologically arranged
collection of portraits of famous
people in British history since
Tudor times.
Special exhibitions also held.
*Shop

ORLEANS HOUSE
GALLERY
Riverside,
Twickenham, Middlesex
892 0221
BR St Margaret's
April–September:
2.00 p.m.–5.30 p.m.
October–March:
2.00 p.m.–4.30 p.m.
Free
Temporary exhibitions held in
gallery attached to the remains
of Orleans House.

THE QUEEN'S GALLERY
Buckingham Palace Road,
SW1
930 4832
✺ Victoria
2.00 p.m.–5.00 p.m.
Admission charge
Features works from the Royal
Collection. Selection is changed
regularly.

RIVERSIDE STUDIOS
Crisp Road, W6
748 3354
✺ Hammersmith
Noon–8.00 p.m.
Free
Exhibitions of contemporary
art. Many items for sale.
*Restaurant *Book shop

THE ROOM
104 Drummond Street, NW1
Enquiries: 267 9549
✺ Euston/Warren Street
3.00 p.m.–6.00 p.m.
Free
Exhibitions of contemporary
paintings and drawings for sale.

ROYAL ACADEMY OF
ARTS
Piccadilly, W1
734 9052
✺ Green Park/Piccadilly
Circus
10.00 a.m.–6.00 p.m.
Admission charge (reduced fee
before 1.45 p.m.)
Variety of important
exhibitions all year with the
Summer Exhibition from May
to August.
*Restaurant *Shop

ROYAL FESTIVAL HALL
FOYER
Belvedere Road, SE1
Recorded information:
938 3002
✺Waterloo/Embankment
10.00 a.m.–10.00 p.m.
Free

Exhibitions of arts and crafts.
Items for sale.
*Restaurant/café *Shops

SERPENTINE GALLERY
Kensington Gardens, W2
402 6075
⊖ South Kensington
April–September:
10.00 a.m.–6.00 p.m.
October–March:
10.00 a.m.–dusk
Free
Exhibitions of contemporary,
often experimental, art.

THE SHOWROOM
44 Bonner Road, E2
980 6636
⊖ Bethnal Green
2.00 p.m.–6.00 p.m.
Free
Temporary exhibitions of
contemporary art.

SOUTH LONDON ART GALLERY
Peckham Road, SE5
703 6120
BR Peckham Rye
3.00 p.m.–6.00 p.m.
Free
Variety of temporary
exhibitions.

TATE GALLERY
Millbank, SW1
821 1313
Recorded information:
821 7128
⊖ Pimlico
2.00 p.m.–5.50 p.m.
Free

National collections of British
paintings, modern sculpture
and foreign art.
Special exhibitions also held.
*Coffee shop *Shop

TUDOR BARN ART GALLERY
Well Hall Pleasaunce, SE9
850 2340
BR Eltham Well Hall
11.00 a.m.–4.15 p.m.
Free
First floor gallery in 16th
Century building showing
contemporary works of art.
*Restaurant

WARWICK ARTS TRUST
33 Warwick Square, SW1
834 7856
⊖ Pimlico/Victoria
10.00 a.m.–5.00 p.m.
Closed during August
Admission charge
Exhibitions of contemporary
art held most of the year.

WHITECHAPEL ART GALLERY
80 Whitechapel High Street,
E1
377 0107
⊖ Aldgate East
11.00 a.m.–5.50 p.m.
Free
Temporary exhibitions of
contemporary art.
*Coffee shop

WOODLANDS ART
GALLERY
90 Mycenae Road, SE3
858 4631
BR Blackheath
2.00 p.m.–6.00 p.m.
Free
Temporary exhibitions of
contemporary art.

HISTORIC
BUILDINGS

APSLEY HOUSE
Hyde Park Corner, W1
499 5676
⊖ Hyde Park Corner
2.30 p.m.–6.00 p.m.
Admission charge
The Duke of Wellington's
house built in 1771–78 by
Robert Adam. Now the
Wellington Museum containing
paintings, trophies, uniforms,
silver and porcelain.

BANQUETING HOUSE
Whitehall, SW1
(opposite Horse Guards
Parade)
Enquiries: 212 4787
⊖ Charing Cross/
Westminster
2.00 p.m.–5.00 p.m.
Admission charge
Built for James I by Inigo Jones
with the ceiling painted by
Rubens. Now used for
ceremonies and government
functions.
*Souvenir shop

CABINET WAR ROOMS
King Charles Street, SW1
930 6961
⊖ Westminster
10.00 a.m.–5.50 p.m.
Admission charge
Underground rooms used by
Winston Churchill and his War
Cabinet during World War II.
*Souvenir shop

CARLYLE'S HOUSE
24 Cheyne Row, SW3
352 7087
⊖ Sloane Square
April–October (only):
11.00 a.m.–5.00 p.m.
Admission charge
Thomas Carlyle's 18th
Century house containing
furniture, paintings, letters,
books, etc.

CHISWICK HOUSE
Burlington Lane, W4
994 3299
BR Chiswick
mid March–mid October:
9.30 a.m.–6.30 p.m.
mid October–mid March:
9.30 a.m.–4.00 p.m.
Admission charge
Palladian villa designed by the
Earl of Burlington in 1725
with octagonal domed saloon
and state rooms decorated by
William Kent.
*Cafeteria

FENTON HOUSE
Hampstead Grove, NW3
435 3471

✪ Hampstead
March–October (only):
2.00 p.m.–6.00 p.m.
Admission charge
Late 17th Century (William
and Mary) house containing
superb collection of early
keyboard instruments, furniture
and porcelain.

HAM HOUSE
at Petersham,
Richmond, Surrey
940 1950
April–September:
2.00 p.m.–6.00 p.m.
October–March:
Noon–4.00 p.m.
Admission charge
Beautifully preserved Stuart
house built in 1610
containing fine 17th Century
furniture.
*Teas/Shop
(April–September)

HAMPTON COURT PALACE
East Molesey, Surrey
977 8441
BR Hampton Court
– STATE APARTMENTS
April–September:
11.00 a.m.–6.00 p.m.
October–March:
2.00 p.m.–5.00 p.m.
Admission charge
– CELLARS AND KITCHENS
April–September (only):
11.00 a.m.–6.00 p.m.

Admission charge
Tudor palace begun by Wolsey
in 1514, enlarged by Henry VIII,
and extensively altered for
William and Mary by Wren.
Fine collection of Italian
paintings, tapestries and
furniture.
*Café/Restaurant

HOGARTH'S HOUSE
Hogarth Lane, W4
994 6757
✪ Turnham Green
Summer: 2.00 p.m.–6.00 p.m.
Winter: 2.00 p.m.–4.00 p.m.
Closed: first two weeks in
September and last three
weeks in December.
Free
The house in which Hogarth
lived. Collection of prints,
paintings and relics.

KEATS' HOUSE
Keats Grove, NW3
435 2062
✪ Hampstead
2.00 p.m.–5.00 p.m.
Free
Keats' Regency house
containing personal
possessions and manuscripts.

KENSINGTON PALACE
Kensington Gardens, W8
Enquiries: 937 9561
✪ High Street Kensington/
Queensway
1.00 p.m.–5.00 p.m.
Admission charge

Late Stuart and Hanoverian State Apartments decorated by William Kent and Grinling Gibbons. Display of Court dress.

KENWOOD HOUSE
– THE IVEAGH BEQUEST
Hampstead Lane, NW3
348 1286/7
● Archway/Golders Green
April–September:
10.00 a.m.–7.00 p.m.
October–March:
10.00 a.m.–5.00 p.m. or dusk
Free
Fine 18th-Century house designed by Robert Adam containing collection of furniture and paintings by the great English and Flemish masters.
*Restaurant

KEW PALACE
Royal Botanic Gardens,
Kew, Richmond, Surrey
Enquiries: 940 3321
● Kew Gardens
April–September (only):
11.00 a.m.–5.30 p.m.
Admission charge
Built by a Dutchman in 1631 and lived in by George III and Queen Charlotte 1802–18.
*Teas/Restaurant in Gardens

LANCASTER HOUSE
Stable Yard, SW1
● Green Park
Easter–mid December (only):
2.00 p.m.–6.00 p.m.

Admission charge
Elaborately decorated rooms now used for government functions.

LINLEY SAMBOURNE
HOUSE
18 Stafford Terrace, W8
Enquiries: 994 1019
● High Street Kensington
March–October (only):
2.00 p.m.–5.00 p.m.
Admission charge
Victorian house lived in by Linley Sambourne, the cartoonist. Contains collection of his and other artists' work.

MARBLE HILL HOUSE
Richmond Road,
Twickenham, Middlesex
892 5115
● Richmond
February–October:
10.00 a.m.–5.00 p.m.
November–January:
10.00 a.m.–4.00 p.m.
Free
Superb example of English Palladian architecture. Contains fine collection of 18th Century furniture and paintings.
*Café

MONUMENT
Monument Street, EC3
● Monument
May–September (only):
2.00 p.m.–5.40 p.m.
Admission charge

Hollow Doric column 202 feet high commemorating the Great Fire of London. Climb 311 steps to the top for panoramic view of London.

OSTERLEY PARK HOUSE
Isleworth, Middlesex
560 3918
⊖ Osterley
April–September:
2.00 p.m.–6.00 p.m.
October–March:
Noon–4.00 p.m.
Elizabethan mansion transformed, decorated and furnished by Robert Adam in 1760–80.
*Teas (summer only)

QUEEN CHARLOTTE'S COTTAGE
Royal Botanic Gardens,
Kew, Richmond, Surrey
Enquiries: 940 3321
⊖ Kew Gardens
April–September (only):
11.00 a.m.–5.30 p.m.
Admission charge
Thatched cottage built in 1772.
*Teas/Restaurant in Gardens

RANGER'S HOUSE
Chesterfield Walk, SE10
853 0035
BR Greenwich/Blackheath
February–October:
10.00 a.m.–5.00 p.m.
November–January:
10.00 a.m.–4.00 p.m.

Free
The 4th Earl of Chesterfield's red brick villa housing the Suffolk Collection of Jacobean and Elizabethan paintings.

SYON HOUSE
Park Road,
Brentford, Middlesex
560 0884
⊖ Gunnersbury
April–October (only):
Noon–5.00 p.m.
Admission charge
Built as a convent in the 15th Century. Interior decorated by Robert Adam 1762–69.
*Café/Restaurant *Shop

THE TOWER OF LONDON
Tower Hill, EC3
709 0765
⊖ Tower Hill
March–October (only):
2.00 p.m.–5.00 p.m.
Admission charge
Very famous Norman and medieval building housing the Crown Jewels, the Herald's Museum and large collection of arms and armour.
*Café

WHITEHALL
Malden Road, Cheam, Surrey
643 1236
2.00 p.m.–5.30 p.m.
Admission charge
16th Century timber-framed house in which Cheam

School began. Exhibits include medieval pottery and local history.
*Café

WIMBLEDON WINDMILL
Windmill Road, SW19
788 7655
Easter–October (only):
2.00 p.m.–5.00 p.m.
Admission charge
Early 19th Century windmill containing exhibition illustrating the history of windmills.

ANIMALS & BIRDS

(P) = Park. Refer to 'Parks' section for further information.

(P) BATTERSEA PARK, SW11
Animal enclosure and children's zoo

(P) BROCKWELL PARK, SE24
Aviary

(P) CLISSOLD PARK, N4
Animal enclosure and aviary

(P) CRYSTAL PALACE PARK, SE19
Children's zoo

(P) DULWICH PARK, SE21
Aviary

FREIGHTLINERS FARM
Sheringham Road, N7
609 0467

✪ Highbury & Islington/ Holloway Road
9.00 a.m.–1.00 p.m.
& 2.00 p.m.–6.00 p.m.
Free (donation appreciated)
City farm with arts and crafts during summer holidays.

(P) GOLDERS HILL, NW11
Animal enclosure

(P) HOLLAND PARK, W8
Wide variety of birds

(P) HORNIMAN GARDENS, SE23
Animal enclosure

INTER-ACTION CITY FARM
1 Cressfield Close, NW5
485 4585
✪ Kentish Town
9.30 a.m.–10.00 p.m.
Free
City farm with pony rides and shop selling farm produce.

THE LONDON BUTTERFLY HOUSE
Syon Park
Brentford, Middlesex
560 7272
✪ Gunnersbury
March–November (only):
Summer (BST):
10.00 a.m.–5.00 p.m.
Winter: 10.00 a.m.–3.30 p.m.
Admission charge
Many exotic butterflies and other insects.
*Shop

LONDON ZOO &
AQUARIUM
Regent's Park, NW1
722 3333
✆ Camden Town
March–October:
9.00 a.m.–6.00 p.m.
November–February:
10.00 a.m.–4.00 p.m. or dusk
if earlier
Admission charge
All kinds of animals, birds and
fish from all over the world.
Also a children's zoo, animal
rides and regular feeding
times throughout the day.
*Restaurant/café *Shop

MUDCHUTE FARM PARK
Pier Street, E14
515 5901
✆ Mile End
Summer: 9.00 a.m.–dusk
Winter: 9.00 a.m.–5.00 p.m.
Free
City farm of 32 acres. Honey
for sale.

(P) REGENT'S PARK, NW1
Wide variety of birds

(P) RICHMOND PARK,
RICHMOND
Deer and many other animals
and birds

(P) ST JAMES'S PARK, SW1
Bird sanctuary

SPITALFIELDS FARM
Buxton Street, E1
247 8762
✆ Whitechapel

10.00 a.m.–5.00 p.m. or dusk
if earlier
Free (donation appreciated)
Educational farm selling
produce and some crafts.

STEPNEY STEPPING
STONES FARM
Stepney High Street, E1
790 8204
✆ Stepney Green
9.30 a.m.–1.00 p.m.
& 2.00 p.m.–6.00 p.m.
Free (donation appreciated)
City farm with variety of
animals.

SURREY DOCKS FARM
Gulliver Street, SE16
231 1010
✆ Surrey Docks
10.00 a.m.–5.00 p.m.
Free
City farm with variety of
animals. Produce for sale.

VAUXHALL CITY FARM
St Oswald's Place, SE11
582 4204
✆ Vauxhall
10.00 a.m.–5.00 p.m.
Admission charge
Small children's zoo and farm
selling produce.

(P) VICTORIA PARK, E9
Animal enclosure

(P) WATERLOW PARK, N6
Aviary

GARDENS & NATURAL HISTORY

(P) = Park. Refer to 'Parks' section for further details.

(P) AVERY HILL PARK, SE9
Winter Garden with many tropical plants.

(P) BATTERSEA PARK, SW11
Flower garden

(P) BROCKWELL PARK, SE24

BROOMFIELD MUSEUM, N13
(see Museums)

CHELSEA PHYSIC GARDEN
Swan Walk, SW3
352 5646
♦ Sloane Square
April–October (only):
2.00 p.m.–5.00 p.m.
Admission charge
Four acres of botanical gardens.

CHISWICK HOUSE, W4
(see Historic Buildings)

(P) CLISSOLD PARK, N4

(P) DULWICH PARK, SE21
Rhododendrons and many trees

GEOLOGICAL MUSEUM, SW7
(see Museums)

HAM HOUSE, RICHMOND
(see Historic Buildings)

HAMPTON COURT PALACE, EAST MOLESEY
(see Historic Buildings)

(P) HOLLAND PARK, W8
19th Century Dutch garden and many other gardens and trees

HORNIMAN MUSEUM, SE23
(see Museums)

MUSEUM OF GARDEN HISTORY, SE1
(see Museums)

NATURAL HISTORY MUSEUM, SW7
(see Museums)

OSTERLEY PARK HOUSE, ISLEWORTH
(see Historic Buildings)

(P) REGENT'S PARK, NW1
Queen Mary's rose garden

ROYAL BOTANIC GARDENS
Kew Road,
Richmond, Surrey
940 1171
♦ Kew Gardens
Summer: 10.00 a.m.–8.00 p.m.
Winter: 10.00 a.m.–4.00 p.m.
Admission charge

The world's best-known botanical gardens with huge variety of plants, trees and shrubs.
*Refreshments

SYON HOUSE,
BRENTFORD
(see Historic Buildings)

WILLIAM CURTIS
ECOLOGICAL PARK
Vine Lane, SE1
403 2078
✪ London Bridge
March–October:
10.00 a.m.–6.00 p.m.
November–February:
10.00 a.m.–dusk
Free
Reclaimed wasteland with many varieties of plants and wildlife.

OTHER OUTINGS

H.M.S. BELFAST
Symons Wharf,
Vine Lane, SE1
407 6434
✪ London Bridge
Summer: 11.00 a.m.–
5.50 p.m.
Winter: 11.00 a.m.–4.30 p.m.
Admission charge
11,500 ton cruiser permanently moored as a floating maritime museum.

CHANGING THE GUARD
at Buckingham Palace,
The Mall, SW1
✪ Victoria/Green Park
Summer: 11.30 a.m. every day
Winter: 11.30 a.m. alternate days (time may vary)
Free
and
at Horse Guards
Whitehall, SW1
✪ Westminster/Charing Cross
10.00 a.m. (time may vary)
Free

CUTTY SARK
King William Walk, SE10
858 3445/853 3589
BR Greenwich
April–September:
2.30 p.m.–6.00 p.m.
October–May:
2.30 p.m.–5.00 p.m.
Admission charge
The best known and fastest of the tea clippers. Museum and collection of figureheads.
*Shop

DAILY EXPRESS and
EVENING STANDARD
Fleet Street, EC4
353 8000
✪ Blackfriars
8.30 p.m.–11.00 p.m.
Free
Maximum 12 people.
Minimum age 16. Must book several months in advance.
2½ hour tour showing every stage of newspaper production.

GIPSY MOTH IV
King William Walk, SE10
858 3445/853 3589
BR Greenwich
April–September (only):
2.30 p.m.–6.00 p.m.
Admission charge
The boat in which Sir Francis
Chichester sailed round the
world.
*Shop

HIGHGATE CEMETERY
Swains Lane, N6
340 1834
⊖ Archway
Summer: 10.00 a.m.–
4.00 p.m.
Winter: 10.00 a.m.–3.00 p.m.
Free
Burial place of many famous
people including Karl Marx
and George Eliot. Guided
tours round Western side.
*Shop

HISTORIC SHIP
COLLECTION
East Basin,
St Katharine's Dock, E1
481 0043
⊖ Tower Hill
10.00 a.m.–5.00 p.m.
Admission charge
The Maritime Trust's
collection of ships ranging from
a Thames tug to H.M.S.
Discovery, in which Scott sailed
to the Antarctic.
*Refreshments *Shop

KENSAL GREEN
CEMETERY
Ladbroke Grove, W10
969 0152
⊖ Kensal Green
2.00 p.m.–6.00 p.m. or dusk if
earlier
Free
Those buried here include
Brunel, Thackeray and
Trollope.

LIGHT FANTASTIC
48 South Row,
The Market, WC2
836 6423
⊖ Covent Garden
11.00 a.m.–6.00 p.m.
Admission charge
Permanent exhibition of
holographs.
*Bookstall

LONDON DUNGEON
28–34 Tooley Street, SE1
403 0606
⊖ London Bridge
Summer: 10.00 a.m.–
5.45 p.m.
Winter: 10.00 a.m.–4.30 p.m.
Admission charge
Display of horrors – torture,
plague and witchcraft with
sound effects. Not for young
children.
*Café *Shop

LONDON LASERIUM
Marylebone Road, NW1
486 1121
Recorded information:
486 2242

◉ Baker Street
6.00 p.m. and 7.30 p.m.
Admission charge
Part of Planetarium
Laser light concerts.

LONDON PLANETARIUM
Marylebone Road, NW1
486 1121
Recorded information:
486 2242
◉ Baker Street
11.00 a.m.–4.30 p.m.
Admission charge
Regular programmes of
projected displays of the
planets and stars.

MADAME TUSSAUD'S
Marylebone Road, NW1
935 6861
◉ Baker Street
Summer: 10.00 a.m.–
6.00 p.m.
Winter: 10.00 a.m.–5.30 p.m.
Admission charge
Wax figures of famous people
and reconstructed historical
scenes.
*Snack bar *Shop

OLD ROYAL
OBSERVATORY
Greenwich Park, SE10
858 1167
BR Greenwich
2.00 p.m.–5.00 p.m.
Admission charge
Collection of telescopes, clocks
and astronomical instruments.
Outside is the meridian line.
*Bookstall

THAMES BARRIER
Barrier Approach, SE7
854 1373
BR Woolwich Dockyard/
Charlton
10.30 a.m.–5.00 p.m.
Free
Thames Barrier Centre puts
on audio-visual presentation and
exhibition illustrating the
construction and operation of
the flood barrier.
*Café *Shop

TOWER BRIDGE
WALKWAY
Tower Bridge, E1
407 0922
◉ Tower Hill
Summer: 10.00 a.m.–
5.45 p.m.
Winter: 10.00 a.m.–4.00 p.m.
Admission charge
Magnificent views of London
from North Tower.
Exhibition and museum
illustrating the history and
operation of the bridge.
*Shop

WEMBLEY STADIUM
Empire Way
Wembley, Middlesex
903 4864/902 8833
◉ Wembley Park
Summer: 10.00 a.m.–
4.00 p.m. tours on the hour
(not 1.00 p.m.)
Winter: 10.00 a.m.–3.00 p.m.
tours on the hour (not 1.00
p.m.)

Admission charge
No tour the day before, after
or during an event.
Tour of the stadium and its
facilities. Audio-visual
presentation of its history.
*Refreshments *Shop

CANAL TRIPS

JASON'S TRIP
Embarkation point opposite
60 Blomfield Road, W9
286 3428
❸ Warwick Avenue
additional pick-up point at
Camden Lock, NW1
❸ Camden Town
Easter–October (only):
at least two trips a day, more
in summer
Approximately 1½ hours on a
narrow boat along Regent's
Canal to Camden Town.
Booking advised.
*Refreshments

JENNY WREN
250 Camden High Street,
NW1
485 4433/6210
❸ Camden Town
Easter–October (only):
at least two trips a day, more
in summer
Approximately 1½ hours on a
narrow boat along Regent's
Canal to Little Venice.
Booking advised.

THE LACE PLATE
Embarkation point opposite
60 Blomfield Road, W9
286 3428
❸ Warwick Avenue
Restaurant boat, seats 12 for
lunch or dinner cruise on
canal lasting 3 hours.
Booking essential.

MY FAIR LADY
250 Camden High Street,
NW1
485 4433/6210
❸ Camden Town
Restaurant boat for traditional
Sunday lunch cruise on canal
lasting 3 hours.
Booking essential.

PORT A BELLA PACKET
Ladbroke Grove, W10
(corner of Kensal Road)
960 5456
❸ Ladbroke Grove
April–October (only):
Various day and evening trips
Narrow boat cruises on Grand
Union and Regent's Canals.
Can disembark at zoo.
Booking advised.
*Bar

ZOO WATERBUS
Delamere Terrace, W2
286 6101
❸ Warwick Avenue
April–September (only):
Frequent service along
Regent's Canal to London Zoo.
Fare includes zoo admission
charge.

Also, June–August: trips to
Camden Lock.

RIVER TRIPS

The layout of this section is
based on the order of the
piers along the Thames,
starting up-river and working
down-river:
Hampton Court Pier
Richmond Pier
Kew Pier
Putney Pier
Westminster Pier
Charing Cross Pier
Festival Pier
Tower Pier
Greenwich Pier
Barrier Pier

Special tours and cruises are
listed after the regular trips
from each pier.

The adult fare on a regular trip
may be £1.00–£4.00.
Cruises with meals, discos, etc.
cost more.

from RICHMOND PIER
Northumberland Place,
Richmond
⊖ Richmond

to Hampton Court Pier
940 2244/8505
Summer: 11.30 a.m.–
3.30 p.m.
Four sailings
Duration: 1½ hours

to Westminster Pier, SW1
940 2244/8505
Summer: 4.45 p.m. & 5.15
p.m.

Circular Cruise
892 0741
to Teddington Lock and return
Summer: 10.30 a.m.–
6.00 p.m.
every 45 minutes

from KEW PIER
Thetis Terrace, Richmond
⊖ Kew Gardens

to Hampton Court Pier
940 3891
Summer: 11.45 a.m.–
1.30 p.m.
every 30 minutes

to Richmond Pier, Richmond
940 3891
Summer: 11.45 a.m.–
1.30 p.m.
every 30 minutes

to Westminster Pier, SW1
940 3891
Summer: 11.45 a.m.–2.45p.m.
every 30 minutes

from PUTNEY PIER
Embankment, SW15
⊖ Putney Bridge

to Hampton Court Pier
788 5104
Summer: 11.00 a.m.–
4.00 p.m.
every 30 minutes
last return boat 1.00 p.m.

to Richmond Pier, Richmond
788 5104
Summer: 11.00 a.m.–
4.00 p.m.
every 30 minutes

to Kew Pier, Richmond
788 5104
Summer: 11.30 a.m.–
4.30 p.m.
every 30 minutes

to Westminster Pier, SW1
788 5104
Summer: Noon–6.00 p.m.
every 30 minutes

from WESTMINSTER PIER
Victoria Embankment, SW1
⊖ Westminster

to Hampton Court Pier
930 2062
Summer: 10.00 a.m.–noon
Three sailings
Duration 4–5 hours

to Richmond Pier, Richmond
930 2062
Summer: 10.00 a.m.–noon
Three sailings
Last return boat 5.00 p.m.
Duration: 2½–3 hours

to Kew Pier, Richmond
930 2062
Summer: 10.30 a.m.–
4.00 p.m.
every 30 minutes
last return boat 5.00 p.m.
Duration: 1½ hours

to Festival Pier, SE1
regular ferry service
Duration: 5–10 minutes

to Tower Pier, EC3
930 4097
Summer: 10.00 a.m.–
5.00 p.m.
every 20 minutes
Winter: 10.00 a.m.–3.00 p.m.
every 30 minutes
Duration: 20 minutes

to Greenwich Pier, SE10
930 4097
Summer: 10.30 a.m.–
5.00 p.m.
every 20 minutes
Winter: 10.00 a.m.–3.00 p.m.
every 30 minutes
Duration: 45 minutes

to Thames Barrier, SE7
740 8263/930 3373
Summer: 10.00 a.m.–
2.45 p.m.
every 1¼ hours
Duration: 1¼ hours

Circular Cruise
839 4859/231 1322
Summer: 11.00 a.m.–
5.00 p.m.
every 30 minutes
Duration: 1 hour

Disco Cruise
722 9132
Summer: 8.00 p.m.
Duration: 4 hours

Evening Cruise
930 4097
Summer: 7.30 p.m. &
8.15 p.m.
Duration: 1¾ hours

Floodlit Supper Cruise
839 2349/3523
to Tower Bridge & Albert
Bridge. With supper and
commentary.
Summer: 9.00 p.m.
Duration: 1½ hours

Luncheon Cruise
839 2349/3523
to Greenwich and return.
With lunch and commentary.
Departure: 12.45 p.m.
Duration: 2 hours

Variety Supper Dance Cruise
839 2349/3523
Supper, music hall show and
dancing.
Departure: 6.30 p.m.
Duration: 3½–4 hours

from CHARING CROSS
PIER
Victoria Embankment, WC2
⊖ Embankment

to Tower Pier, EC3
930 0971
Summer: 10.30 a.m.–
4.30 p.m.
every 30 minutes
Duration: 20 minutes

to Greenwich Pier, SW10
930 0971
some with audio-visual
commentary
Summer: 10.00 a.m.–
4.30 p.m.
every 30 minutes
Duration: 45 minutes

Circular Evening Cruise
930 0971
Summer: 7.30 p.m. &
8.30 p.m.
according to demand
Duration: 1½ hours

Thames Guided Tours
839 3312
to Tower Bridge via Chelsea
with audio-visual
commentary
10.00 a.m.–6.30 p.m.
Four sailings
Duration: 1½ hours

from FESTIVAL PIER
Albert Embankment, SE1
⊖ Waterloo

to Tower Pier, EC3
930 0971
Summer: 10.35 a.m.–
4.35 p.m.
every 30 minutes
Duration: 20 minutes

to Greenwich, SE10
930 0971
some with audio-visual
commentary
Summer: 10.05 a.m.–
4.30 p.m.
every 30 minutes
Duration: 45 minutes

Supper Cruise
722 9132
Summer: 8.00 p.m.
Duration: 2 hours

from TOWER PIER
Tower Hill, EC3
⊖ Tower Hill

to Westminster Pier, SW1
709 9855
Summer: 11.20 a.m.–
5.00 p.m.
every 20–30 minutes
Duration: 20 minutes

to Charing Cross Pier, WC2
930 0971
Summer: 10.30 a.m.–
4.30 p.m.
every 30 minutes
Duration: 20 minutes

to H.M.S. Belfast, SE1
Ferry service
407 6436/709 9855
Summer: 11.00 a.m.–
5.50 p.m.
Winter: 11.00 a.m.–4.30 p.m.
every 20 minutes
Duration: 10 minutes

to Greenwich Pier, SE10
488 0344/709 7967
Summer: 11.30 a.m.–
5.00 p.m.
every 20–30 minutes
Duration: 35 minutes

Audio-visual History Cruise
488 0344
Summer: Lunchtime &
evening
Duration: 2–2½ hours

Circular Cruise
839 3312
to Chelsea and return. With
lunch or dinner.
1.00 p.m. & 7.30 p.m.
Duration: 1½ hours

Thames Guided Tours
839 3312
to Greenwich
Departure: 9.30 a.m.
Duration: 1¼ hours

from GREENWICH PIER
King William Walk, SE10
BR Greenwich

to Charing Cross Pier, WC2
858 3996
10.20 a.m.–5.20 p.m.
every 20 minutes
Duration: 40 minutes

to Tower Pier, EC3
488 0344
Summer: 11.15 a.m.–
5.00 p.m.
every 20–30 minutes
Duration: 30 minutes

from BARRIER PIER
Riverside, SE7
BR Charlton/Woolwich
Dockyard

Circular Cruise
854 5555
10.00 a.m.–4.00 p.m.
every 30 minutes
Duration: 20–30 minutes

WALKS

GUIDED WALKS

Many different routes and
themes (listed in *The Times* and
Time Out) are available from
archaeology to pub walks;
from Roman to Dickens'
London.

Starting from various Underground stations, walks generally last approximately 1½ hours and you will be charged about £2.00.

Guided walks are organized by the following:

CITISIGHTS
12 Alpha Place, SW3
600 3699 Ext. 281

DISCOVERING LONDON
11 Pennyfields, Warley,
Brentwood, Essex
Brentwood (0277) 213704

EXCITING WALKS
624 9981

THE INLAND
WATERWAYS
ASSOCIATION
114 Regent's Park Road, NW1
586 2510/2556
Canal walks

LONDON WALKS
139 Conway Road, N14
882 2763

THE LONDONER
3 Springfield Avenue, N10
883 2656

STREETS OF LONDON
32 Grovelands Road, N13
882 3414/886 9708

NATURE TRAILS

This is a list of Parks with nature trails and/or walks.

Guides may be obtained from the Superintendent for a nominal charge.

See Parks for further details.

BOSTALL HEATH, SE2

CASTLEWOOD &
JACKWOOD, SE18

DULWICH PARK, SE21

ELTHAM PARK, SE9

HORNIMAN GARDENS,
SE23

LESNES ABBEY WOODS,
SE2

OXLEAS WOOD, SE9

COACH TOURS

The companies listed here arrange sightseeing tours round London. The tours vary greatly. Some have a guide or commentary, others don't; some are bookable, others are not; some last 1½ hours, others 4½ hours; and some cost £3.00, others (with lunch) may cost £20.00.

There may be only one tour or several tours daily. Generally, there is a reduced service in winter.

Further information from
London Tourist Boards at
Victoria Station (730 3488
during office hours Monday to
Friday) or direct from the
operators listed here.

CITYRAMA
Silverthorne Road, SW8
720 5971
starts from Grosvenor Gardens
⊖ Victoria

THE CULTURE BUS
844 0880/834 6732
20 stops all round London.
You may get off and reboard
as you please.

EVAN EVANS
27 Cockspur Street, SW1
930 2377
April–October

FRAMES TOURS
11 Herbrand Street, WC1
837 3111/837 6311
April–October

LONDON TRANSPORT
227 3443/222 1234
Wide variety of tours.
Good introductory tour:
Round London Sightseeing
Tour with pick-up points at a
number of places.

POSTAL ZONE INDEX

(p.m.) = open during the
afternoon only

E1

ART GALLERIES
Whitechapel Art Gallery

ANIMALS & BIRDS
Spitalfields Farm
Stepney Stepping Stones Farm

OTHER OUTINGS
Historic Ship Collection
Tower Bridge Walkway

E2

MUSEUMS
Bethnal Green Museum of
Childhood (p.m.)
Geffrye Museum (p.m.)

ART GALLERIES
The Showroom (p.m.)

E4

MUSEUMS
Epping Forest Museum (p.m.)

E9

ANIMALS & BIRDS
Victoria Park

E14

ANIMALS & BIRDS
Mudchute Farm Park

E17

MUSEUMS
William Morris Gallery

EC2

MUSEUMS
The Museum of London
(p.m.)

ART GALLERIES
Barbican Centre Art Gallery

EC3

MUSEUMS
Herald's Museum at the
Tower of London (p.m.)

HISTORIC BUILDINGS
Monument (p.m.)
The Tower of London (p.m.)

RIVER TRIPS
Tower Pier

EC4

MUSEUMS
St Bride's Crypt Museum

OTHER OUTINGS
Daily Express and Evening
Standard (evening)

N4

ART GALLERIES
Black-Art Gallery (p.m.)

ANIMALS & BIRDS
Clissold Park

**GARDENS & NATURAL
HISTORY**
Clissold Park

N6

ART GALLERIES
Lauderdale House

HISTORIC BUILDINGS
Kenwood House – The Iveagh
Bequest

ANIMALS & BIRDS
Waterlow Park

OTHER OUTINGS
Highgate Cemetery

N7

ANIMALS & BIRDS
Freightliners Farm

N13

MUSEUMS
Broomfield Museum

**GARDENS & NATURAL
HISTORY**
Broomfield Museum

NW1

ART GALLERIES
Chalcot Gallery
The Room (p.m.)

ANIMALS & BIRDS
London Zoo & Aquarium
Regent's Park

**GARDENS & NATURAL
HISTORY**
Regent's Park

OTHER OUTINGS
London Laserium (evening)
London Planetarium
Madame Tussaud's

CANAL TRIPS
Jason's Trip
Jenny Wren
My Fair Lady

NW3

ART GALLERIES
Camden Arts Centre (p.m.)

HISTORIC BUILDINGS
Fenton House (p.m.)
Keats' House (p.m.)

NW4

MUSEUMS
Church Farm House Museum
(p.m.)

NW5

ANIMALS & BIRDS
Inter-Action City Farm

NW9

MUSEUMS
Royal Air Force Museum
(p.m.)

NW11

ANIMALS & BIRDS
Golders Hill

SE1

MUSEUMS
Bear Gardens Museum
Imperial War Museum (p.m.)
Museum of Garden History

ART GALLERIES
Bankside Gallery (p.m.)
Hayward Gallery
Royal Festival Hall Foyer

GARDENS & NATURAL HISTORY
Museum of Garden History
William Curtis Ecological Park

OTHER OUTINGS
H.M.S. Belfast
London Dungeon

RIVER TRIPS
Festival Pier

SE2

WALKS
Nature Trails
Bostall Heath
Lesnes Abbey Woods

SE3

ART GALLERIES
Woodlands Art Gallery (p.m.)

SE5

ART GALLERIES
South London Art Gallery
(p.m.)

SE7

OTHER OUTINGS
Thames Barrier

RIVER TRIPS
Barrier Pier

SE9

ART GALLERIES
Tudor Barn Art Gallery

GARDENS & NATURAL HISTORY
Avery Hill Park

WALKS
Nature Trails
Eltham Park
Oxleas Wood

SE10

MUSEUMS
National Maritime Museum (p.m.)

HISTORIC BUILDINGS
Ranger's House

OTHER OUTINGS
Cutty Sark (p.m.)
Gipsy Moth IV (p.m.)
Old Royal Observatory (p.m.)

RIVER TRIPS
Greenwich Pier

SE11

ANIMALS & BIRDS
Vauxhall City Farm

SE16

ANIMALS & BIRDS
Surrey Docks Farm

SE18

MUSEUMS
Rotunda Museum of Artillery (p.m.)

WALKS
Nature Trails
Castlewood & Jackwood

SE19

ANIMALS & BIRDS
Crystal Palace Park

SE21

ART GALLERIES
Dulwich Picture Gallery (p.m.)

ANIMALS & BIRDS
Dulwich Park

GARDENS & NATURAL HISTORY
Dulwich Park

WALKS
Nature Trails
Dulwich Park

SE23

MUSEUMS
Horniman Museum (p.m.)

ANIMALS & BIRDS
Horniman Gardens

GARDENS & NATURAL HISTORY
Horniman Museum (p.m.)

WALKS
Nature Trails
Horniman Gardens

SE24

ANIMALS & BIRDS
Brockwell Park

GARDENS & NATURAL
HISTORY
Brockwell Park

SW1

ART GALLERIES
Canada House
The Crafts Council (p.m.)
Institute of Contemporary Arts
Loggia Gallery (p.m.)
The Queen's Gallery (p.m.)
Tate Gallery (p.m.)
Warwick Arts Trust

HISTORIC BUILDINGS
Banqueting House (p.m.)
Cabinet War Rooms
Lancaster House (p.m.)

ANIMALS & BIRDS
St James's Park

OTHER OUTINGS
Changing the Guard

RIVER TRIPS
Westminster Pier

SW3

MUSEUMS
National Army Museum (p.m.)
Royal Hospital Museum

HISTORIC BUILDINGS
Carlyle's House

GARDENS & NATURAL
HISTORY
Chelsea Physic Garden (p.m.)

SW7

MUSEUMS
Baden-Powell House
Geological Museum (p.m.)
Natural History Museum
(p.m.)
Science Museum (p.m.)
Victoria and Albert Museum
(p.m.)

GARDENS & NATURAL
HISTORY
Geological Museum (p.m.)
Natural History Museum
(p.m.)

SW11

ART GALLERIES
Battersea Arts Centre

ANIMALS & BIRDS
Battersea Park

GARDENS & NATURAL
HISTORY
Battersea Park

SW15

RIVER TRIPS
Putney Pier

SW19

MUSEUMS
Wimbledon Lawn Tennis
Museum (p.m.)

HISTORIC BUILDINGS
Wimbledon Windmill (p.m.)

W1

MUSEUMS
Museum of Mankind (p.m.)
Wallace Collection (p.m.)

ART GALLERIES
Royal Academy of Arts

HISTORIC BUILDINGS
Apsley House (p.m.)

W2

MUSEUMS
London Toy and Model
Museum

ART GALLERIES
Serpentine Gallery

CANAL TRIPS
Zoo Waterbus

W3

MUSEUMS
Gunnersbury Park Museum
(p.m.)

W4

HISTORIC BUILDINGS
Chiswick House
Hogarth's House (p.m.)

GARDENS & NATURAL
HISTORY
Chiswick House

W6

ART GALLERIES
Riverside Studios

W8

MUSEUMS
Commonwealth Institute
(p.m.)

HISTORIC BUILDINGS
Kensington Palace (p.m.)
Linley Sambourne House
(p.m.)

ANIMALS & BIRDS
Holland Park

GARDENS & NATURAL
HISTORY
Holland Park

W9

CANAL TRIPS
Jason's Trip
The Lace Plate

W10

OTHER OUTINGS
Kensal Green Cemetery (p.m.)

CANAL TRIPS
Port A Bella Packet

WC1

MUSEUMS
British Library and Museum
(p.m.)
Jewish Museum

ART GALLERIES
Courtauld Institute Galleries
(p.m.)

WC2

MUSEUMS
London Transport Museum

ART GALLERIES
The National Gallery (p.m.)
National Portrait Gallery
(p.m.)

OTHER OUTINGS
Light Fantastic

RIVER TRIPS
Charing Cross Pier

OUT OF TOWN – BRENTFORD

MUSEUMS
Heritage Motor Museum
Kew Bridge Engines Museum
The Musical Museum (p.m.)

ART GALLERIES
The Art Centre

HISTORIC BUILDINGS
Syon House

ANIMALS & BIRDS
The London Butterfly House

GARDENS & NATURAL
HISTORY
Syon House

OUT OF TOWN – CHEAM

HISTORIC BUILDINGS
Whitehall (p.m.)

OUT OF TOWN – EAST MOLESEY

HISTORIC BUILDINGS
Hampton Court Palace

GARDENS & NATURAL
HISTORY
Hampton Court Palace

RIVER TRIPS
from various piers

OUT OF TOWN – HARROW

MUSEUMS
Kodak Museum (p.m.)

OUT OF TOWN – ISLEWORTH

HISTORIC BUILDINGS
Osterley Park House (p.m.)

GARDENS & NATURAL
HISTORY
Osterley Park House

OUT OF TOWN – RICHMOND

HISTORIC BUILDINGS
Ham House (p.m.)
Kew Palace
Queen Charlotte's Cottage

ANIMALS & BIRDS
Richmond Park

GARDENS & NATURAL HISTORY
Ham House
Royal Botanic Gardens

RIVER TRIPS
Kew Pier
Richmond Pier

OUT OF TOWN – TWICKENHAM

ART GALLERIES
Orleans House Gallery (p.m.)

HISTORIC BUILDINGS
Marble Hill House

OUT OF TOWN – WEMBLEY

OTHER OUTINGS
Wembley Stadium

SPORTS & ACTIVITIES

The first part of this section is an A–Z of sports and activities; the second part is a list of sports centres and health clubs. Within both sections, the listings are arranged by *postal zone*.

Under a particular activity in the A–Z, information may be given in one of three ways:

(a) In full because only one principal activity, e.g. riding, is available.
(b) As a place name only, in which case you should refer to Sports Centres & Health Clubs for further details.
(c) Preceded by (P), in which case you should refer to the 'Parks' section of this book for further details.

HOURS
The times given are the opening hours of the building. Ring to check if what you want to do is available at a specified time.

CHARGES
The amount you will be charged varies considerably. At some places full membership is necessary; at others, you will be charged a nominal sum for day membership or simply an admission or class fee.

ADVANCE BOOKING
If booking is available you are advised, in most cases, to do so. This is especially true of sports such as riding, tennis or squash which you may need to book some days in advance. Membership may give you special booking privileges but in any case ring and check to be certain.

LESSONS
Tuition is generally less frequently available on Sunday. There are exceptions, however, such as riding or ice skating and those activities in which classes are held such as aerobics. Ring and check for details.

PARKS
There are so many parks in London with sports facilities that those listed here are necessarily limited. Included here are the Royal Parks and G.L.C. Parks but, in addition, many of the Borough Parks have excellent facilities. Contact your local council for information on facilities, season tickets, booking procedure etc.

SEASONAL
Obviously some of the sports listed are available on a seasonal basis only. The cricket pitch in a park in summer will be used for rugby in winter. If in doubt, ring and check.

EVENTS
Sporting events are sometimes held at a number of the sports centres listed here. See Press for details, announcements and information about other major sporting events.

AEROBICS

BODY TALK
Onslow Parade,
Hampden Square, N14
368 1113
⊖ Southgate
10.00 a.m.–2.00 p.m.
*Café

Durnsford Community
Sports Centre, N22

Medina Rajneesh
Body Centre, NW3

Belsize Dance Studio, NW6

Lewisham Leisure Centre,
SE13

Body's, SW3

Lillie Road Fitness Centre,
SW6

South London Centre, SW8

CHELSEA DANCE STUDIOS
Chelsea Wharf,
15 Lots Road, SW10
351 5173
☻ Fulham Broadway/Sloane Square
10.00 a.m.–1.30 p.m.
*Café *Shop

Holmes Place Health Club, SW10

Dance Works, W1

PINEAPPLE WEST
60 Paddington Street, W1
487 3444
☻ Baker Street
Noon–5.00 p.m.
Membership necessary
*Health bar *Shop

London Central Y.M.C.A., WC1

DANCE CENTRE
11–12 Floral Street, WC2
836 6544
☻ Covent Garden
Noon–5.00 p.m.
*Snack bar *Shop

Jubilee Hall
Recreation Centre, WC2

ARCHERY

Finsbury Leisure Centre, EC1

Flaxman Sports Centre, SE5

ATHLETICS

(P) King George's Field, E3

(P) Victoria Park, E9

(P) Finsbury Park, N4

New River Sports Centre, N22

(P) Parliament Hill, NW3

Crystal Palace National Sports Centre, SE19

Sands End Community Sports Hall, SW6

(P) Battersea Park, SW11

(P) Wormwood Scrubs, W12

BADMINTON

Wapping Sports Centre, E1

George Sylvester Sports Centre, E8

Eastway Sports Centre, E10

Wanstead Leisure Centre, E11

George Green Sports Centre, E14

Kelmscott Leisure Centre, E17

Finsbury Leisure Centre, EC1

Britannia Leisure Centre, N1

Sobell Sports Centre, N7

EDMONTON GREEN POOL
Knights Lane, N9
807 8725

BR Lower Edmonton
8.00 a.m.–2.10 p.m.
*Café

Picketts Lock Centre, N9

ASHMOLE CENTRE
Burleigh Gardens, N14
368 4984
⊖ Southgate
10.00 a.m.–4.00 p.m.
*Refreshments *Equipment
hire

Langham Sports Centre, N15

Northumberland Park Sports
Centre, N17

Tottenham Sports Centre,
N17

Durnsford Community Sports
Centre, N22

New River Sports Centre, N22

Swiss Cottage Sports Centre,
NW3

Charteris Community Sports
Centre, NW6

Colombo Street Sports &
Community Centre, SE1

Elephant & Castle Recreation
Centre, SE1

Crofton Leisure Centre, SE4

Flaxman Sports Centre, SE5

Lewisham Leisure Centre,
SE13

Plumstead Sports Centre,
SE18

Crystal Palace National Sports
Centre, SE19

Sylvan Sports Centre, SE19

Queen Mother Sports Centre,
SW1

Chelsea Sports Centre, SW3

Eternit Wharf Recreation
Centre, SW6

Sands End Community Sports
Hall, SW6

Wimbledon Recreation
Centre, SW19

Y.M.C.A., SW19

Seymour Hall Leisure Centre,
W1

Chiswick Community Sports
Hall, W4

London Central Y.M.C.A.,
WC1

Jubilee Hall Recreation
Centre, WC2

Harrow Leisure Centre,
Harrow

BASKETBALL

Eastway Sports Centre, E10

Finsbury Leisure Centre, EC1

Picketts Lock Centre, N9

New River Sports Centre, N22

Swiss Cottage Sports Centre,
NW3

Charteris Community Sports Centre, NW6

Flaxman Sports Centre, SE5

Crystal Palace National Sports Centre, SE19

Sylvan Sports Centre, SE19

Jubilee Sports Centre, W10

London Central Y.M.C.A, WC1

Jubilee Hall Recreation Centre, WC2

BOATING

(P) Victoria Park, E9

(P) Finsbury Park, N4

(P) Alexandra Park, N22

(P) Regent's Park, NW1

(P) Thamesmead, SE2

(P) Burgess Park, SE5

(P) Crystal Palace Park, SE19

(P) Dulwich Park, SE21

(P) Battersea Park, SW11

(P) Hyde Park, W2

BOWLS

Wapping Sports Centre, E1

(P) Victoria Park, E9

(P) Finsbury Park, N4

Picketts Lock Centre, N9

(P) Parliament Hill, NW3

(P) Bostall Heath, SE2

(P) Blackheath, SE3

Plumstead Sports Centre, SE18

(P) Dulwich Park, SE21

(P) Battersea Park, SW11

(P) Hyde Park, W2

BRASS RUBBING

ALL-HALLOWS-BY-THE-TOWER
Byward Street, EC3
481 2928
● Tower Hill
11.00 a.m.–5.00 p.m.
*Café (noon–3.00 p.m.)

ST JAMES'S CHURCH
Piccadilly, W1
437 6023
● Piccadilly Circus
Noon–6.00 p.m.

CHESS

CHEQUERS
18 Chalk Farm Road, NW1
485 1696
● Chalk Farm/Camden Town
10.00 a.m.–2.00 a.m.
*Light meals

Y.M.C.A., SW19

CRICKET

N.B. Includes places with nets *and/or* pitches.

(P) Hackney Marsh, E9

(P) Victoria Park, E9

(P) Finsbury Park, N4

Langham Sports Centre, N15

Durnsford Community Sports Centre, N22

(P) Regent's Park, NW1

(P) Parliament Hill, NW3

M.C.C. INDOOR CRICKET SCHOOL
Lord's Cricket Ground
St John's Wood Road, NW8
286 3649
✪ St John's Wood
10.00 a.m.–5.00 p.m.
*Bar/restaurant *Shop

(P) Hampstead Heath Extension, NW11

(P) Archbishop's Park, SE1

(P) Bostall Heath, SE2

(P) Thamesmead, SE2

(P) Blackheath, SE3

(P) Avery Hill Park, SE9

(P) Eltham Park, SE9

(P) Greenwich Park, SE10

Lewisham Leisure Centre, SE13

(P) Crystal Palace Park, SE19

Sylvan Sports Centre, SE19

(P) Dulwich Park, SE21

(P) Battersea Park, SW11

(P) Hyde Park, W2

Chiswick Community Sports Hall, W4

(P) Holland Park, W8

(P) Wormwood Scrubs, W12

(P) Richmond Park, Richmond

CYCLING

EASTWAY CYCLE CIRCUIT
Temple Mills Lane, E15
534 6085
✪ Leyton/Stratford
8.00 a.m.–5.00 p.m.
*Vending machines
*Equipment hire

(P) Crystal Palace Park, SE19

DANCE

ISLINGTON ARTS FACTORY
2 Parkhurst Road, N7
607 0561
✪ Holloway Road/Caledonian Road
10.30 a.m.–7.30 p.m.
*Café

Riviera, NW1

Medina Rajneesh Body
Centre, NW3

Belsize Dance Studio, NW6

Charteris Community Sports
Centre, NW6

Chelsea Dance Studios, SW10
(see Aerobics)

Holmes Place Health Club,
SW10

Metropolitan Club, SW11

Y.M.C.A., SW19

Dance Works, W1

Stripes Squash & Health Club,
W5

Sundance Studios, W6

FOOTWORK DANCE
STUDIO
38 Mount Pleasant, WC1
278 0567
☻ Holborn
Noon–2.00 p.m.
& 3.00 p.m.–6.00 p.m.

London Central Y.M.C.A.,
WC1

Dance Centre, WC2
(see Aerobics)

PINEAPPLE DANCE
STUDIOS
7 Langley Street, WC2
836 4004
☻ Covent Garden
11.00 a.m.–5.00 p.m.
Membership necessary
*Health bar *Shop

URDANG ACADEMY OF
BALLET & PERFORMING
ARTS
20–22 Shelton Street, WC2
836 5709/7010
☻ Covent Garden
Noon–4.30 p.m. (approx.)
*Coffee bar

FISHING

N.B. Fishing in Parks: Permit
from Superintendent
necessary.

In general: Permits, licences
and further information from
THAMES WATER
AUTHORITY
Metropolitan Division,
New River Head,
Rosebery Avenue, EC1
837 3300 Ext. 2420
Office hours Monday to Friday

(P) Victoria Park, E9

(P) Finsbury Park, N4

WALTHAMSTOW
RESERVOIRS
Ferry Lane, N17
Gatehouse: 808 1527
☻ Tottenham Hale/
Blackhorse Road

(P) Alexandra Park, N22

(P) Parliament Hill, NW3

(P) Thamesmead, SE2

(P) Burgess Park, SE5

(P) Crystal Palace Park, SE19

(P) Battersea Park, SW11

BARN ELMS RESERVOIRS
Merthyr Terrace, SW13
Gatehouse: 748 3423
● Hammersmith

(P) Hyde Park, W2

FIVE-A-SIDE FOOTBALL

Eastway Sports Centre, E10

George Green
Sports Centre, E14

Finsbury Leisure Centre, EC1

Picketts Lock Centre, N9

Swiss Cottage
Sports Centre, NW3

Charteris Community
Sports Centre, NW6

Crystal Palace
National Sports Centre, SE19

Sylvan Sports Centre, SE19

Queen Mother
Sports Centre, SW1

Eternit Wharf
Recreation Centre, SW6

Seymour Hall Leisure Centre,
W1

Chiswick Community
Sports Hall, W4

Jubilee Sports Centre, W10

Jubilee Hall
Recreation Centre, WC2

Harrow Leisure Centre,
Harrow

FIVES

Finsbury Leisure Centre, EC1

Jubliee Hall
Recreation Centre, WC2

FOOTBALL

(P) King George's Field, E3

(P) Hackney Marsh, E9

(P) Victoria Park, E9

Wanstead Leisure Centre, E11

Kelmscott Leisure Centre,
E17

(P) Finsbury Park, N4

Picketts Lock Centre, N9

(P) Regent's Park, NW1

(P) Parliament Hill, NW3

(P) Hampstead Heath
Extension, NW11

(P) Abbey Wood Park, SE2

(P) Bostall Heath, SE2

(P) Thamesmead, SE2

(P) Blackheath, SE3

(P) Burgess Park, SE5

Flaxman Sports Centre, SE5

(P) Avery Hill Park, SE9

(P) Eltham Park, SE9

(P) Oxleas Wood, SE9

Lewisham Leisure Centre, SE13

(P) Castlewood & Jackwood, SE18

(P) Crystal Palace Park, SE19

(P) Dulwich Park, SE21

(P) Battersea Park, SW11

Seymour Hall Leisure Centre, W1

(P) Hyde Park, W2

(P) Holland Park, W8

(P) Wormwood Scrubs, W12

(P) Richmond Park, Richmond

GOLF

CHINGFORD GOLF COURSE
Station Road, E4
529 2107
BR Chingford
from 11.00 a.m.

Picketts Lock Centre, N9

GOLF CENTRES
444 High Road, N12
445 0411
◒ East Finchley
10.00 a.m.–10.00 p.m.
*Bar *Equipment hire

TRENT PARK GOLF COURSE
Bramley Road, N14
366 7432
◒ Oakwood
7.00 a.m.–dusk
*Bar *Shop

Mr THOM'S GOLF SCHOOL
Outer Circle,
Regent's Park, NW1
723 4588
◒ St John's Wood
8.30 a.m.–dusk
*Shop *Equipment hire

RICHMOND PARK GOLF COURSE
Roehampton Gate,
Priory Lane, SW15
876 3205
◒ Putney Bridge
7.30 a.m.–dusk
Membership available
*Café *Shop *Equipment hire

BRENT VALLEY MUNICIPAL GOLF COURSE
138 Church Road, W7
567 4230
BR Hanwell
7.30 a.m.–dusk
*Equipment hire

(P) Holland Park, W8
(nets)

GYMNASIUMS

Hyams Gymnasium, E11

Leytonstone Recreation Centre, E11

Wanstead Leisure Centre, E11

George Green Sports Centre, E14

Finsbury Leisure Centre, EC1

Picketts Lock Centre, N9

Tottenham Sports Centre, N17

Flaxman Sports Centre, SE5

Crystal Palace National Sports Centre, SE19

Sylvan Sports Centre, SE19

Queen Mother Sports Centre, SW1

Body's, SW3

Chelsea Sports Centre, SW3

Eternit Wharf Recreation Centre, SW6

Lillie Road Fitness Centre, SW6

Sands End Community Sports Hall, SW6

South London Centre, SW8

Holmes Place Health Club, SW10

Power Station, SW10
Men only

Metropolitan Club, SW11

Wimbledon Recreation Centre, SW19

Burlington Health Club, W1

Grosvenor House Health Club, W1

Hogarth Health Club, W4

Stripes Squash & Health Club, W5

Sundance Studios, W6

Westside Health Club, W8

Jubilee Sports Centre, W10

Kensington New Pools, W11

London Central Y.M.C.A., WC1

The Fitness Centre, WC2

HANDBALL

Wapping Sports Centre, E1

Finsbury Leisure Centre, EC1

London Central Y.M.C.A., WC1

Jubilee Hall Recreation Centre, WC2

HOCKEY

(P) Hackney Marsh, E9

(P) Victoria Park, E9

Wanstead Leisure Centre, E11

Kelmscott Leisure Centre, E17

(P) Finsbury Park, N4

Picketts Lock Centre, N9

(P) Regent's Park, NW1

(P) Parliament Hill, NW3

(P) Avery Hill Park, SE9

(P) Greenwich Park, SE10

(P) Hyde Park, W2

(P) Wormwood Scrubs, W12

ICE SKATING

LEE VALLEY ICE CENTRE
Lea Bridge Road, E10
533 3151
⊖ Leyton
10.00 a.m.–noon &
2.00 p.m.–4.00 p.m.
Hockey: 7.00 p.m.–9.00 p.m.
Membership available
*Equipment hire

Sobell Sports Centre, N7

STREATHAM ICE RINK
386 Streatham High Road,
SW16
769 7861
⊖ Brixton
10.30 a.m.–12.30 p.m. &
2.00 p.m.–5.00 p.m. &
8.30 p.m.–11.00 p.m.
Hockey: 6.15 p.m.
*Café *Shop *Equipment hire

QUEEN'S ICE SKATING
CLUB
17 Queensway, W2
229 0172
⊖ Queensway

10.00 a.m.–noon &
2.00 p.m.–5.00 p.m. &
7.00 p.m.–10.00 p.m.
*Café *Shop *Equipment hire

RICHMOND ICE RINK
Clevedon Road
Twickenham, Middlesex
892 3646
⊖ Richmond
10.00 a.m.–12.30 p.m. &
2.30 p.m.–5.00 p.m. &
7.30 p.m.–10.00 p.m.
*Café *Shop *Equipment hire

JACUZZI

Hyams Gymnasium, E11

Power Station, SW10
Men only

Metropolitan Club, SW11

Grosvenor House Health
Club, W1

Hogarth Health Club, W4

Covent Garden Sauna for
Men, WC2

The Sanctuary, WC2
Women only

KEEP FIT

Islington Arts Factory, N7
(see Dance)

Northumberland Park Sports
Centre, N17

Holmes Place Health Club,
SW10

Dance Works, W1

Seymour Hall Leisure Centre,
W1

Westside Health Club, W8

Jubilee Sports Centre, W10

London Central Y.M.C.A.,
WC1

Jubilee Hall Recreation
Centre, WC2

KITE FLYING

(P) Regent's Park, NW1
(Primrose Hill)

(P) Parliament Hill, NW3

(P) Blackheath, SE3

(P) Kensington Gardens, W2

MARTIAL ARTS
including Judo, Karate, Tai
Chi

George Sylvester Sports
Centre, E8

Eastway Sports Centre, E10

Finsbury Leisure Centre, EC1

Langham Sports Centre, N15

Northumberland Park Sports
Centre, N17

Medina Rajneesh Body
Centre, NW3

Colombo Street Sports &
Community Centre, SE1

Crofton Leisure Centre, SE4

Sands End Community Sports
Hall, SW6

LONDON JUDO SOCIETY
89 Lansdowne Way, SW8
622 0529
● Stockwell
10.30 a.m.–12.30 p.m.
Membership available
*Bar/vending machine *Shop

Chiswick Community Sports
Hall, W4

Jubilee Sports Centre, W10

London Central Y.M.C.A.,
WC1

Harrow Leisure Centre,
Harrow

MASSAGE

J. K. SAUNA
193 Royal College Street,
NW1
485 9380/5554
● Camden Town
Noon–6.00 p.m.
*Refreshments

St James's Health Club, SW1

Burlington Health Club, W1

Dance Works, W1

Hogarth Health Club, W4

Holland Park Sauna for Men, W12

Covent Garden Sauna for Men, WC2

The Sanctuary, WC2
Women only

MODEL BOATING

(P) Victoria Park, E9

(P) Parliament Hill, NW3

(P) Thamesmead, SE2

(P) Blackheath, SE3

(P) Kensington Gardens, W2
(Round Pond)

(P) Richmond Park, Richmond
(Adam's Pond)

NETBALL

(P) Victoria Park, E9

Wanstead Leisure Centre, E11

Kelmscott Leisure Centre, E17

Finsbury Leisure Centre, EC1

(P) Finsbury Park, N4

Picketts Lock Centre, N9

(P) Regent's Park, NW1

(P) Parliament Hill, NW3

Swiss Cottage
Sports Centre, NW3

Charteris Community
Sports Centre, NW6

(P) Hampstead Heath
Extension, NW11

(P) Archbishop's Park, SE1

(P) Burgess Park, SE5

(P) Greenwich Park, SE10

Crystal Palace
National Sports Centre, SE19

Queen Mother
Sports Centre, SW1

Eternit Wharf
Recreation Centre, SW6

(P) Battersea Park, SW11

(P) Hyde Park, W2

Jubilee Sports Centre, W10

(P) Wormwood Scrubs, W12

Jubilee Hall
Recreation Centre, WC2

(P) Richmond Park, Richmond

ORIENTEERING

(P) Bostall Heath, SE2

(P) Lesnes Abbey Woods, SE2

(P) Oxleas Wood, SE9

(P) Castlewood & Jackwood, SE18

PUTTING

(P) Hackney Marsh, E9

(P) Victoria Park, E9

(P) Finsbury Park, N4

(P) Alexandra Park, N22

(P) Golders Hill, NW11

(P) Archbishop's Park, SE1

(P) Thamesmead, SE2

(P) Avery Hill Park, SE9

(P) Eltham Park, SE9

(P) Greenwich Park, SE10

(P) Castlewood, SE18

(P) Dulwich Park, SE21

(P) Horniman Gardens, SE23

(P) Holland Park, W8

RIDING

BARNFIELD RIDING
STABLES
Sewardstone Road, E4
529 5200
BR Chingford
9.00 a.m.–dusk

BURY FARM RIDING
SCHOOL
Bury Road, E4
529 1878
BR Chingford
10.00 a.m.–dusk

QUEEN ELIZABETH
RIDING SCHOOL
97 Forest Side, E4
529 1223
BR Chingford
9.00 a.m.–1.00 p.m.
*Refreshments

LEA BRIDGE RIDING
SCHOOL
Lea Bridge Road, E10
556 2629
◒ Leyton
9.30 a.m.–5.30 p.m.
*Refreshments

SNARESBROOK RIDING
SCHOOL
67–69 Hollybush Hill, E11
989 3256
◒ Snaresbrook
Morning only
*Refreshments

ALDERSBROOK RIDING
SCHOOL
Empress Avenue, E12
530 4648
◒ Wanstead/East Ham
9.00 a.m.–4.00 p.m.
*Refreshments *Shop

LONDON EQUESTRIAN
CENTRE
Lullington Garth, N12
349 1345
◒ Woodside Park/Mill Hill
East
9.00 a.m.–6.30 p.m.
*Refreshments *Shop

TRENT PARK
EQUESTRIAN CENTRE
Bramley Road, N14
363 8630
✪ Oakwood
9.00 a.m.–3.45 p.m.
*Shop

TOTTERIDGE RIDING
SCHOOL
32 Totteridge Common, N20
959 7290
✪ Totteridge & Whetstone
9.30 a.m.–4.30 p.m.
*Bar

BELMONT RIDING
CENTRE
The Ridgeway, NW7
906 1255
✪ Mill Hill East
9.00 a.m.–5.00 p.m.
*Refreshments

MOTTINGHAM FARM
RIDING CENTRE
Mottingham Lane, SE9
857 3003
BR Mottingham
8.00 a.m.–2.00 p.m.

WILLOWTREE RIDING
SCHOOL
Ronver Road, SE12
857 6438
BR Grove Park/Lee
9.00 a.m.–5.30 p.m.

DULWICH RIDING
SCHOOL
Dulwich Common, SE21
693 2944
BR West Dulwich
8.00 a.m.–7.30 p.m.

SOUTH LONDON RIDING
CENTRE
117a Canterbury Grove, SE27
670 0775
BR West Norwood/Streatham
Hill
8.00 a.m.–5.30 p.m.

LILO BLUM'S RIDING
SCHOOL
32a Grosvenor Crescent
Mews, SW1
235 6846
✪ Hyde Park Corner
7.00 a.m.–dusk

BATTERSEA HIPPIC
14a Winders Road, SW11
223 0909
BR Clapham Junction
8.00 a.m.–dusk

ROEHAMPTON GATE
STABLES
Priory Lane, SW15
876 7089
✪ Putney Bridge
7.30 a.m.–dusk

WANDLE RIDING
STABLES
130 Mitcham Road, SW17
947 6749/0931
✪ Tooting Broadway
9.00 a.m.–noon

WIMBLEDON VILLAGE
STABLES
24 High Street, SW19
946 8579
✪ Wimbledon
Dawn–dusk

BATHURST RIDING STABLES
63 Bathurst Mews, W2
723 2812
● Lancaster Gate/Paddington
9.00 a.m.–3.30 p.m.

ROSS NYE'S RIDING ESTABLISHMENT
8 Bathurst Mews, W2
262 3791
● Lancaster Gate/Paddington
10.00 a.m.–2.30 p.m.
Children only

WYNCOTE FARM
Trumpers Way, W7
843 1615
● Boston Manor
9.00 a.m.–5.15 p.m.

ROLLER SKATING

George Sylvester
Sports Centre, E8

Finsbury Leisure Centre, EC1

Picketts Lock Centre, N9

(P) Battersea Park, SW11

(P) Hyde Park, W2

Jubilee Hall Recreation
Centre, WC2

ROUNDERS

(P) Regent's Park, NW1

(P) Golders Hill, NW11

(P) Blackheath, SE3

(P) Dulwich Park, SE21

(P) Wormwood Scrubs, W12

RUGBY

(P) Hackney Marsh, E9

(P) Regent's Park, NW1

(P) Parliament Hill, NW3

(P) Hampstead Heath Extension, NW11

(P) Avery Hill Park, SE9

(P) Hyde Park, W2

(P) Wormwood Scrubs, W12

SAUNA

Hyams Gymnasium, E11

Britannia Leisure Centre, N1

J. K. Sauna, NW1
(see Massage)

Riviera, NW1

Medina Rajneesh
Body Centre, NW3

Elephant & Castle
Recreation Centre, SE1

Dolphin Square
Sports Centre, SW1

St James's Health Club, SW1

Body's, SW3

Chelsea Sports Centre, SW3

Fulham Pools, SW6
Women only
(see Swimming)

Sands End Community
Sports Hall, SW6

South London Centre, SW8

Power Station, SW10
Men only

Metropolitan Club, SW11

Wimbledon Recreation
Centre, SW19

Burlington Health Club, W1

Dance Works, W1

Grosvenor House
Health Club, W1

Hogarth Health Club, W4

Stripes Squash & Health Club,
W5

Sundance Studios, W6

Westside Health Club, W8

Holland Park Sauna for Men,
W12

West London Squash Club,
W12

White City Pool, W12

Covent Garden Sauna for
Men, WC2

The Fitness Centre, WC2

The Sanctuary, WC2
Women only

Harrow Leisure Centre,
Harrow

SELF DEFENCE

Sands End Community
Sports Hall, SW6

South London Centre, SW8

SKI-ING

ALEXANDRA PALACE SKI
CENTRE
Alexandra Park, N22
888 2284
⊖ Wood Green
October–March (only):
10.00 a.m.–6.00 p.m.

Crystal Palace
National Sports Centre, SE19
(October–March only)

SNOOKER

Sobell Sports Centre, N7

Tottenham Sports Centre,
N17

South London Centre, SW8

Harrow Leisure Centre,
Harrow

SOLARIUM

Hyams Gymnasium, E11

Leytonstone Recreation
Centre, E11

Body Talk, N14
(see Aerobics)

Riviera, NW1

Dolphin Square
Sports Centre, SW1

St James's Health Club, SW1

Chelsea Sports Centre, SW3

Lillie Road Fitness Centre,
SW6

South London Centre, SW8

Metropolitan Club, SW11

Wimbledon Recreation
Centre, SW19

Burlington Health Club, W1

Dance Works, W1

Grosvenor House
Health Club, W1

Hogarth Health Club, W4

Stripes Squash & Health Club,
W5

Sundance Studios, W6

Kensington New Pools, W11

Holland Park Sauna for Men,
W12

West London Squash Club,
W12

White City Pool, W12

London Central Y.M.C.A.,
WC1

The Fitness Centre, WC2

The Sanctuary, WC2
Women only

SQUASH

Eastway Sports Centre, E10

Leytonstone Recreation
Centre, E11

Wanstead Leisure Centre, E11

Kelmscott Leisure Centre,
E17

Finsbury Leisure Centre, EC1

Sobell Sports Centre, N7

Langham Sports Centre, N15

Medina Rajneesh
Body Centre, NW3

Swiss Cottage
Sports Centre, NW3

Elephant & Castle
Recreation Centre, SE1

Crofton Leisure Centre, SE4

Flaxman Sports Centre, SE5

Crystal Palace
National Sports Centre, SE19

Dolphin Square
Sports Centre, SW1

Queen Mother
Sports Centre, SW1

Chelsea Sports Centre, SW3

South London Centre, SW8

Metropolitan Club, SW11

Seymour Hall Leisure Centre, W1

Chiswick Community Sports Hall, W4

Hogarth Health Club, W4

Stripes Squash & Health Club, W5

BROADWAY SQUASH CENTRE
Shortlands, W6
741 4640
⊖ Hammersmith
10.00 a.m.–6.00 p.m.
Membership available
*Equipment hire

(P) Holland Park, W8

West London Squash Club, W12

London Central Y.M.C.A., WC1

Harrow Leisure Centre, Harrow

WEMBLEY SQUASH CENTRE
Empire Way,
Wembley, Middlesex
902 9230
⊖ Wembley Park
9.30 a.m.–10.00 p.m.
*Bar *Shop *Equipment hire

SWIMMING

WHISTON ROAD BATHS
Whiston Road, E2
739 7166
8.30 a.m.–1.00 p.m.
*Café *Shop

YORK HALL BATHS
Old Ford Road, E2
980 2243
⊖ Bethnal Green
8.00 a.m.–11.45 a.m.

CENTRAL BATHS
King's Hall
Lower Clapton Road, E5
985 2158
⊖ Bethnal Green
8.00 a.m.–3.00 p.m.
Men only: 3.30 p.m.–5.00 p.m.
*Café

(P) Victoria Park, E9

Leytonstone
Recreation Centre, E11

ROMFORD ROAD BATHS
Romford Road, E15
534 4545
⊖ Stratford
8.00 a.m.–10.45 a.m.

WALTHAM FOREST BATHS
Chingford Road, E17
527 5431
⊖ Walthamstow Central
8.00 a.m.–12.15 p.m.

CALEDONIAN ROAD BATHS
Caledonian Road, N1
837 0852

⊖ Caledonian Road/King's
Cross
9.00 a.m.–noon
*Vending machines

Highgate Ponds, N6
Men only
(see Parliament Hill, NW3)

Kenwood Pond, N6
Women only
(see Kenwood, NW3)

PARK ROAD BATHS
Park Road, N8
348 9484
⊖ Highgate
8.00 a.m.–12.30 p.m. &
1.15 p.m.–3.00 p.m. &
3.45 p.m.–5.15 p.m.

Edmonton Green Pool, N9
(see Badminton)

Picketts Lock Centre, N9

WINCHMORE HILL ROAD
POOL
Winchmore Hill Road, N14
886 4598
⊖ Southgate
8.00 a.m.–4.30 p.m.
*Vending machines

CENTRAL BATHS
Town Hall Approach Road,
N15
808 1000
⊖ Seven Sisters
8.00 a.m.–noon
*Café

CLISSOLD ROAD BATHS
Clissold Road, N16
254 4272

BR Stoke Newington
9.00 a.m.–5.30 p.m.
*Café

Northumberland Park
Sports Centre, N17

WESTERN ROAD BATHS
Western Road, N22
888 3055
⊖ Wood Green
8.00 a.m.–noon
*Vending machines

Hampstead Ponds, NW3
(see Parliament Hill, NW3)

(P) Kenwood, NW3

(P) Parliament Hill, NW3

Swiss Cottage
Sports Centre, NW3

COPTHALL SWIMMING
POOL
Great North Way, NW4
203 4187
⊖ Mill Hill East
9.00 a.m.–4.30 p.m.
*Café

WILLESDEN SPORTS
CENTRE
Donnington Road, NW10
459 6605
⊖ Willesden Green
8.00 a.m.–11.45 a.m.
*Café

Elephant & Castle
Recreation Centre, SE1

(P) Eltham Park, SE9

GREENWICH BATHS
80 Trafalgar Road, SE10
858 0159
BR Maze Hill
8.00 a.m.–11.00 p.m.
*Vending machines

LADYWELL BATHS
Lewisham High Street, SE13
690 2123
BR Ladywell/Lewisham
8.00 a.m.–11.15 a.m.
*Café *Vending machine

ROTHERHITHE BATHS
196 Lower Road, SE16
237 3296
⊖ Surrey Docks
8.30 a.m.–noon
*Vending machine

Crystal Palace
National Sports Centre, SE19

SOUTH NORWOOD POOL
Portland Road, SE25
654 6117
BR Norwood Junction
8.00 a.m.–noon
*Vending machines

Dolphin Square
Sports Centre, SW1

Queen Mother
Sports Centre, SW1

Chelsea Sports Centre, SW3

FULHAM POOLS
Normand Park
Lillie Road, SW6
381 4498/9
⊖ West Kensington/Fulham
Broadway

9.00 a.m.–noon
*Restaurant/bar *Shop

LATCHMERE LEISURE
CENTRE
Burns Road, SW11
350 1588
BR Clapham Junction
7.30 a.m.–9.00 p.m.
*Restaurant

STREATHAM BATHS
384 Streatham High Road,
SW16
769 6971
⊖ Brixton
8.00 a.m.–12.30 p.m.
*Vending machines

BALHAM POOL
Elmfield Road, SW17
871 7196
⊖ Balham
8.15 a.m.–11.15 a.m.
*Vending machines

TOOTING SWIMMING
POOL
Greaves Place, SW17
767 3234
⊖Tooting Broadway
8.30 a.m.–3.00 p.m.
*Vending machine

Wimbledon Recreation
Centre, SW19

Grosvenor House
Health Club, W1

Seymour Hall Leisure Centre,
W1

(P) Hyde Park, W2

The Serpentine, W2
(see Hyde Park, W2)

ACTON BATHS
Salisbury Street, W3
992 9242
✪ Acton Town
8.00 a.m.–11.30 a.m.
*Vending machines

Hogarth Health Club, W4

Jubilee Sports Centre, W10

Kensington New Pools, W11

White City Pool, W12

GURNELL POOL
Ruislip Road East, W13
998 3241
✪ Ealing Broadway
8.00 a.m.–4.00 p.m.
*Vending machines

OASIS
167 High Holborn, WC1
836 9555/3771
✪ Tottenham Court Road/
Covent Garden/Holborn
–INDOOR POOL:
May–September:
9.00 a.m.–5.45 p.m.
October–April:
9.00 a.m.–11.45 a.m.
–OUTDOOR POOL:
May–September (only):
9.00 a.m.–5.45 p.m.

The Sanctuary, WC2
Women only

Harrow Leisure Centre,
Harrow

TABLE TENNIS

Eastway Sports Centre, E10

Wanstead Leisure Centre, E11

George Green
Sports Centre, E14

Finsbury Leisure Centre, EC1

Sobell Sports Centre, N7

Langham Sports Centre, N15

Crofton Leisure Centre, SE4

Lewisham Leisure Centre,
SE13

Plumstead Sports Centre,
SE18

Crystal Palace
National Sports Centre, SE19

Queen Mother
Sports Centre, SW1

Chelsea Sports Centre, SW3

Sands End Community
Sports Hall, SW6

Wimbledon
Recreation Centre, SW19

Y.M.C.A., SW19

Chiswick Community
Sports Hall, W4

Jubilee Sports Centre, W10

London Central Y.M.C.A.,
WC1

Jubilee Hall
Recreation Centre, WC2

Harrow Leisure Centre, Harrow

TEN-PIN BOWLING

MECCA STREATHAM
BOWL
142 Streatham Hill, SW2
674 5251
BR Streatham Hill
11.00 a.m.–9.00 p.m.
*Bar/buffet *Shop
*Equipment hire

TENNIS

(P) King George's Field, E3

(P) Victoria Park, E9

Wanstead Leisure Centre, E11

George Green
Sports Centre, E14

Finsbury Leisure Centre, EC1

Britannia Leisure Centre, N1

(P) Finsbury Park, N4

Picketts Lock Centre, N9

Northumberland Park
Sports Centre, N17

(P) Regent's Park, NW1

(P) Parliament Hill, NW3

Swiss Cottage
Sports Centre, NW3

(P) Golders Hill, NW11

(P) Archbishop's Park, SE1

(P) Thamesmead, SE2

(P) Blackheath, SE3

(P) Burgess Park, SE5

(P) Avery Hill Park, SE9

(P) Eltham Park, SE9

(P) Greenwich Park, SE10

Plumstead Sports Centre,
SE18

Crystal Palace
National Sports Centre, SE19

(P) Crystal Palace Park, SE19

(P) Dulwich Park, SE21

(P) Horniman Gardens, SE23

Queen Mother
Sports Centre, SW1

(P) Battersea Park, SW11

LONDON INDOOR
TENNIS CLUB
Alfred Road, W2
286 1985
⊖ Royal Oak
8.00 a.m.–7.00 p.m.
Membership necessary
*Restaurant/bar *Shop
*Equipment hire

Hogarth Health Club, W4

(P) Holland Park, W8

(P) Wormwood Scrubs, W12

TRAMPOLINE

Eastway Sports Centre, E10

Finsbury Leisure Centre, EC1

Crofton Leisure Centre, SE4

Flaxman Sports Centre, SE5

Sylvan Sports Centre, SE19

Queen Mother
Sports Centre, SW1

Jubilee Sports Centre, W10

TURKISH BATHS

Ladywell Baths, SE13
(see Swimming)

Holmes Place Health Club,
SW10

VOLLEYBALL

Picketts Lock Centre, N9

Queen Mother
Sports Centre, SW1

Eternit Wharf
Recreation Centre, SW6

Jubilee Sports Centre, W10

London Central Y.M.C.A.,
WC1

WEIGHT TRAINING

Eastway Sports Centre, E10

Hyams Gymnasium, E11

Wanstead Leisure Centre, E11

Finsbury Leisure Centre, EC1

Colombo Street Sports &
Community Centre, SE1

Flaxman Sports Centre, SE5

Crystal Palace
National Sports Centre, SE19

Queen Mother
Sports Centre, SW1

Lillie Road Fitness Centre,
SW6

Sands End Community
Sports Hall, SW6

Power Station, SW10
Men only

Y.M.C.A., SW19

Burlington Health Club, W1

Seymour Hall Leisure Centre,
W1

Jubilee Sports Centre, W10

The Fitness Centre, WC2

Jubilee Hall
Recreation Centre, WC2

WORKSHOPS

MERMAID THEATRE
Puddle Dock, EC4
236 5568/9521
● Blackfriars
Molecule Club for children in afternoon

CECIL SHARP HOUSE
2 Regent's Park Road, NW1
485 2206
● Camden Town
11.00 a.m.–5.00 p.m.
Country dance and music
*Canteen

BATTERSEA ARTS CENTRE
Old Town Hall,
176 Lavender Hill, SW11
223 6557/8413
BR Clapham Junction
Family workshops
*Restaurant

Jubilee Hall
Recreation Centre, WC2
Juggling workshop

YOGA

Belsize Dance Studio, NW6

Flaxman Sports Centre, SE5

Holmes Place Health Club, SW10

Metropolitan Club, SW11

Hogarth Health Club, W4

London Central Y.M.C.A., WC1

SPORTS CENTRES & HEALTH CLUBS

E1

WAPPING SPORTS CENTRE
Tench Street
488 9421
● Wapping
9.00 a.m.–8.00 p.m.
Membership available
Badminton, Bowls, Handball
*Shop

E8

GEORGE SYLVESTER SPORTS CENTRE
Wilton Way
985 2105
BR Hackney Central
9.00 a.m.–9.00 p.m.
Badminton, Martial Arts, Roller Skating

E10

EASTWAY SPORTS CENTRE
Quartermile Lane
519 0017
● Leyton
9.00 a.m.–10.30 p.m.

Membership available
Badminton, Basketball,
5-a-side, Martial Arts, Squash,
Table Tennis, Trampoline,
Weight Training
*Licensed bar & snacks *Shop

E11

HYAMS GYMNASIUM
857–861 High Road
558 3138
✆ Leytonstone
10.00 a.m.–2.30 p.m.
Membership available
Gymnasium, Jacuzzi, Sauna,
Solarium, Weight Training
*Shop

LEYTONSTONE
RECREATION CENTRE
Cathall Road
539 8343
✆ Leyton/Leytonstone
9.00 a.m.–noon
& 2.15 p.m.–5.15 p.m.
Gymnasium, Solarium (women
only), Squash, Swimming
*Vending machines, *Shop
*Equipment hire

WANSTEAD LEISURE
CENTRE
Redbridge Lane West
989 1172/3
✆ Wanstead/Redbridge
9.00 a.m.–10.30 p.m.
Membership available
Badminton, Football,
Gymnasium, Hockey, Netball,
Squash, Table Tennis,

Tennis, Weight Training
*Licensed bar *Equipment
hire

E14

GEORGE GREEN SPORTS
CENTRE
Manchester Road
515 5154
✆ Mile End
10.30 a.m.–5.30 p.m.
Badminton, 5-a-side,
Gymnasium,
Table Tennis, Tennis
*Café *Equipment hire

E17

KELMSCOTT LEISURE
CENTRE
Markhouse Road
520 7464
✆ Blackhorse Road
10.00 a.m.–6.00 p.m.
Badminton, Football, Hockey,
Netball, Squash
*Licensed bar *Vending area
*Equipment hire

EC1

FINSBURY LEISURE
CENTRE
Norman Street
253 2346
✆ Old Street
10.00 a.m.–10.00 p.m.
Archery, Badminton,
Basketball, 5-a-side, Fives,
Gymnasium, Handball,

Martial Arts, Netball, Roller
Skating, Squash, Table
Tennis, Tennis, Trampoline,
Weight Training

N1

BRITANNIA LEISURE
CENTRE
40 Hyde Road
729 4485
⊖ Old Street
9.00 a.m.–10.00 p.m.
Badminton, Sauna, Tennis
*Café *Equipment hire

N7

SOBELL SPORTS
CENTRE
Hornsey Road
607 1632
⊖ Finsbury Park/Holloway
Road
10.00 a.m.–9.30 p.m.
Membership available
Badminton, Ice Skating,
Snooker, Squash, Table
Tennis
*Café *Equipment hire

N9

PICKETTS LOCK
CENTRE
Picketts Lock Lane
803 4756
BR Lower Edmonton
9.00 a.m.–930 p.m.
Membership available

Badminton, Basketball, Bowls,
5-a-side, Football, Golf,
Gymnasium, Hockey, Netball,
Roller Skating, Swimming,
Tennis, Volleyball
*Café *Shop *Equipment hire

N15

LANGHAM SPORTS
CENTRE
Langham Road
889 5111
⊖ Turnpike Lane
9.00 a.m.–10.30 p.m.
Badminton, Cricket, Martial
Arts, Squash, Table Tennis
*Vending machines

N17

NORTHUMBERLAND
PARK SPORTS CENTRE
Northumberland Park
801 9964
BR Northumberland Park/
White Hart Lane
8.00 a.m.–6.00 p.m.
Badminton, Keep Fit, Martial
Arts, Swimming, Tennis
*Vending machines
*Equipment hire

TOTTENHAM SPORTS
CENTRE
703 High Road
801 6401
BR White Hart Lane
9.00 a.m.–9.00 p.m.
Badminton, Gymnasium,
Snooker
*Refreshments

N22

DURNSFORD
COMMUNITY SPORTS
CENTRE
Rhodes Avenue
881 3610
⊖ Bounds Green
9.00 a.m.–10.30 p.m.
Aerobics, Badminton, Cricket
*Vending machines
*Equipment hire

NEW RIVER SPORTS
CENTRE
White Hart Lane
881 1926
⊖ Wood Green
9.00 a.m.–6.00 p.m.
Athletics, Badminton,
Basketball
*Vending machines
*Equipment hire

NW1

RIVIERA
122 Kentish Town Road
482 3118
⊖ Kentish Town/Camden
Town
10.30 a.m.–1.30 p.m.
& 4.30 p.m.–7.30 p.m.
Membership available
Dance, Sauna, Solarium
*Refreshments *Shop

NW3

MEDINA RAJNEESH
BODY CENTRE
81 Belsize Park Gardens
722 6404/8220

⊖ Belsize Park/Swiss Cottage
8.00 a.m.–10.30 p.m.
Membership available
Aerobics, Dance, Martial Arts,
Sauna, Squash
*Restaurant

SWISS COTTAGE
SPORTS CENTRE
Winchester Road
586 5989
⊖ Swiss Cottage
8.00 a.m.–6.00 p.m.
Badminton, Basketball,
5-a-side, Netball, Squash,
Swimming, Tennis
*Café *Shop

NW6

BELSIZE DANCE STUDIO
244 Belsize Road
328 9403
⊖ Kilburn Park
10.00 a.m.–12.15 p.m.
Aerobics, Dance, Yoga
*Coffee bar

CHARTERIS
COMMUNITY SPORTS
CENTRE
Charteris Road
625 6451
⊖ Queen's Park
11.00 a.m.–10.00 p.m.
Badminton, Basketball, Dance,
5-a-side, Netball
*Café

SE1

COLOMBO STREET SPORTS & COMMUNITY CENTRE
Colombo Street
261 1658
✪ Blackfriars/Waterloo
10.00 a.m.–4.00 p.m.
Membership available
Badminton, Martial Arts,
Weight Training
*Café *Equipment hire

ELEPHANT & CASTLE RECREATION CENTRE
22 Elephant & Castle
582 5505
✪ Elephant & Castle
9.00 a.m.–10.00 p.m.
Badminton, Sauna, Squash,
Swimming
*Bar & vending machines
*Equipment hire

SE4

CROFTON LEISURE CENTRE
Manwood Road
690 0273
BR Crofton Park/Catford
9.00 a.m.–5.00 p.m.
Membership available
Badminton, Martial Arts,
Squash, Table Tennis,
Trampoline
*Vending machines *Shop
*Equipment hire

SE5

FLAXMAN SPORTS CENTRE
Carew Street
737 3273
✪ Brixton/Oval
9.00 a.m.–10.30 p.m.
Archery, Badminton,
Basketball, Football,
Gymnasium, Squash,
Trampoline, Weight Training,
Yoga
*Vending machines
*Equipment hire

SE13

LEWISHAM LEISURE CENTRE
Rennell Street
318 4421
BR Lewisham
9.0 a.m.–6.00 p.m.
Membership available
Aerobics, Badminton, Cricket,
Football, Table Tennis
*Café & licensed bar
*Equipment hire

SE18

PLUMSTEAD SPORTS CENTRE
Speranza Street
854 9217
BR Plumstead
9.00 a.m.–9.00 p.m.
Membership available
Badminton, Bowls, Table
Tennis, Tennis
*Vending machines
*Equipment hire

SE19

CRYSTAL PALACE NATIONAL SPORTS CENTRE
Norwood
778 0131
BR Crystal Palace
9.00 a.m.–5.00 p.m.
Membership available
Athletics, Badminton,
Basketball, 5-a-side,
Gymnasium, Netball, Ski-ing,
Squash, Swimming, Table
Tennis, Tennis, Weight
Training
*Restaurant & bar *Shop
*Equipment hire

SYLVAN SPORTS CENTRE
Maberley Road
771 0366
BR Crystal Palace
10.00 a.m.–6.00 p.m.
Membership available
Badminton, Basketball,
Cricket, 5-a-side, Gymnasium,
Trampoline
*Licensed bar *Equipment
hire

SW1

DOLPHIN SQUARE SPORTS CENTRE
Dolphin Square
838 1681
⊖ Pimlico
9.30 a.m.–6.00 p.m.
Sauna, Solarium, Squash,
Swimming
*Restaurant & bar *Shop

QUEEN MOTHER SPORTS CENTRE
223 Vauxhall Bridge Road
834 4725/6/7
⊖ Victoria/Pimlico
8.00 a.m.–6.00 p.m.
Badminton, 5-a-side,
Gymnasium, Netball, Squash,
Swimming, Table Tennis,
Tennis, Trampoline,
Volleyball, Weight Training
*Café & licensed bar
*Equipment hire

ST JAMES'S HEALTH CLUB
7 St James's Street
930 5870
⊖ Green Park/Piccadilly
Circus
Noon–10.00 p.m.
Men only
Massage, Sauna, Solarium
*Snack bar

SW3

BODY'S
250 King's Road
351 5682
⊖ South Kensington/Sloane
Square
10.30 a.m.–2.00 p.m.
Membership available
Aerobics, Gymnasium, Sauna
*Café & bar *Shop

CHELSEA SPORTS CENTRE
Chelsea Manor Street
352 6985

❂ South Kensington/Sloane
Square
8.30 a.m.–11.15 a.m.
Badminton, Gymnasium,
Sauna, Solarium, Squash,
Swimming, Table Tennis
*Vending machines
*Equipment hire

SW6

ETERNIT WHARF
RECREATION CENTRE
Stevenage Road
381 5266
❂ Putney Bridge/
Hammersmith
10.00 a.m.–5.00 p.m.
Membership available
Badminton, 5-a-side,
Gymnasium, Netball, Volleyball
*Vending machines
*Equipment hire

LILLIE ROAD FITNESS
CENTRE
Lillie Road
385 5360
❂ Hammersmith/Fulham
Broadway
10.30 a.m.–5.00 p.m.
Membership available
Aerobics, Gymnasium,
Solarium, Weight Training
*Vending machines *Shop

SANDS END
COMMUNITY SPORTS
HALL
59–61 Broughton Road
736 1504

❂ Fulham Broadway
11.00 a.m.–3.00 p.m.
Membership available
Athletics, Badminton,
Gymnasium, Sauna, Self
Defence, Table Tennis,
Weight Training
*Shop *Equipment hire

SW8

SOUTH LONDON
CENTRE
124–130 Wandsworth Road
622 6866
❂ Vauxhall
9.00 a.m.–10.30 p.m.
Membership available
Aerobics, Gymnasium, Sauna,
Self Defence, Snooker,
Solarium, Squash
*Refreshments *Shop

SW10

HOLMES PLACE HEALTH
CLUB
188a Fulham Road
352 9452
❂ Gloucester Road/Fulham
Broadway
10.00 a.m.–5.00 p.m.
Membership necessary
Aerobics, Dance, Gymnasium,
Keep Fit, Turkish Baths,
Yoga
*Refreshments

POWER STATION
533 King's Road
351 5718

⊖ Fulham Broadway
10.00 a.m.–7.00 p.m.
Men only
Membership necessary
Gymnasium, Jacuzzi, Sauna,
Weight Training

SW11

METROPOLITAN CLUB
Sheepcote Lane
228 4400
BR Clapham Junction
8.30 a.m.–11.00 p.m.
Membership necessary
Dance, Gymnasium, Jacuzzi,
Sauna, Solarium, Squash, Yoga
*Restaurant *Shop
*Equipment hire

SW19

WIMBLEDON
RECREATION CENTRE
Latimer Road
542 1330
⊖ South Wimbledon
8.30 a.m.–9.30 p.m.
Badminton, Gymnasium,
Sauna, Solarium, Swimming,
Table Tennis
*Vending machines

Y.M.C.A.
200 The Broadway
540 7255
⊖ Wimbledon/South
Wimbledon
2.00 p.m.–10.00 p.m.
Membership necessary
Badminton, Chess, Dance,
Table Tennis, Weight Training
*Buffet *Equipment hire

W1

BURLINGTON HEALTH
CLUB
23 Old Bond Street
493 2265
⊖ Green Park
1.00 p.m.–midnight
Men only
Membership available
Gymnasium, Massage, Sauna,
Solarium, Weight Training
*Refreshments

DANCE WORKS
16 Balderton Street
629 6183
⊖ Bond Street
Noon–6.00 p.m.
Membership necessary
Aerobics, Dance, Keep Fit,
Massage, Sauna, Solarium

GROSVENOR HOUSE
HEALTH CLUB
Grosvenor House,
Park Lane
499 6363
⊖ Marble Arch/Hyde Park
Corner
7.00 a.m.–10.00 p.m.
Membership necessary
Gymnasium, Jacuzzi, Sauna,
Solarium, Swimming
*Buffet & licensed bar

SEYMOUR HALL
LEISURE CENTRE
Bryanston Place
723 8018
⊖ Marylebone/Baker Street

9.00 a.m.–1.00 p.m.
Membership available
Badminton, 5-a-side, Football,
Keep Fit, Squash, Swimming,
Weight Training
*Licensed bar *Equipment
hire

W4

CHISWICK COMMUNITY SPORTS HALL
Burlington Lane
995 4067
✆ Turnham Green
9.00 a.m.–10.30 p.m.
Badminton, Cricket, 5-a-side,
Martial Arts, Squash, Table
Tennis
*Vending machines
*Equipment hire

HOGARTH HEALTH CLUB
1a Airedale Avenue
995 4600
✆ Stamford Brook
10.00 a.m.–10.00 p.m.
Membership necessary
Gymnasium, Jacuzzi, Massage,
Sauna, Solarium, Squash,
Swimming, Tennis, Yoga
*Restaurant & bar *Shop
*Equipment hire

W5

STRIPES SQUASH & HEALTH CLUB
Town Square,
Ealing Broadway Centre
579 9433/4

✆ Ealing Broadway
10.00 a.m.–10.30 p.m.
Membership necessary
Dance, Gymnasium, Sauna,
Solarium, Squash
*Restaurant & bar *Shop
*Equipment hire

W6

SUNDANCE STUDIOS
Galena House,
Galena Road
741 8536
✆ Hammersmith
10.00 a.m.–4.00 p.m.
Membership necessary
Dance, Gymnasium, Sauna,
Solarium
*Restaurant *Shop

W8

WESTSIDE HEALTH CLUB
201–207 Kensington High
Street
937 5386
✆ High Street Kensington
10.30 a.m.–4.30 p.m.
Membership necessary
Gymnasium, Keep Fit, Sauna
*Restaurant

W10

JUBILEE SPORTS CENTRE
Caird Street
960 5512

✪ Westbourne Park/Queen's
Park
9.00 a.m.–1.00 p.m.
Membership available
Basketball, 5-a-side,
Gymnasium, Keep Fit,
Martial Arts, Netball,
Swimming, Table Tennis,
Trampoline, Volleyball,
Weight Training
*Café *Equipment hire

W11

KENSINGTON NEW
POOLS
Walmer Road
727 9923
✪ Ladbroke Grove
8.30 a.m.–noon
Gymnasium, Solarium,
Swimming
*Vending machine

W12

HOLLAND PARK SAUNA
FOR MEN
156 Shepherd's Bush Centre
743 3264/3473
✪ Shepherd's Bush
11.30 a.m.–11.00 p.m.
Men only
Massage, Sauna, Solarium

WEST LONDON SQUASH
CLUB
99a Devonport Road
743 1016

✪ Shepherd's Bush
9.45 a.m.–7.15 p.m.
Membership necessary
Sauna, Solarium, Squash
*Restaurant & bar *Shop
*Equipment hire

WHITE CITY POOL
Bloemfontein Road
743 3401
✪ White City
9.00 a.m.–noon
Sauna, Solarium, Swimming
*Café/restaurant

WC1

LONDON CENTRAL
Y.M.C.A.
112 Great Russell Street
637 8131
✪ Tottenham Court Road
10.00 a.m.–9.30 p.m.
Membership necessary
Aerobics, Badminton,
Basketball, Dance, Gymnasium,
Handball, Keep Fit, Martial
Arts, Solarium, Squash,
Table Tennis, Volleyball, Yoga
*Buffet

WC2

COVENT GARDEN
SAUNA FOR MEN
29 Endell Street
836 2236
✪ Covent Garden
11.30 a.m.–11.00 p.m.
Men only
Jacuzzi, Massage, Sauna
*Coffee bar

THE FITNESS CENTRE
11 Floral Street
379 6613
✪ Covent Garden
10.00 a.m.–6.00 p.m.
Membership necessary
Gymnasium, Sauna, Solarium,
Weight Training
*Café/bar

JUBILEE HALL
RECREATION CENTRE
Covent Garden
836 2799/4835
✪ Covent Garden
10.00 a.m.–5.00 p.m.
Membership available
Aerobics, Badminton,
Basketball, 5-a-side, Fives,
Handball, Keep Fit, Netball,
Roller Skating, Table Tennis,
Weight Training, Workshop
*Vending machines
*Equipment hire

THE SANCTUARY
11–12 Floral Street
240 2744
✪ Covent Garden
Noon–8.00 p.m.
Women only
Membership available
Jacuzzi, Massage, Sauna,
Solarium, Swimming
*Healthfood bar *Shop

OUT OF TOWN – HARROW

HARROW LEISURE
CENTRE
Christchurch Avenue,
Harrow, Middlesex
863 5611
✪ Harrow & Wealdstone
9.00 a.m.–11.00 p.m.
Membership available
Badminton, 5-a-side, Martial
Arts, Sauna, Snooker, Squash,
Swimming, Table Tennis
*Bar *Equipment hire

PARKS

There are literally hundreds of parks, gardens and open spaces in London. Obviously they can't all be included in this book. The ones listed here are those referred to elsewhere in the text and/or the best known and most popular places for a Sunday afternoon walk or picnic.

If a park is mentioned elsewhere it will be in one, or more, of the following categories:

ENTERTAINMENT
JAUNTS & EXCURSIONS
SPORTS & ACTIVITIES

These headings, where applicable, are included in the Parks Index. They act as a general guide only; if you are looking for something in particular, you should refer to the relevant section of this book to find out in which park it may be available.

PARKS INDEX

Many parks cover such a wide expanse that, strictly speaking, the information given should include a number of streets, post zones and Underground or rail stations. For simplicity, this is condensed to the name of the park (listed alphabetically) followed by one street name, a post zone, a telephone number (the Park Superintendent) and the nearest station.

OPENING HOURS

Some parks are open from dawn to dusk, while others are open 24 hours. The opening and closing times are generally posted at the entrance along with the rules and regulations regarding dogs, facilities etc.

CHILDREN
Many parks have a children's area, playground and/or paddling pool. Special events and entertainments may be arranged throughout the year and you should contact your local council or the G.L.C. (see below) for further information.

BOOKING OF FACILITIES
It is often possible to book sports facilities in advance. Contact the appropriate Parks Office for further details.

FURTHER INFORMATION
Most of the parks listed here are run by either the Department of the Environment (D.O.E.) or the Greater London Council (G.L.C.) as indicated. For general enquiries and further information call the number given below during office hours, Monday to Friday.

      D.O.E. – 212 3434
      G.L.C. – 633 1708 for sports facilities
      G.L.C. – 633 1707 for other facilities

OTHER PARKS
In addition to those parks listed here there are numerous parks in the various London boroughs, many with excellent sports facilities, children's events, etc. To find out more, contact your local council during office hours, Monday to Friday.

PARKS INDEX

CLAPHAM COMMON
The Avenue, SW4
⊖ Clapham Common/
Clapham South

CLISSOLD PARK
(G.L.C.)
Green Lanes, N4
800 1021
⊖ Manor House
Jaunts & Excursions

CRYSTAL PALACE PARK
(G.L.C.)
Crystal Palace Parade, SE19
778 7148
Children's Zoo (summer only
11.00 a.m.–5.30 p.m.):
778 4487
BR Crystal Palace
Entertainment
Jaunts & Excursions
Sports & Activities
*Refreshments (summer only)

CUTTY SARK GARDENS
(G.L.C.)
King William Walk, SE10
Messroom: 858 8609
BR Greenwich/Maze Hill
Entertainment

DULWICH PARK
(G.L.C.)
College Road, SE21
693 5737
BR North Dulwich/West
Dulwich
Jaunts & Excursions
Sports & Activities
*Refreshments (summer only)

ELTHAM PARK
(G.L.C.)
Glenesk Road, SE9
850 2031
Swimming: 850 9890
BR Eltham Park
Jaunts & Excursions
Sports & Activities

EPPING FOREST
Woodford New Road, E17
BR Wood Street

FINSBURY PARK
(G.L.C.)
Seven Sisters Road, N4
800 4743
⊖ Finsbury Park
Entertainment
Sports & Activities
*Refreshments

GOLDERS HILL
(G.L.C.)
West Heath Avenue, NW11
455 5183
⊖ Golders Green
Jaunts & Excursions
Sports & Activities
*Refreshments

GREEN PARK, SW1
(see St James's Park)

GREENWICH PARK
(D.O.E.)
Greenwich, SE10
858 2608
BR Maze Hill
Entertainment
Sports & Activities

HACKNEY MARSH
(G.L.C.)
Homerton Road, E9
985 8206
✪ Leyton
Sports & Activities

HAMPSTEAD HEATH,
NW3
(see Golders Hill/Hampstead
Heath Extension/Kenwood/
Parliament Hill)

HAMPSTEAD HEATH
EXTENSION
(G.L.C.)
Hampstead Way, NW11
458 4548
✪ Golders Green
Sports & Activities

HOLLAND PARK
(G.L.C.)
Holland Walk, W8
602 2226/6016
Squash Court: 727 9276
✪ Holland Park/High Street
Kensington
Entertainment
Jaunts & Excursions
Sports & Activities
*Refreshments

HORNIMAN GARDENS
(G.L.C.)
London Road, SE23
699 8924
BR Forest Hill
Jaunts & Excursions
Sports & Activities
*Refreshments (summer only)

HYDE PARK
(D.O.E.)
Bayswater Road, W2
262 5484
Serpentine Lido: 262 3751
✪ Hyde Park Corner/
Knightsbridge/
Lancaster Gate/Marble Arch
Entertainment
Jaunts & Excursions
Sports & Activities
*Refreshments

KENSINGTON GARDENS
(D.O.E.)
Bayswater Road, W2
723 3509
✪ High Street Kensington/
Lancaster Gate/Queensway
Entertainment
Sports & Activities

KENWOOD
(G.L.C.)
Hampstead Lane, NW3
340 5303
Ladies Pond: 348 1033
✪ Archway/Golders Green
Sports & Activities
*Refreshments

KING GEORGE'S FIELD
(G.L.C.)
Leith Road, E3
980 1885
East London Stadium:
980 2579
✪ Mile End
Sports & Activities
*Refreshments

LESNES ABBEY WOODS
(G.L.C.)
Abbey Road, SE2
310 2777
BR Abbey Wood
Jaunts & Excursions
Sports & Activities
*Refreshments (summer only)

OXLEAS WOOD
(G.L.C.)
Welling Way, SE9
BR Falconwood
Jaunts & Excursions
Sports & Activities
*Refreshments (summer only)

PARLIAMENT HILL
(G.L.C.)
Hampstead Heath, NW3
485 4491
Athletics Track: 435 8998
Hampstead Bathing Pond:
435 2366
Highgate Bathing Pond:
340 4044
The Lido: 485 3873
BR Gospel Oak
Entertainment
Sports & Activities
*Refreshments (summer only)

PUTNEY HEATH
Telegraph Road, SW15
⊖ East Putney

RAVENSCOURT PARK
Paddenswick Road, W6
741 2051
⊖ Stamford Brook
Entertainment
*Refreshments

REGENT'S PARK
(D.O.E.)
Park Road, NW1
486 7905
Tennis: 935 8556
⊖ Baker Street/Camden
Town
Entertainment
Jaunts & Excursions
Sports & Activities
*Refreshments

RICHMOND PARK
(D.O.E.)
Richmond, Surrey
948 3209
⊖ Richmond
Jaunts & Excursions
Sports & Activities
*Refreshments

ST JAMES'S PARK
(D.O.E.)
Birdcage Walk, SW1
930 1793
⊖ St James's Park
Entertainment
Jaunts & Excursions

SHOOTERS HILL, SE18
(see Castlewood & Jackwood/
Eltham Park/Oxleas Wood)

THAMESMEAD
(G.L.C.)
Hartslock Drive, SE2
310 0472
BR Abbey Wood
Sports & Activities

VICTORIA PARK
(G.L.C.)
Victoria Park Road, E9
985 1957

Athletics Track: 985 8065
The Lido: 985 6774
● Mile End/Bethnal Green
Entertainment
Jaunts & Excursions
Sports & Activities
*Refreshments

WATERLOW PARK
Swains Lane, N6
272 2825
● Archway/Highgate
Entertainment
Jaunts & Excursions
*Refreshments (summer only)

WIMBLEDON COMMON
Windmill Road, SW19
788 7655

WORMWOOD SCRUBS
and West London Stadium
(G.L.C.)
Du Cane Road, W12
749 5505/743 4030
● East Acton
Sports & Activities
*Refreshments

SHOPS

This section is divided into a number of categories and, where appropriate, split into sub-divisions. Under these headings (see below) the shops are listed alphabetically by postal zone.

BOOKS, RECORDS & VIDEOS
CHEMISTS
CLOTHES & FOOTWEAR
D.I.Y. SHOPS
ELECTRICAL GOODS
FLOWERS
FOOD & DRINK
  Supermarket
  Delicatessen
  Baker/Confectioner
  Butcher
  Fishmonger
  Dairy & Ice Cream
  Freezer Centre
  Coffee
  Pasta
  Wholefoods
  Off-Licence

FURNITURE & FURNISHINGS
  Bedroom
  Bathroom
  Kitchen
  General
  Antiques
GARDEN CENTRES
GIFTS
MARKETS & AUCTIONS
NEWSPAPERS & STATIONERY
OPTICIANS
PET SHOPS
SPORTS EQUIPMENT
TOBACCONISTS
TOYS, GAMES & JOKES

CREDIT CARDS ACCEPTED

AC = Access
AX = American Express
BC = Barclaycard (Visa)
DC = Diners Club

BOOKS, RECORDS & VIDEOS

Many museums, galleries etc. have shops or bookstalls. See Jaunts & Excursions.

N1

PHILLIPS
72–73 Chapel Market
837 2440
◉ Angel
9.30 a.m.–2.00 p.m.
General record shop

RECKLESS RECORDS
79 Upper Street
359 0501
◉ Angel
10.00 a.m.–7.00 p.m.
Records bought, sold or exchanged

N4

TREHANTIRI GREEK RECORD SHOP
365–367 Green Lanes
802 6530
◉ Manor House
10.30 a.m.–9.00 p.m.
Newspapers, records and computer software

NW1

KAYS IRISH MUSIC CENTRE
161 Arlington Road
485 4880
◉ Camden Town
10.30 a.m.–1.30 p.m.
Records, sheet music etc. – mainly Irish folk

RECORD, TAPE & VIDEO EXCHANGE
229 Camden High Street
267 1898
◉ Camden Town
10.00 a.m.–8.00 p.m.
Records and cassettes bought, sold or exchanged

RHYTHM RECORDS
281 Camden High Street
267 0123
◉ Camden Town
10.30 a.m.–5.30 p.m.
New and second-hand records
*AC BC

SEA OF TUNES
3 Buck Street
482 1784
◉ Camden Town
11.00 a.m.–4.00 p.m.
Records

SE10

BOOK BOAT
Cutty Sark Gardens,
King William Walk
853 4383
BR Greenwich
10.00 a.m.–5.00 p.m.
Mainly children's books for sale on a painted barge

SW1

KNIGHTS VIDEO
118 Knightsbridge
581 0568

✪ Knightsbridge
Noon–7.00 p.m.
Video cassettes and machines
for sale or rental
*AC AX BC DC

SW7

GLOUCESTER ROAD
BOOKSHOP
123 Gloucester Road
370 3503
✪ Gloucester Road
10.30 a.m.–6.30 p.m.
Mainly second-hand books
*AC AX BC

WATERSTONE'S
99–101 Old Brompton Road
581 8523
✪ South Kensington
Noon–7.00 p.m.
Books
*AC BC

SW10

THE PAN BOOKSHOP
158 Fulham Road
373 4997
✪ South Kensington
2.00 p.m.–8.00 p.m.
Mainly paperback books
*AC BC

VIDEO SHUTTLE
309 Fulham Road
352 7986
✪ South Kensington
10.00 a.m.–10.00 p.m.
Cassette hire
*AC AX BC DC

W1

GROOVE RECORDS
52 Greek Street
439 8231
✪ Tottenham Court Road
2.00 p.m.–6.00 p.m.
Records
*AC

HAROLD MOORE'S
RECORDS
2 Great Marlborough Street
437 1576
✪ Oxford Circus
Noon–6.30 p.m.
Classical records
*AC BC

OUR PRICE RECORDS
5 Coventry Street
734 2240
and
27 Shaftesbury Avenue
437 3294
✪ Piccadilly Circus
11.00 a.m.–9.30 p.m.
Records
*AC

PICCADILLY RARE
BOOKS
30 Sackville Street
437 2135
✪ Piccadilly Circus
10.00 a.m.–6.00 p.m.
Antiquarian books
*AC AX BC

THE PRICE BUSTERS
50 Rupert Street
434 1278
✪ Piccadilly Circus

3.00 p.m.–9.00 p.m.
Records and video games
*AC BC

RECKLESS RECORDS
30 Berwick Street
437 4271
✪ Piccadilly Circus
10.00 a.m.–7.00 p.m.
Records bought, sold or
exchanged

WATERSTONE'S
88 Regent Street
734 0713/4
✪ Piccadilly Circus
Noon–7.00 p.m.
Books, records and cassettes
*AC BC

W2

OUR PRICE RECORDS
117–119 Queensway
229 8346
✪ Bayswater
11.00 a.m.–9.30 p.m.
Records
*AC

W8

WATERSTONE'S
191–195 Kensington High
Street
937 8432/3
✪ High Street Kensington
Noon–7.00 p.m.
Books, records and cassettes
*AC BC

W10

HONEST JON'S RECORDS
278 Portobello Road
969 9822
✪ Ladbroke Grove
11.00 a.m.–5.00 p.m.
Mainly jazz and latin, new and
second-hand
*AC AX BC

W11

**RECORD, TAPE & VIDEO
EXCHANGE**
38 Notting Hill Gate
727 3539
and
29 Pembridge Road
727 3538
✪ Notting Hill Gate
10.00 a.m.–8.00 p.m.
Records and cassettes bought,
sold or exchanged

W12

**RECORD, TAPE & VIDEO
EXCHANGE**
90 Goldhawk Road
749 2930
✪ Goldhawk Road
10.00 a.m.–8.00 p.m.
Records and cassettes bought,
sold or exchanged

WC1

ARTHUR PAGE
29 Museum Street
636 8206
✪ Tottenham Court Road

11.30 a.m.–6.00 p.m.
Antiquarian books
*AC BC

GAY'S THE WORD
66 Marchmont Street
278 7654
● Russell Square
Noon–6.00 p.m.
Books, records and cassettes
for the gay community
*AC AX BC DC

WC2

HOLBORN BOOKS
14 Charing Cross Road
240 2337
● Leicester Square
11.00 a.m.–7.00 p.m.
Second-hand books

CHEMISTS

NW6

BLISS CHEMISTS
54 Willesden Lane
624 8000
● Kilburn
open 24 hours
*AC AX BC

NW11

WARMAN FREED
45 Golders Green Road
455 4351/7779
● Golders Green
8.00 a.m.–midnight

SW1

UNDERWOODS
15 Lower Regent Street
930 0405
● Piccadilly Circus
10.00 a.m.–7.00 p.m.
and
86 Victoria Street
828 0293
● Victoria
10.00 a.m.–6.00 p.m.
Chemist and general goods
*AC AX BC

SW3

MARKHAM PHARMACY
138 King's Road
589 0071
● Sloane Square
10.00 a.m.–5.00 p.m.
*AC AX BC DC

UNDERWOODS
205 Brompton Road
584 5391
● South Kensington/
Knightsbridge
10.00 a.m.–6.00 p.m.
and
60 King's Road
589 3234
● Sloane Square
10.00 a.m.–6.00 p.m.
Chemist and general goods
*AC AX BC

SW5

W. W. BRUNTON
240 Earls Court Road
373 5078

✪ Earls Court
10.00 a.m.–10.00 p.m.
*AC BC

SW7

UNDERWOODS
120 Gloucester Road
370 2824
✪ Gloucester Road
10.00 a.m.–9.00 p.m.
Chemist and general goods
*AC AX BC

SW15

UNDERWOODS
109 Putney High Street
788 4345
✪ East Putney/Putney Bridge
10.00 a.m.–6.00 p.m.
Chemist and general goods
*AC AX BC

W1

UNDERWOODS
96 Baker Street
486 6852
✪ Baker Street
11.00 a.m.–7.00 p.m.
and
201 Piccadilly
437 5572
✪ Piccadilly Circus
10.00 a.m.–8.00 p.m.
and
62 Shaftesbury Avenue
434 3647
✪ Piccadilly Circus/Leicester
Square
11.00 a.m.–10.00 p.m.

and
267 Tottenham Court Road
580 1686
✪ Tottenham Court Road
11.00 a.m.–8.00 p.m.
Chemist and general goods
*AC AX BC

W2

UNDERWOODS
75 Queensway
229 9266
✪ Bayswater
10.00 a.m.–10.00 p.m.
and
114 Queensway
229 4819/5126
✪ Bayswater
10.00 a.m.–10.00 p.m.
Chemist and general goods
*AC AX BC

W8

UNDERWOODS
174 Kensington High Street
937 1646
✪ High Street Kensington
11.0 a.m.–6.00 p.m.
Chemist and general goods
*AC AX BC

WC2

THE BODYSHOP
Unit 13 The Market
836 2183
✪ Covent Garden
11.00 a.m.–6.00 p.m.
Beauty products and gifts
*AC BC

NEAL'S YARD
APOTHECARY
2 Neal's Yard
379 7222
● Covent Garden
11.00 a.m.–4.00 p.m.
Natural, herbal and
homoeopathic cures and
cosmetics
*BC

UNDERWOODS
137 Charing Cross Road
734 1879
● Tottenham Court Road
11.00 a.m.–8.00 p.m.
and
352 Strand
379 3469
● Covent Garden
11.00 a.m.–6.00 p.m.
Chemist and general goods
*AC AX BC

CLOTHES & FOOTWEAR

E15

DICKIE DIRTS
146–148 The Grove
519 1915
● Stratford
10.00 a.m.–10.00 p.m.
Jeans

NW1

KINGSLEY
25 Chalk Farm Road
267 9403

● Chalk Farm/Camden
Town
11.00 a.m.–5.30 p.m.
Clothes for men
*Credit cards

SIREN
285 Camden High Street
267 5581
● Camden Town
10.00 a.m.–7.00 p.m.
Second-hand 40's, 50's and
60's clothes

SPATZ
4 Castlehaven Road
482 3785
● Camden Town/Chalk
Farm
11.00 a.m.–6.30 p.m.
1920's to 1950's clothes

W2

DICKIE DIRTS
58a Westbourne Grove
229 1466
● Bayswater
10.00 a.m.–10.00 p.m.
Jeans

HOTLINE
36–38 Westbourne Grove
221 7782
● Bayswater
Noon–7.00 p.m.
Casual clothes for men and
women
*Credit cards

WC2

ACCESSORIZE
Unit 22 The Market
240 2107
☻ Covent Garden
Noon–6.00 p.m.
Accessories, jewellery and
footwear
*Credit cards

BERTIE
Unit 15 The Market
836 9147
☻ Covent Garden
11.30 a.m.–4.30 p.m.
Accessories and footwear
*Credit cards

CONNECTIONS
12 James Street
836 0522
☻ Covent Garden
Noon–5.00 p.m.
'French Connection' clothes
for women

S. FISHER
Unit 18 The Market
836 2576
☻ Covent Garden
Noon–5.00 p.m.
Classic clothing – mostly
knitwear for men
*Credit cards

FLIP
125 Long Acre
836 9851
☻ Covent Garden
Noon–7.00 p.m.
American clothes, some
second-hand
*Credit cards

HOBBS
Unit 17 The Market
836 9168
☻ Covent Garden
Noon–5.00 p.m.
Clothes and shoes for women;
shoes for men

MONSOON
Unit 23 The Market
836 9140
☻ Covent Garden
Noon–6.00 p.m.
Fashionable Indian clothes for
women
*Credit cards

OUT OF TOWN – TWICKENHAM

SPECIAL EFFECTS
367 Richmond Road
Twickenham, Middlesex
892 0116
☻ Richmond
phone for opening hours
Victorian–1960's second-
hand clothes

D.I.Y. SHOPS

E4

B & Q RETAIL LTD
Deacon Way,
North Circular Road
523 1133
BR Angel Road
10.00 a.m.–6.00 p.m.
*AC BC

E10

B & Q RETAIL LTD
19 Heybridge Way
558 4817
BR St James Street
Walthamstow
and
798 High Road
539 1141
✪ Walthamstow Central
10.00 a.m.–6.00 p.m.
*AC BC

NW2

B & Q D.I.Y. SUPER
CENTRE
Staples Corner,
1000 North Circular Road
208 0739
10.00 a.m.–6.00 p.m.
*AC BC

SE27

B & Q RETAIL LTD
304–322 Norwood Road
761 1236
BR West Norwood
10.00 a.m.–6.00 p.m.
*AC BC

SW6

QUADRANT D.I.Y.
MARKET
355 North End Road
381 0445
✪ Fulham Broadway
9.30 a.m.–4.30 p.m.

SW19

B & Q RETAIL LTD
Alexandra Road
879 3322
✪ Wimbledon
10.00 a.m.–6.00 p.m.
*AC BC

W3

B & Q D.I.Y. SUPER
CENTRE
3 King Street
992 1182
✪ Acton Town
10.00 a.m.–6.00 p.m.
*AC BC

ELECTRICAL GOODS

W1

LONDON PHONE
COMPANY
The Trocadero,
Piccadilly Circus
437 9921
✪ Piccadilly Circus
1.00 p.m.–7.30 p.m.
Telephones, answering
machines, etc.

W2

LASKY'S
7–9 Queensway
229 6425
✪ Queensway

11.00 a.m.–7.00 p.m.
Televisions, videos, hi-fi,
computers, etc.

FLOWERS

You will generally find fresh
flowers being sold near
hospitals.

NW1

CHATTELS
53 Chalk Farm Road
267 0877
⊖ Chalk Farm
Noon–5.00 p.m.
Dried flowers and baskets

SW6

FAST FLOWERS
25 Vanston Place
381 6422
⊖ Fulham Broadway
10.00 a.m.–5.00 p.m.
Fresh flowers and plants.
Can arrange local deliveries

SW8

PATIO
155 Battersea Park Road
622 8262
BR Battersea Park
9.30 a.m.–6.00 p.m.
Dried flowers and terracotta
pots and window boxes

SW15

MISTER BUTTERCUPS
118a Upper Richmond Road
785 6606
⊖ East Putney
9.00 a.m.–2.30 p.m.
(hours may vary)
Fresh flowers

FOOD & DRINK

In all parts of London you will
almost certainly find a nearby
shop selling food, drink,
cigarettes, etc. but they are
too numerous to include here.

E1

Supermarket

THE LIFE RAFT
Ivory House,
St Katharine's Dock
488 2292
⊖ Tower Hill
Summer: 9.00 a.m.–8.00 p.m.
Winter: 9.00 a.m.–7.30 p.m.

Delicatessen

ROGG
137 Cannon Street Road
488 3368
⊖ Aldgate East
7.00 a.m.–2.00 p.m.
Jewish deli – herrings, bagels,
smoked meat, olives, cheese,
etc.

Baker/Confectioner

A. GRODZINSKI & CO.
235 Whitechapel Road
247 8516
⊖ Whitechapel
8.00 a.m.–1.00 p.m.

Off-Licence

THE NOBLE GRAPE
26 The Highway
488 4788
⊖ Tower Hill
Summer: 10.00 a.m.–
7.00 p.m.
Winter: 10.00 a.m.–5.00 p.m.
Wine and wide variety of beers.
Purchase by the case only.

E5

Baker/Confectioner

A. GRODZINSKI & CO.
170 Clapton Common
800 2535
⊖ Manor House
8.00 a.m.–6.00 p.m.

N1

Supermarket

THE MARKET
213–215 Upper Street
359 5386
⊖ Angel/Highbury &
Islington
9.00 a.m.–9.00 p.m.

Delicatessen

MR J. R.'s CONTINENTAL
DELI
52 Penton Street
278 4960
⊖ Angel
open 24 hours

OLGA STORES
30 Penton Street
837 5467
⊖ Angel
11.00 a.m.–1.00 a.m.
Continental food

N6

Supermarket

THE MARKET
32–34 Highgate High Street
348 2422
⊖ Highgate/Archway
9.00 a.m.–9.00 p.m.

Wholefoods

EARTH EXCHANGE
213 Archway Road
340 6407
⊖ Highgate
11.00 a.m.–7.00 p.m.
Also sells herbal remedies,
shampoos and soaps, books and
some crafts.

Off-Licence

SOUTHWOOD'S VILLAGE
NURSERIES
Townsend Yard
Highgate High Street
340 1041

◉ Archway
10.00 a.m.–1.00 p.m.
Wine warehouse attached to
garden centre
*AC AX BC

N8

Baker/Confectioner

THE QUEEN OF TARTS
173 Priory Road
340 1854
◉ Wood Green
9.00 a.m.–5.00 p.m.

N15

Baker/Confectioner

A. GRODZINSKI & CO.
Overbury Road
802 4161
◉ Manor House
8.00 a.m.–1.00 p.m.

Off-Licence

MAJESTIC WINE
WAREHOUSE
Colina Mews
889 9380
◉ Turnpike Lane
10.00 a.m.–8.00 p.m.
Purchase by the case only.
Also sells coffee, oils, herbs,
etc.
*AC BC

N16

Baker/Confectioner

A. GRODZINSKI & CO.
91 Dunsmure Road
802 4161
BR Stoke Newington
and
34 Stamford Hill
802 4161
BR Stamford Hill
8.00 a.m.–1.00 p.m.

NW1

Delicatessen

CAMDEN WINE AND
CHEESE CENTRE
214 Camden High Street
482 2553
◉ Camden Town
11.00 a.m.–4.30 p.m.
Wines (11.00 a.m.–2.00 p.m.),
cheeses and delicatessen

MIRANDY ET FILLES
3 Park Road
262 1906
◉ Baker Street
10.00 a.m.–5.00 p.m.
Delicatessen, chocolates and
afternoon tea

NW3

Supermarket

THE MARKET
165 Haverstock Hill
722 6521

◉ Belsize Park
9.00 a.m.–11.00 p.m.

Delicatessen

PROVENÇAL
167 Haverstock Hill
586 7987
◉ Belsize Park
9.00 a.m.–9.00 p.m.

Baker/Confectioner

A. GRODZINSKI & CO.
161 Haverstock Hill
722 7688
◉ Belsize Park
8.00 a.m.–5.30 p.m.
and
9 Northways Parade
Finchley Road
722 4944
◉ Finchley Road
8.00 a.m.–1.00 p.m.

LOUIS PÂTISSERIE
12 Harben Parade,
Finchley Road
722 8100
◉ Swiss Cottage
and
32 Heath Street
435 9908
◉ Hampstead
9.30 a.m.–6.00 p.m.

RUMBOLD'S
45 South End Road
435 4998
◉ Hampstead/Belsize Park
10.00 a.m.–4.00 p.m.

Dairy & Ice Cream

MARINE ICES
8 Haverstock Hill
485 5298
◉ Chalk Farm
11.00 a.m.–10.00 p.m.
All flavours of ice cream by the
tub or gallon.

NW4

Baker/Confectioner

A. GRODZINSKI & CO.
62 Vivian Avenue
202 6092
◉ Hendon Central
8.00 a.m.–1.00 p.m.

MAISON BOUQUILLON
22 Vivian Avenue
202 3354
◉ Hendon Central
9.00 a.m.–1.00 p.m.

NW6

Delicatessen

OSAKA
17 Goldhurst Terrace
624 4983
◉ Swiss Cottage/Finchley
Road
11.00 a.m.–7.00 p.m.
Eastern food – Indian,
Chinese, Malaysian etc.

Baker/Confectioner

ALEXIS
272 West End Lane
794 2617

➌ West Hampstead
9.30 a.m.–1.30 p.m.

Off-Licence

THE GROG BLOSSOM
253 West End Lane
794 7808
➌ West Hampstead
Noon–2.00 p.m.
& 7.00 p.m.–10.00 p.m.
Also real ale specialists

NW8

Delicatessen

RIAS ALTAS
97 Frampton Street
262 4340
➌ Edgware Road
10.00 a.m.–2.00 p.m.
Spanish delicatessen

Pasta

THE PASTA MACHINE
51a St John's Wood High
Street
722 0977
➌ St John's Wood
10.00 a.m.–2.00 p.m.
Fresh pasta and sauces; ice
cream etc.

NW10

Delicatessen

SAB-RAS
263 High Road
459 0340

➌ Dollis Hill
12.30 p.m.–9.15 p.m.
Indian food – pulses, spices,
cakes, etc.

Baker/Confectioner

A. GRODZINSKI & CO.
2 High Road
459 2380
➌ Willesden Green/Dollis
Hill
8.00 a.m.–11.00 a.m.

NW11

Baker/Confectioner

A. GRODZINSKI & CO.
867 Finchley Road
455 9370
➌ Golders Green
and
223 Golders Green Road
458 3654
➌ Brent Cross/Golders
Green
8.00 a.m.–6.00 p.m.
and
3 Hallswelle Parade,
Finchley Road
455 7242
➌ Golders Green
and
45 Market Place
455 0470
➌ East Finchley
8.00 a.m.–1.00 p.m.

Freezer Centre

**KOSHER FREEZER
CENTRE**
235 Golders Green Road
455 1429
⊖ Brent Cross
8.00 a.m.–6.00 p.m.

SE11

Fishmonger

BOB WHITE
1 Kennington Lane
735 1931
⊖ Kennington/Elephant &
Castle
7.00 a.m.–5.00 p.m.
and stall at The Oval.
Fish, shellfish and game birds

Off-Licence

**MAJESTIC WINE
WAREHOUSE**
Arch 84, Goding Street
587 1830
⊖ Vauxhall
10.00 a.m.–4.00 p.m.
Purchase by the case only.
Also sells coffee, oils, herbs,
etc.
*AC BC

SE16

Off-Licence

**ADHOC WINE
WAREHOUSE**
753 Enid Street
231 9113

⊖ London Bridge
10.00 a.m.–2.00 p.m.
Also sell wine on draught –
take your own bottle to be
filled

SW1

Delicatessen

PARTRIDGES
132–134 Sloane Street
730 0651
⊖ Sloane Square/
Knightsbridge
8.30 a.m.–9.00 p.m.
Wide range of groceries, wines
and spirits

**VINEGAR JOE'S
DELICATESSEN**
46 Pimlico Road
730 0176/9357
⊖ Victoria/Sloane Square
8.00 a.m.–10.00 p.m.
Also supermarket and hot take
away food

Off-Licence

ANDRÉ SIMON WINES
50 Elizabeth Street
730 8108
⊖ Sloane Square/Victoria
Noon–2.00 p.m.
Also cigarettes, chocolates,
books, etc.

SW3

Delicatessen

THE MIDNIGHT SHOP
223 Brompton Road
589 7788
◉ South Kensington/
Knightsbridge
9.00 a.m.–midnight
Deli and general groceries

Wholefoods

NEAL'S YARD
WHOLEFOOD
WAREHOUSE
Chelsea Farmers Market,
Sydney Street
352 6006
◉ Sloane Square
11.00 a.m.–5.00 p.m.
Wide variety – mostly dried
fruit, nuts, grains, pulses,
honeys, etc.

SW4

Delicatessen

HERE IS FOOD
26 The Pavement
622 4051
◉ Clapham Common
10.00 a.m.–9.00 p.m.

SW5

Delicatessen

OLD BROMPTON
COLONIAL
255 Old Brompton Road
373 9131
◉ Earls Court
9.00 a.m.–9.00 p.m.

STAR DELICATESSEN
176 Earls Court Road
370 3064
◉ Earls Court
Deli and general groceries

SW6

Supermarket

THE MARKET
700 Fulham Road
736 4348
◉ Parsons Green/Putney
Bridge
9.00 a.m.–9.00 p.m.

SW7

Pasta

PRONTO PASTA &
CHEESE
66 Old Brompton Road
589 1760
◉ South Kensington
Noon–8.00 p.m.
Fresh pasta and sauces, ice
cream, cakes, wine, etc.

Off-Licence

LA VIGNERONNE
105 Old Brompton Road
589 6113
◉ South Kensington
Noon–2.00 p.m.
& 7.00 p.m.–10.30 p.m.
Wine merchant

SW10

Off-Licence

LONDON WINE BROKERS
15 Lots Road
352 5843
✪ Fulham Broadway
11.00 a.m.–5.00 p.m.
Purchase by the case only

SW11

Delicatessen

ACQUIRED TASTE
9 Battersea Rise
223 9942
✪ Clapham Common
11.00 a.m.–8.00 p.m.
Also wines, beers, wholefood,
snacks, etc.

PUDDLEDUCKS
4 Battersea Rise
228 2231
✪ Clapham Common
9.00 a.m.–9.00 p.m.

Fishmonger

**ALBERT WHARF FISH
MARKET**
22 Hester Road
10.00 a.m.–2.00 p.m.
Fish, shellfish and smoked fish

Off-Licence

**MAJESTIC WINE
WAREHOUSE**
Albion Wharf,
Hester Road
223 2983

10.00 a.m.–10.00 p.m.
Purchase by the case only.
Also sells coffee, oils, herbs,
etc.
*AC BC

SW15

Butcher

ST MARCUS
1 Rockingham Close
878 1898
✪ East Putney
11.00 a.m.–7.00 p.m.
Also fine foods

W1

Supermarket

THE GREAT WALL
31–37 Wardour Street
437 7963
✪ Piccadilly Circus/Leicester
Square
11.00 a.m.–8.00 p.m.
Chinese supermarket

**LOON FUNG
SUPERMARKET**
42–44 Gerrard Street
437 7332
✪ Leicester Square
10.00 a.m.–8.30 p.m.
Huge range of oriental food

Delicatessen

WELSS DELICATESSEN
110–112 Baker Street
486 8444
✪ Baker Street

8.00 a.m.–11.00 p.m.
Indian food and off-licence

Baker/Confectioner

A. GRODZINSKI & CO.
53 Goodge Street
636 0561
☻ Goodge Street
8.00 a.m.–1.00 p.m.

MAISON BERTAUX
28 Greek Street
437 6007
☻ Tottenham Court Road
9.30 a.m.–1.00 p.m.

PASTICCERIA AMALFI
31 Old Compton Street
437 7284
☻ Leicester Square
9.00 a.m.–12.30 p.m.
*AC AX BC DC

RICHOUX
172 Piccadilly
493 2204
☻ Green Park/Piccadilly
Circus
and
41a South Audley Street
629 5228
☻ Green Park/Hyde Park
Corner
10.00 a.m.–11.00 p.m.
Cakes and superb chocolates
*AC AX BC DC

Off-Licence

THE VINTAGE HOUSE
42 Old Compton Street
437 5112

☻ Leicester Square/Piccadilly
Circus
Noon–2.00 p.m. &
7.00 p.m.–10.00 p.m.

W2

Supermaret

THE MARKET
12 Craven Road
723 6965
☻ Paddington/Lancaster Gate
9.00 a.m.–11.00 p.m.

24-HOUR SUPERMARKET
68 Westbourne Grove
727 4927
☻ Bayswater
open 24 hours

Delicatessen

ATHENIAN GROCERY
16a Moscow Road
229 6280
☻ Bayswater/Queensway
9.30 a.m.–1.00 p.m.
Greek, Middle Eastern and
Indian foods

THAI SHOP
3 Craven Terrace
723 2358
☻ Lancaster Gate
Noon–4.00 p.m.
Fresh and dried oriental food

Baker/Confectioner

MAISON BOUQUILLON
45 Moscow Road
727 4897

⊖ Bayswater
8.00 a.m.–1.00 p.m.
French pâtisserie and
charcuterie

W4

Baker/Confectioner

OLD HEIDELBERG
PÂTISSERIE
270 Chiswick High Road
994 6621
⊖ Turnham Green
2.30 p.m.–5.30 p.m.
*AC BC DC

W6

Off-Licence

BARRETT'S
LIQUORMART
46 Shepherd's Bush Road
603 2924
⊖ Goldhawk Road/
Hammersmith
Noon–2.00 p.m.
& 7.00 p.m.–9.00 p.m.

W9

Supermarket

SUPERFOODS
21/23 Clifton Road
286 1668
⊖ Warwick Avenue
9.00 a.m.–9.00 p.m.

W11

Delicatessen

MR CHRISTIAN'S
11 Elgin Crescent
229 0501
⊖ Ladbroke Grove
9.30 a.m.–2.00 p.m.

W12

Off-Licence

BARRETT'S
LIQUORMART
76 Goldhawk Road
⊖ Goldhawk Road
Noon–2.00 p.m.

W13

Off-Licence

MAJESTIC WINE
WAREHOUSE
West Ealing Station,
Hastings Road
567 9251
BR West Ealing
10.00 a.m.–5.00 p.m.
Purchase by the case only.
Also sells coffee, oils, herbs,
etc.
*AC BC

W14

Supermarket

BUY LATE FOODS
99 Hammersmith Road
603 2300

⊖ Hammersmith
9.00 a.m.–9.00 p.m.

Off-Licence

QUEEN'S CLUB WINES
2 Charleville Road
385 3582
⊖ West Kensington
Noon–2.00 p.m.
& 7.00 p.m.–9.00 p.m.
Wine merchants

WC2

Supermarket

CHEON LEEN
SUPERMARKET
4–10 Tower Street
836 5378
⊖ Leicester Square/Covent
Garden
Noon–5.00 p.m.
Chinese food and kitchen
equipment

ENDELL SUPERMARKET
28–30 Endell Street
379 0756
⊖ Covent Garden
7.30 a.m.–1.00 p.m.
Supermarket and newsagent

Dairy & Ice Cream

NEAL'S YARD DAIRY
9 Neal's Yard
379 7646
⊖ Covent Garden
11.00 a.m.–4.00 p.m.
Dairy produce

Coffee

MONMOUTH COFFEE
HOUSE
27 Monmouth Street
836 5272
⊖ Covent Garden/Tottenham
Court Road
11.00 a.m.–5.00 p.m.
Pure coffee beans

Wholefoods

NEAL'S YARD FARM
SHOP
1 Neal's Yard
836 1066
⊖ Covent Garden
11.00 a.m.–5.00 p.m.
Fresh fruit and vegetables,
organically grown

NEAL'S YARD
WHOLEFOOD
WAREHOUSE
21–23 Shorts Gardens
836 5151
⊖ Covent Garden
10.00 a.m.–5.00 p.m.
Wide variety – mostly dried
fruit, nuts, grains, pulses,
honeys, etc.

Off-Licence

SEVEN DIALS WINE
COMPANY
17 Shorts Gardens
836 2189
⊖ Covent Garden
Noon–2.30 p.m.
Also wine and beer available
on draught – take your own
bottle to be filled

OUT OF TOWN – BRENTFORD

Wholefoods

HUNZA WHOLEFOODS
Syon Park,
Brentford, Middlesex
847 2140
⊖ Gunnersbury
10.00 a.m.–5.00 p.m.

FURNITURE & FURNISHINGS

EC2

Bedroom

CITY PINE
311 Old Street
739 3665
⊖ Old Street
11.00 a.m.–3.00 p.m.
Pine beds and furniture

EC3

General

HOUNDSDITCH
WAREHOUSE
123 Houndsditch
283 3131
⊖ Liverpool Street/Aldgate
9.30 a.m.–2.00 p.m.

N2

General

FURNISHINGS & DESIGN
5 Lincoln Parade,
Lincoln Road
444 7249
⊖ East Finchley
11.00 a.m.–4.00 p.m.

N10

Bedroom

MUSWELL PINE
Viaduct Workshops,
St James's Lane
883 4811
⊖ Highgate
11.00 a.m.–4.00 p.m.
Pine beds

N15

Bathroom

BRITISH BATHROOM
CENTRE
602–604 Seven Sisters Road
802 6696/6493
⊖ Seven Sisters
9.00 a.m.–2.00 p.m.
All kinds of suites and decor

N16

Bathroom

SOUTHERN HEATING
278–286 Stamford Hill
809 3211

⊖ Seven Sisters
9.00 a.m.–1.00 p.m.
Suites

NW1

Bedroom

DREAMS
34 Chalk Farm Road
267 8194
⊖ Chalk Farm
10.30 a.m.–6.00 p.m.
Brass bedsteads, headboards,
bedding, etc.

General

CANE WORKSHOP
Unit 29 Camden Lock
485 2350
⊖ Camden Town
10.00 a.m.–5.00 p.m.
Cane furniture

CASA CATALAN
15–16 Chalk Farm Road
485 3975
⊖ Chalk Farm/Camden
Town
10.00 a.m.–6.00 p.m.
Huge range of European tiles,
fabrics, furniture, exotic plants,
etc.

KERMESSEE
23 Camden Lock
267 1530
⊖ Camden Town/Chalk
Farm
11.00 a.m.–5.30 p.m.
New and reproduction pine
furniture

MOORHOUSE
ASSOCIATES
240 Camden High Street
267 9714
⊖ Camden Town
10.00 a.m.–6.00 p.m.
Designers and printers of
fabric

PATCHWORK DOG &
CALICO CAT
21 Chalk Farm Road
485 1239
⊖ Camden Town
10.00 a.m.–6.00 p.m.
Patchwork, fabric,
haberdashery and antique
quilts

THE PINE VILLAGE
19 Chalk Farm Road
485 4034
⊖ Chalk Farm/Camden
Town
10.00 a.m.–6.00 p.m.
Pine furniture

THE POSTER SHOP
1 Chalk Farm Road
267 6985
⊖ Camden Town
10.30 a.m.–6.30 p.m.
Wide selection of posters.
Picture framing service

NW6

Bedroom

FUTON BARRELL
134 West End Lane
328 3495
⊖ West Hampstead

11.00 a.m.–3.00 p.m.
Japanese mattresses

General

THE PINE SHOP
176–184 West End Lane
435 4462/1044
✆ West Hampstead
10.00 a.m.–1.30 p.m.
Pine furniture

NW9

General

SACHELLE STUDIOS
246 Church Lane
200 6697
✆ Kingsbury/Wembley Park
10.00 a.m.–1.00 p.m.
Bathroom tiles, kitchen
appliances, carpets, mirrors,
lights, whirlpools

SW1

General

DESIGN CENTRE SHOP
28 Haymarket
839 8000
✆ Piccadilly Circus
1.00 p.m.–6.00 p.m.
China, kitchen goods, linen,
furniture, etc.

SW3

General

THE REJECT SHOP
245 Brompton Road
584 7611

✆ South Kensington
and
234 King's Road
352 2750/2820/2917
✆ South Kensington/Sloane
Square
11.00 a.m.–5.00 p.m.
All kinds of goods including
furniture, kitchen equipment,
lighting, etc.

SW6

General

THE PINE VILLAGE
162 Wandsworth Bridge Road
736 2753
✆ Fulham Broadway
10.00 a.m.–6.00 p.m.
Pine furniture

SW12

General

THE KILIM WAREHOUSE
28a Pickets Street
675 3122
✆ Clapham South
11.00 a.m.–2.00 p.m.
Kilims and flat weave Turkish
rugs

SW14

General

THE PINE VILLAGE
195 Upper Richmond Road
West
876 4053

BR Mortlake
10.00 a.m.–6.00 p.m.
Pine furniture

W2

General

THE PINE VILLAGE
1 Pembridge Villas
221 7044
✪ Notting Hill Gate
10.00 a.m.–6.00 p.m.
Pine furniture

W7

General

WORLD OF PINE
167 Uxbridge Road
840 5303
✪ Boston Manor
10.00 a.m.–4.00 p.m.
Pine beds and furniture

W9

Bedroom

BIG TABLE FURNITURE
CO.
56 Great Western Road
221 5058
✪ Westbourne Park
2.00 p.m.–5.00 p.m.
Pine beds and mattresses

WC2

Kitchen

COVENT GARDEN
KITCHEN SUPPLIES
Unit 3 The Market
836 9167
✪ Covent Garden
11.30 a.m.–4.30 p.m.
(may vary – call and check)
Kitchen equipment.

OUT OF TOWN – RICHMOND

Antiques

MOLLIE EVANS
84 Hill Rise
948 0182
✪ Richmond
2.30 p.m.–5.30 p.m.

GARDEN CENTRES

N6

SOUTHWOOD'S VILLAGE
NURSERIES
Townsend Yard,
Highgate High Street
340 1041/9117
✪ Archway
10.00 a.m.–1.00 p.m.
*AC AX BC

N10

PETER ADAMS
Cranley Gardens
883 5880/0821
⊖ Highgate
10.00 a.m.–1.00 p.m.
*AC BC

NW1

CAMDEN GARDEN
CENTRE
66 Kentish Town Road
485 8468
⊖ Camden Town
10.15 a.m.–5.00 p.m.
*AC BC

SW3

JACK BEANSTALK
GARDEN & LEISURE
CENTRE
Chelsea Farmers Market,
Sydney Street
352 5656/5657
⊖ Sloane Square
10.00 a.m.–5.00 p.m.
*AC BC

SW6

CRABTREE GARDENS
42–46 Crabtree Lane
385 6280/5451
⊖ Hammersmith
Summer: 10.00 a.m.–
6.00 p.m.
Winter: 10.00 a.m.–5.00 p.m.
*AX DC

WATERFORD GARDEN
CENTRE
108–116 Waterford Road
731 4717/736 2262
⊖ Fulham Broadway
10.00 a.m.–5.00 p.m.
*AC BC

SW7

CROMWELL GARDEN
CENTRE
Lenthal Place,
Gloucester Road
373 5264
⊖ Gloucester Road
10.00 a.m.–5.00 p.m.
*AC AX BC DC

SW10

WORLD'S END
NURSERIES
441–457 King's Road
351 3343
⊖ Sloane Square
10.00 a.m.–5.00 p.m.

SW17

BRYAN'S GARDEN
CENTRE
100 Tooting Bec Road
672 2251
⊖ Tooting Bec
9.00 a.m.–5.15 p.m.
*AC BC

SW18

NEAL'S NURSERIES
Heathfield Road
874 2037

BR Earlsfield
10.00 a.m.–4.00 p.m.
*AC BC

W2

CLIFTON NURSERIES
The Colonnades,
Bishop's Bridge Road
402 9834
✪ Paddington
10.00 a.m.–4.00 p.m.
*AC BC

W9

CLIFTON NURSERIES
5a Clifton Villas
289 6851/286 9888
✪ Warwick Avenue
9.30 a.m.–1.30 p.m.
*AC BC

WC2

CLIFTON NURSERIES
16 Russell Street
379 6878
✪ Covent Garden
Noon–5.00 p.m.
*AC BC

OUT OF TOWN – BRENTFORD

SYON PARK NURSERY
Syon Park,
Brentford, Middlesex
568 0134
✪ Gunnersbury
9.00 a.m.–5.00 p.m.
*AC BC DC

OUT OF TOWN – TWICKENHAM

SQUIRES GARDEN
CENTRE
Sixth Cross Road,
Twickenham, Middlesex
977 1054
BR Fulwell
8.30 a.m.–5.30 p.m.
*AC BC

GIFTS

Refer to other sections under
the relevant heading.
Chocolates, for example, will
be found under Food–Baker/
Confectioner.

NW1

THE LOCK SHOP
Camden Lock
485 3450
✪ Camden Town/Chalk
Farm
10.30 a.m.–6.00 p.m.
British crafts – clothes, glass,
pottery, jewellery, knitwear,
etc.

ROSE ELLIOTT DESIGN
Stairway Studios,
Camden Lock
485 8292
✪ Chalk Farm/Camden
Town
10.00 a.m.–6.00 p.m.

Hand-painted clothes, batik
from Bali, etc. Accepts
commissions from her
portfolio.

WC2

DICKENS OLD
CURIOSITY SHOP
13–14 Portsmouth Street
405 9891
✪ Holborn
9.30 a.m.–5.00 p.m.
Antiques, books, souvenirs,
etc.

GUANGHWA
7–9 Newport Place
437 3737
✪ Leicester Square
11.00 a.m.–7.00 p.m.
Oriental goods, Chinese art
materials, books, cards, etc.

MARKETS & AUCTIONS

Street markets may cover a
number of streets with many
stalls selling a wide variety of
goods.

The opening hours given here
can only be used as a rough
guide but generally the earlier
you get there, the better.

E1

BRICK LANE
and nearby streets
✪Aldgate/Liverpool Street
6.30 a.m.–12.30 p.m.
Street market. All kinds of
goods – furniture, electricals,
fruit, vegetables, clothes,
bicycles, records, etc.

PETTICOAT LANE
and nearby streets
✪ Aldgate/Liverpool Street
6.30 a.m.–12.30 p.m.
Street market. All kinds of
goods – clothes, kitchen
goods, fruit, plants, vegetables,
jewellery, etc.

E2

COLUMBIA ROAD
✪ Old Street/Bethnal Green
9.00 a.m.–1.00 p.m.
Street market. Garden plants
and flowers.

E3

ROMAN ROAD
✪ Bethnal Green
8.30 a.m.–1.00 p.m.
Street market. All kinds of
general goods.

E4

LEA VALLEY VIADUCT
BR Angel Road
9.00 a.m.–2.00 p.m.
Market. All kinds of goods –
clothes, household goods,
camping kit, games, etc.

N1

CHAPEL MARKET
✪ Angel
8.00 a.m.–12.30 p.m.
Street market. Fruit,
vegetables, clothes,
household goods, etc.

NW1

CAMDEN LOCK
Camden High Street and
Chalk Farm Road
✪ Camden Town
9.00 a.m.–6.00 p.m.
Street market. Mainly arts and
crafts plus antiques, jewellery,
clothes, records, etc.

ODDITY'S MARKET
72–73 Chalk Farm Road
267 0152
✪ Chalk Farm/Camden
Town
10.00 a.m.–7.00 p.m.
Covered market selling new
and second-hand clothes,
antiques, bric a brac etc.

ROUNDHOUSE
Chalk Farm Road
✪ Chalk Farm
9.00 a.m.–6.00 p.m.
A few stalls selling bric a brac,
plants, books etc.

SE1

BOROUGH AUCTIONS
6 Park Street
407 9577
✪ London Bridge

Viewing from 10.00 a.m.
Sale at 2.00 p.m.
Antiques, jewellery, silver,
household goods etc.

SE5

FRANKLIN'S ANTIQUE MARKET
161 Camberwell Road
703 8089
✪ Elephant & Castle
1.00 p.m.–6.00 p.m.
Covered market. Second-hand
furniture bought and sold.
*AC BC

SE10

GREENWICH ANTIQUE MARKET
Greenwich High Street
BR Greenwich
June–September (only):
8.00 a.m.–4.00 p.m.
Open air market. Antiques,
bric a brac, clothes, etc.

SE11

THE OVAL
Kennington Oval
✪ Oval/Vauxhall
8.00 a.m.–12.30 p.m.
Street market selling clothes,
household goods, bric a brac,
etc.

SE17

EAST STREET
off Walworth Road
✪ Elephant & Castle

8.00 a.m.–1.00 p.m.
Street market. All kinds of
goods – fruit, vegetables,
plants, records, clothes,
household goods, sports
equipment etc.

WESTMORELAND ROAD
off Walworth Road
⊖Kennington/Elephant &
Castle
8.00 a.m.–1.00 p.m.
Street market selling antiques,
bric a brac, records, clothes,
fruit, vegetables, etc.

SW6

EARLS COURT MARKET
Lillie Road
⊖ Earls Court
8.30 a.m.–12.30 p.m.
Mainly household goods plus
electricals, clothes, fabric,
food, etc.

SW11

BATTERSEA ARTS
CENTRE
Old Town Hall
176 Lavender Hill
223 6557/8413
BR Clapham Junction
11.00 a.m.–6.00 p.m.
Craft market – handmade
goods, pottery, knitting, etc.
to buy and/or sell.

W1

GREEN PARK RAILINGS
Piccadilly
⊖ Green Park

all day
Open air display of arts, crafts,
pictures and paintings for
sale.

W2

HYDE PARK RAILINGS
Bayswater Road
⊖ Lancaster Gate/Queensway
9.00 a.m.–1.00 p.m.
Open air display of souvenirs,
pictures and paintings for sale.

W10

PORTABELLA DOCK
Kensal Road/Ladbroke Grove
⊖ Ladbroke Grove
all day
Mainly arts and crafts market
plus clothes, antiques etc.

WC2

JUBILEE MARKET
Covent Garden
⊖ Covent Garden
9.00 a.m.–4.30 p.m.
Arts and crafts market.

OUT OF TOWN –
WEMBLEY

WEMBLEY STADIUM CAR
PARK
Empire Way,
Wembley, Middlesex
⊖ Wembley Park
9.00 a.m.–1.30 p.m.
Large open air market selling
clothes, jewellery, household
goods, groceries, records,
fabrics, etc.

NEWSPAPERS & STATIONERY

There are too many newsagents in London to list here. Most are open on Sunday for at least part of the day and are likely to sell stationery, including greetings cards, as well as a wide variety of sundry goods.

24 hour newsagent

REGENCY
243 Old Brompton Road, SW5
● Earls Court
Huge range of magazines, newspapers, cards, etc.

Saturday night Sunday papers

Sunday newspapers can be bought on Saturday evening from about 10.30 p.m. from various places including the following:

Earls Court
Underground Station, SW5

Coventry Street, W1

King's Cross Station, N1

Piccadilly Circus, W1

Shaftesbury Avenue, W1
(corner of Denman Street)

Strand WC2
(corner of Villiers Street)

Victoria Station, SW1

OPTICIANS

WC2

FOR EYES
21 James Street
240 1760
● Covent Garden
Noon–5.00 p.m.
*Credit cards

PET SHOPS

N3

COLLEGE FARM
45 Fitzalan Road
349 0690
● Finchley Central
10.00 a.m.–6.00 p.m.
Mainly feed, tack etc. for horses and riding.

SW3

PET CARE OF CHELSEA
Chelsea Farmers Market
Sydney Street
351 3025
● Sloane Square
11.00 a.m.–4.00 p.m.
All kinds of things for pets – coats, food, toys, etc.

SPORTS EQUIPMENT

You should refer to Sports & Activities where those places selling equipment are clearly marked: *Shop.

Riding kit is also available from College Farm, N3 (see Pet Shops).

TOBACCONISTS

Cigarettes etc. are widely available from supermarkets, petrol stations, pubs, newsagents, etc.

TOYS, GAMES & JOKES

NW1

KRISTIN BAYBARS
stall in Camden Lock Market
⊖ Camden Town
9.15 a.m.–5.30 p.m.
British craft toys, rocking horses, miniatures, etc.

SW1

OSCAR'S DEN
15 Buckingham Palace Road
828 9300
⊖ Victoria
10.00 a.m.–6.00 p.m.
Wooden toys, hand-painted children's furniture, children's party shop, etc.

WC2

KNUTZ
1 Russell Street
836 3117
⊖ Covent Garden
Noon–6.00 p.m.
(most Sundays – ring to check)
Whole range of toys and jokes mainly for adults.

PLACES OF WORSHIP

There are literally thousands of cathedrals, churches, chapels, halls, etc. in London – far too many to include in this book.

This is a list, by denomination, of places of worship which can, at least, be taken as a starting point for further enquiries.

It is hoped that the service times given here are reasonably accurate but you must check to be sure. The service times of some churches are printed on the Court and Social pages of *The Times* and the *Daily Telegraph* on Saturdays.

To find out about service times and local churches, call the number given. Further information is available certainly during office hours from Monday to Friday, and many of the telephones are manned on Sundays as well. You will also find the telephone directories useful – look up either the name of the church, e.g. St James's, or the denomination.

Armenian

ARMENIAN CHURCH OF ST SARKIS
Iverna Gardens, W8
937 0152
✪ High Street Kensington
10.00 a.m. & 11.00 a.m.

Austrian

AUSTRIAN CATHOLIC CENTRE
29 Brook Green, W6
603 2697
✪ Hammersmith
8.00 p.m.

Baptist

BLOOMSBURY CENTRAL BAPTIST CHURCH
Shaftesbury Avenue, WC2
240 0544
✪ Tottenham Court Road/ Leicester Square
11.00 a.m. & 6.30 p.m.

WESTBOURNE PARK BAPTIST CHURCH
Porchester Road, W2
727 0979
✪ Royal Oak
11.00 a.m. & 6.40 p.m.

Belgian

NOTRE DAME DE HAL
165 Arlington Road, NW1
485 2727
● Camden Town
8.00 a.m. 10.00 a.m.
11.00 a.m.
Noon 5.00 p.m. 6.30 p.m. &
7.30 p.m.

Chinese

services held at the
WELSH METHODIST
CHURCH
82a Chiltern Street, W1
686 0592/935 7842
● Baker Street
2.00 p.m. (Mandarin) &
3.30 p.m. (English)

Christian Science

FIRST CHURCH OF
CHRIST SCIENTIST
Sloane Terrace
730 8584
● Sloane Square
11.00 a.m & 7.00 p.m.

Church of England

ALL SAINTS
Margaret Street, W1
636 1788
● Oxford Circus
8.00 a.m. 10.20 a.m.
11.00 a.m. 5.15 p.m. &
6.00 p.m.

THE CHAPEL ROYAL
St James's Palace, SW1
● Green Park

October–Easter (only):
8.00 a.m. & 11.15 a.m.

THE CHAPEL ROYAL OF
ST PETER-AD-VINCULAR
Tower of London, EC3
709 0765
● Tower Hill
11.00 a.m.

ST BRIDE'S
Bride Lane,
Fleet Street, EC4
353 1301
● Blackfriars
8.30 a.m. 11.00 a.m. &
6.00 p.m.

ST CLEMENT DANES
Strand, WC2
242 8282
● Embankment/Holborn
8.30 a.m. 11.00 a.m.
12 15 p.m. & 3.30 p.m.

ST GEORGE'S, HANOVER
SQUARE
St George Street, W1
629 0874
● Oxford Circus
8.15 a.m. & 11.00 a.m.

ST JAMES'S, PICCADILLY
Piccadilly, W1
734 5244
● Piccadilly Circus/Green
Park
8.15 a.m. 9.15 a.m. 11.00 a.m.
& 6.00 p.m.

ST MARGARET'S,
WESTMINSTER
Parliament Square, SW1
222 6382

✆ Westminster
1st Sunday: 8.15 a.m. &
11.00 a.m.
Other Sundays: 11.00 a.m. &
12.15 p.m.

ST MARTIN-IN-THE-FIELDS
Trafalgar Square, WC2
930 0089
✆ Leicester Square/Charing Cross
8.00 a.m. 9.45 a.m. 11.15 a.m.
4.15 p.m. & 6.30 p.m.

ST PAUL'S, COVENT GARDEN
Bedford Street, WC2
836 5221
✆ Covent Garden
11.00 a.m.

ST PAUL'S CATHEDRAL
St Paul's Churchyard, EC4
248 2705
✆ St Paul's/Mansion House
8.00 a.m. 10.30 a.m.
11.30 a.m. & 3.15 p.m.

SOUTHWARK CATHEDRAL
Borough High Street, SE1
407 2939
✆ London Bridge
9.00 a.m. 11.00 a.m. &
3.30 p.m.

THE TEMPLE CHURCH
Inner Temple Lane, EC4
353 8559
✆ Blackfriars

8.30 a.m. 11.15 a.m. &
(1st Sunday) 12.30 p.m.
No services August/
September

WESTMINSTER ABBEY
Broad Sanctuary, SW1
222 5152
✆ Westminster/St James's Park
8.00 a.m. 10.30 a.m.
11.40 a.m. 3.00 p.m. &
6.30 p.m.

Church of Scotland

CROWN COURT CHURCH
Russell Street, WC1
836 5643/584 2321
✆ Tottenham Court Road/
Holborn
11.15 a.m. & 6.30 p.m.

ST COLUMBA'S
Pont Street, SW1
584 2321
✆ Knightsbridge
11.00 a.m. & 6.30 p.m.

Danish Church

THE DANISH CHURCH
4 St Katherine's Precinct,
NW1
935 7584
✆ Camden Town
1st Sunday: 11.00 a.m.
Other Sundays: 4.00 p.m.

Dutch Church

THE DUTCH CHURCH
Austin Friars, EC2
588 1684
✜ Bank
11.00 a.m.

Finnish

FINNISH SEAMAN'S
CHURCH
33 Albion Street, SE16
237 4668/1261
✜ Rotherhithe
1st Sunday: 11.00 a.m.
Other Sundays: 7.30 p.m.

French

FRENCH PROTESTANT
CHURCH
9 Soho Square, W1
437 5311
✜ Tottenham Court Road
11.00 a.m.

NOTRE DAME DE
FRANCE
5 Leicester Place, WC2
437 9363
✜ Leicester Square
10.00 a.m. 11.15 a.m.
12.15 p.m. & 6.30 p.m.

German

GERMAN CHRIST
CHURCH
19 Montpelier Place, SW7
589 5303/876 6366
✜ Knightsbridge
11.00 a.m. & (1st Sunday)
6.30 p.m.

GERMAN LUTHERAN
CHURCH OF
ST MARY-LE-SAVOY
10 Sandwich Street,WC1
794 4207
✜ Euston/Russell Square
1st & 3rd Sundays: 11.00 a.m.
Other Sundays: 4.00 p.m.

Greek Orthodox

ALL SAINTS
Pratt Street, NW1
485 2149
✜ Camden Town
9.00 a.m. & 1.00 p.m.

ST SOPHIA'S
Moscow Road, W2
723 4787
✜ Bayswater/Notting Hill
Gate
10.00 a.m.

Hindu

THE HINDU CENTRE
39 Grafton Terrace, NW5
485 8200
✜ Chalk Farm/Belsize Park
1st Sunday: 4.00 p.m.

Hungarian

HUNGARIAN REFORMED
CHURCH
17 St Dunstan's Road, W6
748 8858
✜ Baron's Court
5.00 p.m.

Independent Evangelical

WESTMINSTER CHAPEL
Buckingham Gate, SW1
834 1731
⊖ St James's Park/Victoria
11.00 a.m. & 6.30 p.m.

Italian

ST PETER'S
Back Hill, EC1
837 1528
⊖ Farringdon
9.00 a.m. 10.00 a.m.
11.00 a.m.
& 12.15 p.m.

Jehovah's Witnesses

WATCH TOWER HOUSE
The Ridgeway, NW7
906 2211
⊖ Mill Hill East
3.00 p.m.

Jewish

CENTRAL SYNAGOGUE
(Orthodox)
Great Portland Street, W1
580 1355
⊖ Oxford Circus/Great
Portland Street
8.00 a.m.

WEST END GREAT
SYNAGOGUE
21 Dean Street, W1
437 9157/1873
⊖ Tottenham Court Road/
Leicester Square
8.30 a.m.

Liberal Catholic Church

ST PETER'S CHAPEL
52 Victoria Road, W8
387 3260
⊖ High Street Kensington/
Gloucester Road
11.00 a.m.

Lithuanian

ST CASIMIR'S
21 The Oval
Hackney Road, E2
739 8735
⊖ Bethnal Green
9.00 a.m. & 11.00 a.m.

Lutheran

ST ANNE and ST AGNES
Gresham Street, EC2
606 4986/904 2849
⊖ St Paul's/Mansion House
11.00 a.m. (English) &
1st & 3rd Sundays: 4.14 p.m.
(Estonian)
2nd & 4th Sundays: 5.00 p.m.
(Latvian)

ST JOHN'S
8 Collingham Gardens, SW5
373 1141
⊖ Earls Court/Gloucester
Road
6.30 p.m.

Methodist

CENTRAL HALL
Storey's Gate, SW1
222 8010/7472
⊖ Westminster
11.00 a.m. & 4.30 p.m.

KINGSWAY HALL
Kingsway, WC2
405 3246
⊖ Holborn
11.00 a.m. & 6.30 p.m.

Muslim

LONDON CENTRAL MOSQUE
146 Park Road, NW8
723 7613
⊖ Baker Street/St John's Wood

LONDON MOSQUE
16 Gressenhall Road, SW18
874 6298
⊖ Southfields

Norwegian

ST OLAV'S (Lutheran)
1 Albion Street, SE16
237 5587
⊖ Rotherhithe
11.00 a.m.

Pentecostal

ASSEMBLIES OF GOD
141 Harrow Road, W2
286 9261
⊖ Edgware Road/Warwick Avenue
11.00 a.m. & 6.30 p.m.

Polish

ST ANDREW BOBOLA'S
1 Leysfield Road, W12
743 8848
⊖ Goldhawk Road/Stamford Brook
9.00 a.m. 10.00 a.m.
11.00 a.m. Noon & 5.30 p.m.

Presbyterian

REGENT SQUARE PRESBYTERIAN CHURCH
Regent Square, WC1
837 6523
⊖ Russell Square
11.00 a.m. & 6.30 p.m.

Roman Catholic

BROMPTON ORATORY
Brompton Road, SW7
589 4811
⊖ South Kensington/Knightsbridge
7.00 a.m. 8.00 a.m. 9.00 a.m.
10.00 a.m. 11.00 a.m.
12.30 p.m. 4.30 p.m. & 7.00 p.m.

CHURCH OF THE IMMACULATE CONCEPTION
(Farm Street Church)
114 Mount Street, W1
493 7811
⊖ Green Park/Bond Street
7.30 a.m. 8.30 a.m. 10.00 a.m.
11.00 a.m. 12.15 p.m.
4.15 p.m. & 6.15 p.m.

ST ETHELREDA'S
Ely Place, EC1
405 1061

⊕ Farringdon
8.00 a.m. 11.00 a.m. &
6.00 p.m.

ST GEORGE'S CATHEDRAL
St George's Road, SE1
928 5256
⊕ Lambeth North
7.00 a.m. 8.00 a.m. 9.30 a.m.
10.30 a.m. 12.30 p.m.
5.30 p.m. & 6.30 p.m.

ST PATRICK'S
Soho Square, W1
437 2010
⊕ Tottenham Court Road
8.00 a.m. 9.00 a.m. 10.30 a.m.
Noon 2.00 p.m. 5.00 p.m. &
6.00 p.m.

WESTMINSTER CATHEDRAL
Ashley Place, SW1
834 7452/828 4732
⊕ Victoria
7.00 a.m. 8.00 a.m. 9.00 a.m.
10.30 a.m. Noon 5.30 p.m. &
7.00 p.m.

Romanian

ST DUNSTAN-IN-THE-WEST
183 Fleet Street, EC4
405 1929
⊕ Blackfriars
10.00 a.m.

Russian

ALL SAINTS
Ennismore Gardens, SW7
584 0096
⊕ Knightsbridge
11.00 a.m.

RUSSIAN ORTHODOX CHURCH IN EXILE
Emperor's Gate, SW7
748 4232
⊕ Gloucester Road
10.00 a.m.

Salvation Army

MARYLEBONE HALL
Bell Street, W1
723 8553
⊕ Edgware Road
10.45 a.m. 3.00 p.m. &
6.45 p.m.

REGENT HALL
275 Oxford Street, W1
629 5424
⊕ Oxford Circus
11.00 a.m. 3.00 p.m. &
6.30 p.m.

Serbian

SERBIAN ORTHODOX CHURCH
89 Lancaster Road, W11
727 8367
⊕ Ladbroke Grove
11.00 a.m.

Seventh-Day Adventists

NEW GALLERY CENTRE
123 Regent Street, W1
734 8888
✪ Piccadilly Circus
6.30 p.m.

Society of Friends (Quakers)

FRIENDS HOUSE
173 Euston Road, NW1
387 3601
✪ Euston Square/Euston
11.00 a.m.

WESTMINSTER
MEETING HOUSE
52 St Martin's Lane, WC2
836 7204
✪ Leicester Square
11.00 a.m.

Spanish

SPANISH CATHOLIC
CHAPLAINCY
47 Palace Court, W2
229 8815
✪ Queensway/Notting Hill
Gate
Noon & 6.00 p.m.

Spanish & Portuguese

SPANISH &
PORTUGUESE
SYNAGOGUE
9 Lauderdale Road, W9
286 4189/2153
✪ Maida Vale
8.00 a.m.

Swedish

THE SWEDISH CHURCH
6 Harcourt Street, W1
723 5681
✪ Marylebone/Edgware Road
11.00 a.m.

SWEDISH SEAMAN'S
CHURCH
120 Lower Road, SE16
237 1644
✪ Surrey Docks
7.30 p.m.

Swiss

THE SWISS CHURCH IN
LONDON
79 Endell Street, WC2
340 9740/836 1418
✪ Covent Garden/Tottenham
Court Road
11.00 a.m. (French) &
except 4th Sunday: 10.00 a.m.
(Dutch & German)

Ukrainian

UKRAINIAN CATHOLIC
CATHEDRAL
Duke Street, W1
629 1534
✪ Bond Street
10.30 a.m.

Unitarian

THE UNITARIAN
CHURCH
112 Palace Gardens Terrace,
W8
221 6514

✪ Notting Hill Gate
11.00 a.m.

United Reformed

CITY TEMPLE
Holborn Viaduct, EC1
583 5532/8701
✪ Farringdon/St Paul's
11.00 a.m. & 6.30 p.m.

Welsh

ST BENET GUILD
CHURCH
Paul's Walk
Queen Victoria Street, EC4
723 3104
✪ Blackfriars/Mansion House
10.45 a.m. & 3.30 p.m.

TRAVEL & TRANSPORT

The information in this section is split into various categories and only where appropriate is it sub-divided into postal zones.

AIRLINES & AIRPORTS

Many airlines operate a booking service on Sundays and most of the information you will need can be found either under 'Airlines' in Yellow Pages or 'British Airports Authority' in the A-D telephone directory.

BUSES

An extensive service, slightly reduced from that run during the week, is operated on Sunday and many special deals are available on fares and passes.

London Bus Maps are available from London Transport Travel Enquiry Offices (see Information) or by post from:

Public Relations Officer
London Transport
55 The Broadway
London SW1H 08D

For further information call 222 1234 at any time, day or night.

COACHES

A nationwide service operates from:

VICTORIA COACH STATION
164 Buckingham Palace Road, SW1
730 0436

TAXIS

Black cabs can be ordered from the following ranks:

EC2 – Moorgate
606 4526

N1 – Liverpool Road
    837 2394

NW1 – Baker Street
    Underground
    935 2553

SW1 – St George's Square
    834 1014

    – Sloane Square
    730 2664

SW7 – Harrington Road
    589 5242

W2 – Lancaster Gate
    723 9907

W8 – Wrights Lane
    937 0736

W9 – Warwick Avenue
    286 2566

WC1 – Russell Square
    636 1247

or from the following radio cab companies:

Computer Cab: 286 0286
London-Wide Radio Taxis:
286 6010
Radio Taxi Service: 286 4848/
6128
Radio Taxicabs: 272 3030

MINI-CABS

See Yellow Pages or call Teledata (200 0200) for a list of local companies.

THE UNDERGROUND

A reduced service is operated on Sundays and the following stations are closed:

Aldwych, WC2
Barbican, EC1
Cannon Street, EC4
Chancery Lane, WC1
Kensington – Olympia, W14
(except during exhibitions)
Mornington Crescent, NW1
Ravenscourt Park, W6
Shadwell, E1
Shoreditch, E1
Temple, WC2
West Brompton, SW5

There are some cheaper fares and passes available on Sundays.

For further information ring 222 1234 at any time, day or night.

BRITISH RAIL

Main line stations and the area they serve are listed here together with the number to ring for further information.

CHARING CROSS, WC2
Southern Region
928 5100

EUSTON, NW1
London Midland Region
387 7070

KING'S CROSS, NW1
Eastern Region
278 2477

LIVERPOOL STREET, EC3
Eastern Region
283 7171

MARYLEBONE, NW1
London Midland Region
387 7070

PADDINGTON, W2
Western Region
262 6767

ST PANCRAS, NW1
London Midland Region
387 7070

VICTORIA, SW1
Southern Region
928 5100

WATERLOO, SE1
Southern Region
928 5100

Recorded information is
available for some services. See
'British Rail' in the A–D
telephone directory.

RIVER & CANAL TRIPS

see Jaunts & Excursions

ROADS

Constitution Hill and The
Mall running from Hyde Park
Corner to Horse Guards are
closed to traffic on Sundays.

CAR HIRE

This is a list of companies from
which you can hire a car, either
chauffeur-driven or self-drive
as indicated.

Many firms will arrange
collection or delivery in
various parts of London.

AA CAR HIRE SERVICE
13 Craven Terrace, W2
262 2223
⊖ Lancaster Gate
8.00 a.m.–12.30 p.m.
Self-drive
*Credit cards

ACTON CAR RENTAL
LTD
Courtesy House
184 Acton Lane, W4
747 1404/994 7422
⊖ Chiswick Park
Self-drive

AVIS RENT-A-CAR
35 Headfort Place, SW1
245 9862
⊖ Hyde Park Corner
7.00 a.m.–8.00 p.m.
Self-drive
*AC AX BC DC

CENTRAL RENT-A-CAR
28 Queensway, W2
727 7812/9479
229 7211/7212
⊖ Bayswater
8.00 a.m.–8.00 p.m.
Self-drive
*AC AX DC

COLMANS CAR HIRE
93–113 Park Road, N8
340 7902/9280/8614
⊖ Highgate
Self-drive. Also minibuses and
vans.
*AC AX BC

CONNAUGHT SELF-
DRIVE
202 Carlisle Lane, SE1
928 1885
⊖ Lambeth North/Waterloo
Self-drive

D. V. H. SELF-DRIVE
224 Garratt Lane, SW18
870 0707/1943
⊖ Tooting Broadway
9.00 a.m.–noon
Self-drive. Also minibuses and
vans.
*AC AX BC

E. & P. SELF-DRIVE
Sloane Avenue Mansions
Garage,
Sloane Avenue, SW3
581 2255/6
⊖ South Kensington
9.00 a.m.–1.00 p.m.
Self-drive
*AC AX BC DC

GODFREY DAVIS
Davis House,
Wilton Road, SW1
834 8484
⊖ Victoria Station
open 24 hours
*AC AX BC DC

GUY SALMON
7–23 Bryanston Street, W1
408 1255 (self-drive)
730 8571 (chauffeur-driven)
⊖ Marble Arch
8.30 a.m.–4.00 p.m.
Self-drive or chauffeur-driven
*AC AX BC DC

KENNING
84–90 Holland Park Avenue,
W11
727 0123
⊖ Holland Park
8.00 a.m.–4.00 p.m.
Self-drive
*AC AX BC DC

LONDON LIMOUSINE
CO.
Carriage House,
Burrell Street, SE1
928 9280
⊖ Blackfriars
open 24 hours
Chauffeur-driven
*AC AX BC DC

MOTEX
N.C.P. Car Park,
Cadogan Place, SW1
235 9507
⊖ Sloane Square/
Knightsbridge
Self-drive
*Credit cards

PATRICK BARTHROPP
1 Dorset Mews, SW1
245 9171
⊖ Victoria/Hyde Park Corner
8.00 a.m.–6.00 p.m.
Chauffeur-driven
*AX

PAUL HUXFORD
101 Farm Lane, SW6
385 2248
⊖ Fulham Broadway
8.00 a.m.–6.00 p.m.
Chauffeur-driven
*AC AX BC DC

PETROL STATIONS

All of those listed here are
open 24 hours a day.

E1

CITY PETROLEUM
Whitechapel Road
247 0263
*AC AX BC

E3

CITY PETROLEUM
24–26 Bow Road
980 8556
*AC AX BC

E4

CITY PETROLEUM
Walthamstow Avenue
527 8656
*AC AX BC

E7

CITY PETROLEUM
176 Romford Road
534 8835
*AC AX BC

E8

THAMES SERVICE
STATION
139 Mare Street
985 2463
*AC BC

E10

ORIENT SERVICE
STATION
209–219 Lea Bridge Road
*AC BC

E14

STEPNEY SERVICE
STATION
640 Commercial Road
*AC BC

E15

THREE MILLS SERVICE
STATION
Carpenter's Road
534 9306
and
High Street
519 3824
*AC BC

WHITEFIELDS SERVICE
STATION
610–624 Barking Road
*AC BC

E16

SILVERTOWN WAY
SERVICE STATION
Silvertown Way
474 5746
*AC BC

N1

CITY PETROLEUM
276 Upper Street
226 2480
*AC AX BC

COSMO SERVICE
STATION
109–113 York Way
*AC AX BC DC

ST JOHN'S SERVICE
STATION
East Road, Shoreditch
*AC BC

N2

LYTTELTON GARAGE
Lyttelton Road
458 7581
*AC AX BC DC

N7

CITY PETROLEUM
104–116 Holloway Road
607 8567
*AC AX BC

OLYMPIC SELF-SERVICE
Holloway Road
*AC BC

N10

CITY PETROLEUM
Colney Hatch Lane
883 1897
*AC AX BC

N15

CITY PETROLEUM
109 High Road
800 5181
*AC AX BC

N22

LORDSHIP LANE
SERVICE STATION
255 Lordship Lane
*AC AX BC DC

NW1

CAMDEN ROAD SERVICE
STATION
196 Camden Road
485 7144
*AC BC

NW2

CITY PETROLEUM
Staples Corner
721 North Circular Road
452 1388
*AC AX BC

NW3

HAMPSTEAD SERVICE
STATION
104a Finchley Road
722 4976
*AC AX BC DC

NW6

KILBURN SERVICE
STATION
409 Kilburn High Road
624 4801
*AC AX BC DC

NW7

OBSERVATORY SERVICE
STATION
520–522 Watford Way
959 2277
*AC BC

NW9

CITY PETROLEUM
Kingsbury Circle
204 5758
*AC AX BC

HERON SERVICE
STATION
2 Blackbird Hill
205 8070
*AC BC

NW10

CHAMBERLAYNE ROAD
SERVICE STATION
Banister Road
969 1349
*AC AX BC DC

RUCKLEDGE SERVICE
STATION
139–154 High Street
961 6060
*AC BC

NW11

CASTLE SERVICE
CENTRE
713 Finchley Road
458 8175/3416
*AC AX BC DC

SE1

CITY PETROLEUM
233 Old Kent Road
237 4718
*AC AX BC

SE2

THAMESMEAD
MOTORING CENTRE
84–89 Harrow Manor Way
310 5930
*AC AX BC DC

SE5

PECKHAM SERVICE
STATION
37–41 Peckham Road
703 2033
*AC AX BC DC

SE9

CITY PETROLEUM
51 Sidcup Road
857 6262
*AC AX BC

SE10

CITY PETROLEUM
25 High Road
692 5892
*AC AX BC

SE12

CLIFTON SERVICE
STATION
59 Sidcup Road
859 5775
*AC BC

SE13

LOAMPIT SERVICE
STATION
56–60 Loampit Hill
692 4259
*AC BC

SE15

PECKHAM SERVICE
STATION
95 Peckham Road
703 2555
*AC AX BC DC

SE17

CITY PETROLEUM
137 Walworth Road
703 9585
*AC AX BC

SE18

CITY PETROLEUM
125 Woolwich High Street
854 6688/855 6155
*AC AX BC

SE19

CITY PETROLEUM
4 Crystal Palace Parade
670 6322
*AC AX BC

SE21

AVENUE PARK FILLING
STATION
17 Thurlow Park Road
*AC AX BC DC

SE23

CITY PETROLEUM
163 Stanstead Road
699 4070
*AC AX BC

SE25

CITY PETROLEUM
123 Portland Road
654 7111
*AC AX BC

SW1

CITY PETROLEUM
132 Grosvenor Road
834 8054
*AC AX BC

SW2

ACRE LANE FILLING
STATION
47 Acre Lane
274 7698
*AC BC

BRIXTON HILL
SERVICE STATION
124–128 Brixton Hill
*AC AX BC DC

SW3

- CHELSEA CLOISTERS
FILLING STATION
Sloane Avenue
*AC AX BC DC

SW6

CITY PETROLEUM
Wandsworth Bridge Road
(corner of Townmead Road)
736 2491
*AC AX BC

FOUR SEASONS
601–615 King's Road
*AC BC

SW8

CITY PETROLEUM
326 Queenstown Road
622 0328
*AC AX BC

NINE ELMS SERVICE
STATION
54 Wandsworth Road
622 7202
*AC BC

SW9

INGARFIELD SERVICE
STATION
243 Brixton Road
737 4353
*AC BC

SW10

STAMFORD BRIDGE
SERVICE STATION
459 Fulham Road
352 3307
*AC BC

SW11

PARKGATE SERVICE
STATION
15–25 Parkgate Road
223 1926
*AC AX BC DC

SW12

CITY PETROLEUM
67 Balham Hill
673 4030
*AC AX BC

SW16

CITY PETROLEUM
1270 London Road
764 3205
*AC AX BC

SW17

CITY PETROLEUM
Plough Lane
946 1473
*AC AX BC

SW19

CITY PETROLEUM
159–165 High Street
543 8350
*AC AX BC

SW20

OBIN HOOD SERVICE STATION
Coombe Lane West
942 3257
*AC BC

W2

CAPITAL SERVICE STATION
482–490 Edgware Road
*AC BC

W4

CHISWICK FLYOVER SERVICE STATION
1 Great West Road
994 1119/747 1728
*AC BC

CHISWICK SERVICE STATION
361–365 Chiswick High Road
995 4306
*AC AX BC DC

W5

GUNNERSBURY PARK SELF-SERVICE
Gunnersbury Avenue
992 9980
*AC AX BC DC

NORTH EALING SELF-SERVICE
35 Hanger Lane
998 4213
*AC AX BC DC

W6

CROMWELL ROAD FILLING STATION NORTH and SOUTH
Great West Road
*AC AX BC DC

FULHAM PALACE SERVICE STATION
168 Fulham Palace Road
385 1660/0386
*AC BC

W7

HERON SERVICE STATION
144 Uxbridge Road
567 9993
*AC BC

W9

MAIDA VALE SERVICE STATION
115 Maida Vale
286 7321
*AC BC

W14

ALCO SELF-SERVICE
112 North End Road
385 0761
*AC AX BC DC

CITY PETROLEUM
181 Warwick Road
370 1345
*AC AX BC

WC1

RUSSELL COURT
SERVICE STATION
Woburn Place
837 7315
*AC AX BC DC

SPARE PARTS & ACCESSORIES

Most of the garages listed under Petrol Stations also sell spares and accessories.

The centres listed here will supply and fit batteries, exhausts, radiators, shock absorbers or tyres for most makes of car.

Ring to check that what you want is available.

E10

KWIK-FIT-EURO
344 High Road
539 6118
10.00 a.m.–4.00 p.m.
*AC BC

E12

KWIK-FIT-EURO
409 High Street North
472 4744/6686
10.00 a.m.–4.00 p.m.
*AC BC

E13

KWIK-FIT-EURO
301 Barking Road
476 6813
10.00 a.m.–4.00 p.m.
*AC BC

E15

KWIK-FIT-EURO
1 Park Lane
519 4535
10.00 a.m.–4.00 p.m.
*AC BC

EC1

KWIK-FIT-EURO
250 Old Street
251 3310
10.00 a.m.–4.00 p.m.
*AC BC

N8

KWIK-FIT-EURO
163 Tottenham Lane
340 0629
10.00 a.m.–4.00 p.m.
*AC BC

N14

KWIK-FIT-EURO
Tudor Way
886 7328
and
Winchmore Hill Road
886 3753
10.00 a.m.–4.00 p.m.
*AC BC

N16

KWIK-FIT-EURO
3 Stamford Hill
800 1629/802 1370
10.00 a.m.–4.00 p.m.
*AC BC

N17

KWIK-FIT-EURO
2 Ferry Lane
801 8405
10.00 a.m.–4.00 p.m.
*AC BC

NW1

CAMDEN EXHAUST
CENTRE
107 Parkway
267 5364
9.00 a.m.–3.00 p.m.
*AC AX BC DC

NW3

KWIK-FIT-EURO
1 Northways Parade
Finchley Road
722 8541
10.00 a.m.–4.00 p.m.
*AC BC

NW9

KWIK-FIT-EURO
Edgware Road
(corner of Annesley Avenue)
205 4805
10.00 a.m.–4.00 p.m.
*AC BC

NW11

KWIK-FIT-EURO
177 Golders Green Road
458 9926
10.00 a.m.–4.00 p.m.
*AC BC

SE5

KWIK-FIT-EURO
123 Denmark Hill
733 7274
10.00 a.m.–4.00 p.m.
*AC BC

SE6

KWIK-FIT-EURO
1a Brownhill Road
698 3033
10.00 a.m.–4.00 p.m.
*AC BC

SE9

KWIK-FIT-EURO
701 Sidcup Road
857 5147
and
727 Sidcup Road
857 0033
10.00 a.m.–4.00 p.m.
*AC BC

SE17

SUPERDRIVE MOTORING
CENTRE
120–129 Walworth Road
703 8744
10.00 a.m.–1.00 p.m.
*AC AX BC DC

SE20

KWIK-FIT-EURO
2a Marlow Road
778 1119/4745
10.00 a.m.–4.00 p.m.
*AC BC

SW6

KWIK-FIT-EURO
763 Fulham Road
736 1114
10.00 a.m.–4.00 p.m.
*AC BC

SW16

SUPERDRIVE MOTORING
CENTRE
1270 London Road
679 6409
and
43 Mitcham Lane
677 1083
10.00 a.m.–1.00 p.m.
*AC AX BC DC

SW17

KWIK-FIT-EURO
769 Garratt Lane
947 3413
10.00 a.m.–4.00 p.m.
*AC BC

SUPERDRIVE MOTORING
CENTRE
187 Mitcham Road
767 7001
10.00 a.m.–1.00 p.m.
*AC AX BC DC

SW18

KWIK-FIT-EURO
Armoury Way
871 1364/874 1197
10.00 a.m.–4.00 p.m.
*AC BC

SW19

KWIK-FIT-EURO
221 The Broadway
542 1479/2661
10.00 a.m.–4.00 p.m.
*AC BC

W5

KWIK-FIT-EURO
48 The Mall
567 2861
10.00 a.m.–4.00 p.m.
*AC BC

W10

KWIK-FIT-EURO
617 Harrow Road
960 5563
10.00 a.m.–4.00 p.m.
*AC BC

W12

KWIK-FIT-EURO
4 Wood Lane
743 5446/749 1844
10.00 a.m.–4.00 p.m.
*AC BC

CAR WASH

A number of the garages listed under Petrol Stations have car washing machines.

The ones listed here provide a hand car-wash/valet service.

KENSINGTON CAR WASH
Russell Road, W14
603 7191/2
9.00 a.m.–7.00 p.m.

STARWASH
Harriet Walk, SW1
235 6429
8.00 a.m.–6.00 p.m.

WELLINGTON CAR WASH
28–32 Wellington Road, NW8
586 5386
9.00 a.m.–5.00 p.m.

BREAKDOWN

Many garages operate a 24-hour breakdown and recovery service.

See Yellow Pages or call Teledata (200 0200) for a list of local companies.

SERVICES

ACCOMMODATION

LONDON TOURIST BOARD ACCOMMODATION BUREAU
National Tourist Information Centre,
Victoria Station, SW1
9.00 a.m.–8.30 p.m.
(July & August:
8.30 a.m.–10.00 p.m.)
Information and reservation service for all types of accommodation

BALLOONS

see Deliveries

BANKS & BUREAUX DE CHANGE

There are bureaux de change at many rail and central underground stations. They are generally open until about 10.00 p.m. for travellers cheques, cash and foreign currency.

SW1

AMERICAN EXPRESS
6 Haymarket
930 4411
⊖ Piccadilly
10.00 a.m.–6.00 p.m.

LENLYN LTD
by Platform 15,
Victoria Station
828 2010
⊖ Victoria
6.00 a.m.–10.00 p.m.

SW5

CHEQUEPOINT
236 Earls Court Road
370 3239
⊖ Earls Court
open 24 hours

W1

BANK OF CREDIT & COMMERCE
25 Park Lane
629 4927
and
141 Park Lane
499 6881
⊖ Marble Arch
9.00 a.m.–5.00 p.m.

CHEQUEPOINT
37–38 Coventry Street
839 3772
☻ Piccadilly Circus/Leicester
Square
open 24 hours

ERSKINE BUREAU
3–5 Coventry Street
437 7167
☻ Piccadilly Circus/Leicester
Square
open 24 hours
and
13 Shaftesbury Avenue
734 1400
☻ Piccadilly Circus
8.00 a.m.–8.00 p.m.

W2

CHEQUEPOINT
126 Bayswater Road
727 4212
☻ Bayswater
open 24 hours

ERSKINE BUREAU
22 Leinster Terrace
402 6305
☻ Bayswater
8.00 a.m.–8.00 p.m.

WC2

CREDIT CHANGE
7 Grand Buildings,
Trafalgar Square
930 4247
☻ Charing Cross
9.00 a.m.–9.00 p.m.

TOWN TOURS &
TICKETS
corner Long Acre/James
Street
836 0528/9
☻ Covent Garden
9.30 a.m.–10.00 p.m.

COFFEE

see Deliveries

DELIVERIES

Companies who will deliver on
Sundays include:

BALLOONS OVER
LONDON
Unit 2,
Parkfield Industrial Estate,
Culvert Place, SW11
622 7566
☻ Clapham Junction
Bunches of balloons in all
shapes, sizes and colours.
Best to order in advance.
*AC AX BC

HOTWHEELS
95 Fulham Palace Road, W6
748 0777
☻ Hammersmith
5.00 p.m.–11.00 p.m.
Deliver various meals and
menus within a three mile
radius from Hammersmith
Broadway.

PERFECT PIZZA
51 Fulham Broadway, SW6
381 2042
● Fulham Broadway
11.30 a.m.–midnight
Pizzas

PIZZA MIA
189 New King's Road, SW6
736 1145
● Parsons Green
Noon–midnight
Pizzas

RICHARD HART COFFEE
876 3955
8.00 a.m.–midnight
Ground coffee or beans at
wholesale prices delivered.

ESTATE AGENTS

Opening hours may vary.

N1

GOLDSCHMIDT,
HOWLAND, CASSELLS
338 Upper Street
226 0272
● Angel
2.00 p.m.–4.00 p.m.

NW1

BAIRSTOW EVES
82 Park Way
485 6767
● Camden Town
11.00 a.m.–3.30 p.m.

NW3

BAIRSTOW EVES
1 Holly Hill
431 2328
● Hampstead
11.00 a.m.–3.00 p.m.

GOLDSCHMIDT,
HOWLAND, CASSELLS
15 Heath Street
435 4404
● Hampstead
11.00 a.m.–4.00 p.m.

JOHN ENGLAND &
PARTNERS
8 Village Mount
Perrins Court
435 2271
● Hampstead
10.00 a.m.–2.00 p.m.

NW8

BRIAN LACK & CO.
4–6 St Ann's Terrace
586 3088/5929
● St John's Wood
11.00 a.m.–5.00 p.m.

GILLAND & CO.
12 Finchley Road
586 8001/8005
● St John's Wood
Noon–2.00 p.m.

SE19

SOUTH LONDON
PROPERTY CENTRE
81 Church Road
771 1218

BR Crystal Palace
10.00 a.m.–2.00 p.m.

SW6

APPLEGREEN ESTATES
288 Munster Road
381 4755
◒ Fulham Broadway
10.00 a.m.–3.00 p.m.

SW16

HOMEHUNTERS
PROPERTY SHOP
423 Streatham High Road
679 6477
BR Norbury
10.00 a.m.–4.00 p.m.

SW17

HOMEHUNTERS
PROPERTY SHOP
5 Upper Tooting Road
672 6681
◒ Tooting Bec
10.00 a.m.–4.00 p.m.

JOHN P. DENNIS & CO.
16a The Boulevard,
Balham High Road
673 8881
◒ Balham
11.00 a.m.–4.00 p.m.

W1

STUART WILSON & CO.
18 Seymour Place
724 0241
◒ Marble Arch
10.00 a.m.–2.00 p.m.

W2

JOHN ENGLAND &
PARTNERS
1 Craven Terrace
402 2333
◒ Lancaster Gate
10.00 a.m.–2.00 p.m.

KENWOOD
23 Spring Street
258 3931
◒ Paddington
10.00 a.m.–2.00 p.m.

W4

WHITMAN PORTER
273 Chiswick High Road
995 2345/3333
and
45 Turnham Green Terrace
994 5432
◒ Turnham Green
10.00 a.m.–2.00 p.m.

W5

WHITMAN PORTER
2 Haven Lane
997 5000
◒ Ealing Broadway
10.00 a.m.–2.00 p.m.

W6

WHITMAN PORTER
172 King Street
748 4256
◒ Stamford Brook/
Hammersmith
10.00 a.m.–2.00 p.m.

W11

BRIAN LACK & CO.
8 Ladbroke Grove
229 8881
⊖ Holland Park
2.00 p.m.–5.00 p.m.

FARON SUTARIA
89 Notting Hill Gate
243 8521
⊖ Notting Hill Gate
10.00 a.m.–5.00 p.m.

FOXTONS
91–95 Notting Hill Gate
221 3534
⊖ Notting Hill Gate
10.00 a.m.–5.00 p.m.

JOHN WILCOX & CO.
13 Addison Avenue
602 2352
⊖ Holland Park
11.00 a.m.–1.00 p.m.

WHITMAN PORTER
44 Royal Crescent
603 1133
⊖ Shepherd's Bush
10.00 a.m.–2.00 p.m.

FILM PROCESSING

SNAPPY SNAPS
66 Queensway, W2
221 3782
⊖ Bayswater
8.00 a.m.–10.00 p.m.
Express service for developing
and enlargements.

FOOD

see Deliveries

HIRE SERVICES

CARS – see Travel &
Transport

VIDEOS – see Shops, Books
etc.

LAUNDRETTES

There are many in London and
they are mostly open on
Sundays. If you don't find one
nearby, ask locally.

MASSAGE

see Sports & Activities

NURSING SERVICES

BRITISH NURSING
ASSOCIATION
470 Oxford Street, W1
629 9030

PASSPORT PHOTOGRAPHS

There are photograph machines in many Underground stations including:

Baker Street, NW1
Earls Court, SW5
Green Park, W1
Knightsbridge, SW1
South Kensington, SW7

POST OFFICE

POST OFFICE
24 William IV Street, WC2
930 9580
● Leicester Square
10.00 a.m.–5.00 p.m.

PRINTING AND PHOTOCOPYING

KALL-KWIK PRINTING
54 Notting Hill Gate, W11
727 8836
● Notting Hill Gate
5.00 p.m.–8.00 p.m.

SAFE DEPOSIT

BERKELEY SAFE DEPOSIT
The Forecourt,
Victoria Station, SW1
828 0053

● Victoria
8.00 a.m.–midnight

PARK LANE SAFE DEPOSIT CENTRE
3 Park Street, W1
409 1516
● Marble Arch
open 24 hours

SAFE DEPOSIT CENTRE
146 Brompton Road, SW3
581 1212
● Knightsbridge
9.30 a.m.–7.30 p.m.

ST JOHN'S WOOD SAFE DEPOSIT CENTRE
16–18 Circus Road
586 9431
● St John's Wood
9.30 a.m.–7.30 p.m.

SECRETARIAL SERVICES

PIKE & FULTON
118 Beaufort Street, SW3
225 0707
● South Kensington
8.00 a.m.–11.00 p.m.
Typing, telex, photocopying, answering service, translations, etc.
*AC AX BC DC

POLAIRE
134 Lots Road, SW10
351 4333/352 4731
Typing, telex, book-keeping, research, etc.

TATTOOISTS

SAINT MARC
201 Portobello Road, W11
727 8211
✪ Notting Hill Gate/
Ladbroke Grove
Noon–10.00 p.m.

TERRY MACLAREN
673 Fulham Road, SW6
731 6008
✪ Parsons Green/Fulham
Broadway

TICKET AGENTS

NATIONAL TOURIST
INFORMATION CENTRE
Victoria Station, SW1
9.00 a.m.–8.30 p.m.
(July & August:
8.30 a.m.–10.00 p.m.)

TOWN TOURS &
TICKETS
corner Long Acre/James
Street
836 0528/9
✪ Covent Garden
9.30 a.m.–10.00 p.m.

INFORMATION

RECORDED INFORMATION

The following information is available on the telephone 24 hours a day.

For other 'Guidelines', see the Telephone Dialling Codes book.

CHILDREN'S LONDON
246 8007
Weekly summary of events and entertainments for children.

LEISURELINE
English: 246 8041
French: 246 8043
German: 246 8045
Daily information of events, entertainments and exhibitions

SPORTSLINE
246 8020
Results of sporting events

TIMELINE
123
The Speaking Clock will tell you the time precisely.

TRAVELINE
London: 246 8021
Rail: 246 8030
Road: 246 8031
Sea: 246 8032

Air: 246 8033
Travel information

WEATHERLINE
246 8091
Weather forecasts

INFORMATION SERVICES

GAY SWITCHBOARD
837 7324
24 hour telephone service. Information on gay clubs, restaurants, bars, etc.

LONDON TRANSPORT TRAVEL ENQUIRY OFFICES
are situated in the following Underground stations:
Charing Cross, EC4
Euston, NW1
King's Cross, NW1
Oxford Circus, W1
Piccadilly Circus, W1
Victoria, SW1
Waterloo, SE1
They are open from 8.30 a.m. to 9.30 p.m. and will supply free bus and tube maps and answer your questions about travelling on London Transport.

**LONDON TRANSPORT
24-HOUR
INFORMATION SERVICE
222 1234**
Calls are answered in rotation
so be prepared to wait.

**RESTAURANT
SWITCHBOARD
444 0044**
10.00 a.m.–10.00 p.m.
Information on restaurants
throughout London

**TELEDATA
200 0200**
24-hour information service.
Supply local information about
practically anything. Useful for
mini-cabs, plumbers,
locksmiths etc. needed in a
hurry on Sunday.

TOURIST INFORMATION CENTRES

Greenwich:
Cutty Sark Gardens, SE10
858 6376

BR Greenwich
June–August:
11.00 a.m.–5.00 p.m.
September–May:
11.00 a.m.–4.00 p.m.

Tower of London:
West Gate,
Tower of London, EC3
● Tower Hill
April–October:
2.00 p.m.–5.00 p.m.

Victoria:
The Forecourt,
Victoria Station, SW1
● Victoria
9.00 a.m.–8.30 p.m.
(July & August:
8.30 a.m.–10.00 p.m.)

All kinds of tourist
information, guidebooks,
maps, tickets, etc.

EMERGENCIES

AMBULANCE, FIRE, POLICE

Telephone emergency service:
Dial 999
No coins necessary

ANIMALS

BEAUMONT ANIMALS
HOSPITAL
Royal Veterinary College,
Royal College Street, NW1
387 8134
✪ Camden Town
24-hour emergency service.
Only for those who cannot
afford private veterinary
treatment.

THE ELIZABETH STREET
VETERINARY CLINIC
55 Elizabeth Street, SW1
730 9102
✪ Sloane Square/Victoria
24-hour emergency service

PEOPLE'S DISPENSARY
FOR SICK ANIMALS
(P.D.S.A.)
North & West London:
203 2090
South London: 686 3972
East London: 550 6644

24-hour emergency service.
Only for those who cannot
afford private veterinary
treatment.

ROYAL SOCIETY FOR
THE PREVENTION OF
CRUELTY TO ANIMALS
(R.S.P.C.A.)
North London: 272 6214
South London: 789 8252
24-hour emergency service

CAR BREAKDOWN

see Travel & Transport

CHEMISTS

BLISS CHEMISTS
54 Willesden Lane, NW6
624 8000
✪ Kilburn
open 24 hours

Your local police station will
have a list of chemists in your
area.

CRISIS & COUNSELLING

AL-ANON
403 0888
Help for alcoholics, their
friends and relations

**ALCOHOLICS
ANONYMOUS**
834 8202
10.00 a.m.–10.00 p.m.
Help for alcoholics, their
friends and relations

CITY ROADS
278 8671
24-hour telephone service.
Help for those suffering as a
result of drug abuse

GAY SWITCHBOARD
837 7324
24-hour advice and
information service for gay men
and women

**NATIONAL SOCIETY FOR
THE PREVENTION OF
CRUELTY TO CHILDREN
(N.S.P.C.C.)**
580 8812
24-hour telephone service

**NATIONAL WOMEN'S
AID FEDERATION**
251 6429
24-hour telephone service for
battered women

RAPE CRISIS CENTRE
837 1600
24-hour telephone service for
rape victims

RELEASE
603 8654
24-hour emergency service
providing legal advice

SAMARITANS
283 3400/626 9000
24-hour telephone service
providing help and
counselling for the depressed

Other numbers throughout
London – see telephone book
or call the above numbers.

DENTAL TREATMENT

**EMERGENCY DENTAL
SERVICE**
584 1008
24-hour recorded information
giving you a number to call

**PRIVATE DENTAL
EMERGENCY SERVICE**
749 5704
24-hour recorded information
giving you a number to call

**RADIO EMERGENCY
DENTAL SERVICE**
834 8345/828 5621
24-hour emergency service.
Ring, give your name and
phone number and they will
contact you

EYE HOSPITALS

These hospitals are open 24 hours for emergencies.

MOORFIELDS EYE
HOSPITAL
City Road, EC1
253 3411
⊖ Old Street

MOORFIELDS EYE
HOSPITAL
High Holborn, WC1
836 6611
⊖ Holborn

WESTERN OPHTHALMIC
HOSPITAL
Marylebone Road, NW1
402 4211
⊖ Marylebone

HOSPITALS

All of these hospitals are open 24 hours for Accidents & Emergencies.

E1

THE LONDON HOSPITAL
Whitechapel Road
247 5454
⊖ Whitechapel

E2

QUEEN ELIZABETH
HOSPITAL
FOR CHILDREN
Hackney Road
739 8422

E9

HACKNEY HOSPITAL
230 Homerton High Street
985 5555

E11

WHIPPS CROSS
HOSPITAL
Whipps Cross Road
539 5522
BR Wood Street

E15

QUEEN MARY'S
HOSPITAL
West Ham Lane
476 1400
⊖ Plaistow

EC1

ST BARTHOLOMEW'S
HOSPITAL
West Smithfield
600 9000
⊖ St Paul's

N18

NORTH MIDDLESEX
HOSPITAL
Sterling Way
807 3071
⊖ Seven Sisters

NW3

ROYAL FREE HOSPITAL
Pond Street
794 0500
⊖ Hampstead

NW10

**CENTRAL MIDDLESEX
HOSPITAL**
Acton Lane
965 5733
✪ North Acton/Park Royal

SE1

GUY'S HOSPITAL
St Thomas Street
407 7600
✪ London Bridge

ST THOMAS' HOSPITAL
Lambeth Palace Road
928 9292
✪ Westminster/Waterloo

SE5

**KING'S COLLEGE
HOSPITAL**
Denmark Hill
274 6222
✪ Elephant & Castle

MAUDSLEY HOSPITAL
Denmark Hill
703 6333
BR Denmark Hill

SE10

**GREENWICH DISTRICT
HOSPITAL**
Vanbrugh Hill
858 8141
BR Maze Hill

SE13

LEWISHAM HOSPITAL
Lewisham High Street
690 4311
BR Ladywell

SE18

**BROOK GENERAL
HOSPITAL**
Shooters Hill Road
856 5555
BR Blackheath

SE26

CHILDREN'S HOSPITAL
321 Sydenham Road
778 7031
BR Lower Sydenham

SW1

**WESTMINSTER
CHILDREN'S HOSPITAL**
56 Vincent Square
828 9811
✪ Pimlico

**WESTMINSTER
HOSPITAL**
Dean Ryle Street
828 9811
✪ Westminster/Pimlico

SW9

**BELGRAVE HOSPITAL
FOR CHILDREN**
1 Clapham Road
274 6222
✪ Oval/Kennington

SW10

ST STEPHEN'S
HOSPITAL
369 Fulham Road
352 8161

SW12

ST JAMES'S HOSPITAL
Sarsfeld Road
672 1222
⊖ Tooting Bec

SW15

QUEEN MARY'S
HOSPITAL
Roehampton Lane
789 6611
⊖ Putney Bridge

SW17

ST GEORGE'S HOSPITAL
Blackshaw Road
672 1255
⊖ Tooting Broadway

W1

MIDDLESEX HOSPITAL
Mortimer Street
636 8333
⊖ Goodge Street

W2

PADDINGTON GREEN
CHILDREN'S HOSPITAL
Paddington Green
723 1081
⊖ Edgware Road

ST MARY'S HOSPITAL
Praed Street
262 1280
⊖ Paddington

W6

NEW CHARING CROSS
HOSPITAL
Fulham Palace Road
748 2040
⊖ Hammersmith

W12

HAMMERSMITH
HOSPITAL
Du Cane Road
743 2030
⊖ East Acton

LOCKSMITHS

See Yellow Pages or call
Teledata (200 0200)

MONEY

see Services

PETROL

see Travel & Transport

PLUMBERS

See Yellow Pages or call
Teledata (200 0200).

POLICE

Emergencies: dial 999

For your local station, see
under 'Police' in the phone
book.

To: Joanna Whitaker
    'LONDON ON SUNDAY'
    Granada Publishing Ltd
    8 Grafton Street, London W1X 3LA

CATEGORY: ....

NAME: ....

ADDRESS & POST ZONE: ....

....

PHONE: ....

HOURS: ....

GOODS/SERVICES/FACILITIES etc. ....

....

....

From: Name:
      Address:

      Date:

To: Joanna Whitaker
    'LONDON ON SUNDAY'
    Granada Publishing Ltd
    8 Grafton Street, London W1X 3LA

CATEGORY: ....

NAME: ....

ADDRESS & POST ZONE: ....

....

PHONE: ....

HOURS: ....

GOODS/SERVICES/FACILITIES etc. ....

....

....

From: Name:
      Address:

      Date: